What Can You Do
PERSONAL ESSAYS & TRAVEL WRITING

ALSO BY EDWARD HOWER

NOVELS

The New Life Hotel
Wolf Tickets
Night Train Blues
Queen of the Silver Dollar
Shadows and Elephants
A Garden of Demons
The Storms of May
Slick

STORIES

Voices in the Water

FOLKLORE

The Pomegranate Princess and other Tales from India

FOR CHILDREN

The Hiccup

What Can You Do

PERSONAL ESSAYS & TRAVEL WRITING

For Carol Rubenstein

Edward Hower

with best wishes
—Edward

Cayuga Lake Books

Cayuga Lake Books
Ithaca, NY USA

What Can You Do:
Personal Essays & Travel Writing
by Edward Hower

Copyright © 2014 Edward Hower
ALL RIGHTS RESERVED

First Printing – August 2014
ISBN: 978-1-60047-980-9

With gratitude to the Fulbright Program,
and to the Virginia Center for the Creative Arts
Author photo by Phyllis Rose

NO PART OF THIS BOOK MAY BE REPRODUCED IN
ANY FORM, BY PHOTOCOPYING OR BY ANY ELECTRONIC
OR MECHANICAL MEANS, INCLUDING INFORMATION
STORAGE OR RETRIEVAL SYSTEMS, WITHOUT PERMISSION
IN WRITING FROM THE COPYRIGHT OWNER/AUTHOR

www.edwardhower.com

Printed in the U.S.A.

0 1 2 3 4 5 6

For

Bill and Dana Kennedy

TABLE OF CONTENTS

WHAT CAN YOU DO 1
ECHOES 21
GRATITUDE 37
WRITING DANGEROUSLY 53
BELIZE: BRITAIN'S LAID-BACK COLONY IN CENTRAL
AMERICA 63
EL SAPITO 83
QUEENS, DEMONS, AND SAINTS: INDIA'S FOLKLORE
HERITAGE 89
    The Princess and the Witches 102
    The Song of Naina Bai 104
    The Flying Prince 108
ANANDA'S DOVE 113
THE WITCH TEMPLE 125
THE VILLAGE ARTIST 139
CHILDREN OF THE MAZE 149
SCANDALS 163
EXPLORERS OF THE SPIRIT WORLD 179
ALONG SOUTH INDIA'S COROMANDEL COAST 193
A VILLAGE ON THE BAY OF BENGAL 199
FORESTS OF THE NIGHT 205
AFTERWORD 285

WHAT CAN YOU DO

Shoulders hunched, I burned a hole in the floor with my stare and tried to hide in it. But a familiar shape was drifting my way, a hot air balloon in a purple cable-knit sweater. The man's massive height, his roiling confusion of black curls, his loafers squashed down at the heels but so brightly polished that even the tassels looked enthusiastic—this was Ollie O'Flanagan. We'd met a year earlier when I'd returned to Ithaca to take a high school teaching job that hadn't been renewed.

"Hey, you're looking great, pal!" he lied. I hadn't shaved in a week and badly needed a haircut.

"Thanks, Ollie." I shook his huge mitt. "You do, too." His face was puffy, with deep lines around his eyes. We didn't ask each other why we were standing here—house rules at Unemployment Compensation offices. Ollie just shrugged, a gesture I remembered well: his head bonking over to one side, his palms up—as if to say: This is life, what can you do?

After we'd collected our checks, we skidded on snowy sidewalks to a nearby diner. Ollie ordered coffees and a big plate of doughnuts. "Still writing books, are you?" he asked, chewing.

"Not…lately." My first novel had turned out to be a letter in a bottle floated out on the tide in a vain search of readers, my agent had dumped me, and I hadn't finished another project in a very long time.

"Well, then, you could come in on this new business of mine." He beamed and tossed a card onto the table. Under his name I read, REGIONAL MANAGER: ALL-AMERICAN MEAT &

POULTRY, INC. On top was a smiling cartoon turkey, the company logo. Ollie showed me a printed ice list for cuts of meat a customer could buy frozen, a six-months supply at a time. "We help clients sign up for a major credit card, for the payments. It's a breeze!" His hand made a soothing wave in the air. "Just now, I'm expanding the sales force. I figure you could ace a job like this."

"Me? Come on—I've never been in any kind of business!" At Cornell, the university at the top of the hill I now sat at the bottom of, I'd majored in English.

"Just think it over—Ollie reached across the table and gave my shoulder a squeeze.

I spent the next three weeks trying to keep from thinking over Ollie's offer. All day, grayish snow piled on my apartment window sills, trying to seal me in. I scribbled late into the nights, filled my waste basket with wadded-up paper. Finally I read my bank book. It had the most appalling plot I'd ever seen.

The All-American Meat & Poultry company's sign was on a road in corn-stubbled country where farmhouses leaned precariously against the frozen sky. Once the sign had announced the titles of drive-in movies, and the screen still stood high on a snow-dusted field, a blank billboard. Rows of rusted speaker-poles stood like an orchard of denuded dwarf trees. The popcorn stand had been replaced by a low cinderblock building. In Ollie's office, a semi-circle of folding chairs waited around his desk.

"Take a look at this beauty! It just came today." He pointed to a black-dialed steel safe set like an altar against the wall. It squatted waist-high on four sturdy legs, the door locked tight.

I tapped the top with my knuckles. "Solid," I said.

"For sure." Ollie stood up and lumbered toward the door. "Come on, I'll show you your office."

It was one of six cinderblock cubes furnished with metal desks and chairs he'd picked up at an auction for a terrific price. Through the window, Ollie pointed to the storage building. Its lockers would fill up as soon as the sales force began bringing in orders.

"Where is everybody?" I asked. It was very quiet out here.

"The fellows I interviewed, well, they haven't called back yet. So just for now, it's you and me—straight commission." Ollie handed me a some brochures with photos of steaks, chops, chickens and of course, golden roast turkeys. "Start with questions." He pointed to the phone on my desk. "It's a survey. You ask, 'Do you like steak? Would you like to save money?' Get them answering 'yes' over and over, so when you ask them if they'd like to set up an appointment, 'yes' is the first word that jumps into their mind."

Learning the pitch was easy. I dialed Mrs. Aadling, the first name in the directory, picturing a plump Scandinavian housewife with a long, blonde braid. "I got a load in the dryer," she said. Clunk, bzzzzzzzzzz: the lady vanished. I dialed the next name, Aalvag, and a man said he had a cousin who'd lost his shirt with a wholesale food outfit in Arizona. A few people told me to go fuck myself before hanging up. Clunk! Clunk! Bzzz! Dial tones swarmed, hornets scraping my eardrums raw with their wings. Then, startlingly, a man said he'd be willing to "hear me out" at his house, but for "not a millisecond" longer than fifteen minutes. Smiling, I leaned back in my chair, holding the phone as if I were shaking a maraca in a dance band.

I figured that only professors used words like "millisecond." Damn—suppose he'd taught me years ago and now asked me why someone with my education was selling frozen meat? To his house I wore ironed slacks and a sports jacket no one could tell came from a thrift shop. My rusted car, which looked as if it had a bad case of eczema, stayed parked well out of sight as I walked up the man's drive with my Get-Acquainted Special Gift package of bacon. He really was a professor, but fortunately I'd never taken his courses. In his Danish modern living room, he tried for two hours to prove my deals were phony, and when he couldn't, left my contract unsigned and showed me out, chuckling. "Well, a pleasure meeting you."

"The pleasure was all yours," I said, and stepped off his doorstep into the slush.

That week, though, I closed two deals. I was on the team, which had expanded; Ollie hired three more "associates," as he called us. "Smart-dressing quality guys—like you!" He gave my forearm a squeeze.

My clients weren't dissatisfied with the meat they'd already been buying, so I needed to convince them that their whole lives would improve significantly if they signed up with AAMP Inc. A Chilean graduate student liked my price lists he could check off without having to stumble over English words at the supermarket. An elderly piano teacher loved having food delivered to her home in treacherous winter weather. On my appointments, when I saw sports equipment in a house, I talked about hockey games I'd made a point of reading about in the morning paper. I studied the TV schedule, too, though I didn't own a set, so I could ask people with big-screen consoles how they'd liked a show the night before. It was fun playing new characters in different scenarios.

The new salesmen liked sitting around the office talking and munching sugar doughnuts. "I guess I ought to boot these fellows out on the road," Ollie said. "But Charlie's just lost custody of both his kids. And Bob's wife's had to go back for more chemo." He sighed. "You got to give the sales force some encouragement. Isn't that what we all need?"

It was what a new guy called Lester needed, Ollie told me one day. Lester was a spade-faced man in a pale green sports jacket with matching socks. He'd worked in truck sales, but not for a few years. "I need you to show him the ropes," Ollie said. "You're my number one closer."

"I didn't know that!" And after only a month I was being trusted to train a new man. I said I'd do it.

On the evening Lester and I were to go out on an appointment together, he rattled up to the office in an old car finned like an overweight space ship. Stepping out, Lester combed back his hair into a duck-tail the way kids in an early rock-'n'-roll movies did. Close up, though, he looked about forty-five, with pitted skin. My car's dashboard lights turned his jacket the tint of pond algae. As we rode along, his lips moved silently as if he were having an argument with himself that he wasn't winning.

"What was it like selling trucks?" I asked finally.

"Who told you I sold trucks?" His eyes darted sideways at me. "It was truck accessories."

I said I didn't know what "truck accessories" were. For twenty minutes, he told me. They were the big rubber mud guards embossed with silhouettes of kneeling naked girls that swung behind the back tires of eighteen wheelers. They were the orange flame decals on the sides of the cabs. They were those funny bumper stickers that said, If you don't like my driving, dial 1-800-FUCK YOU. (Lester said "F-blank-blank-blank you.") "That's what truck accessories are, man."

We rode on in silence. The marbled sky stained iced-over fields a purplish red. Then they vanished as the sun burrowed behind a long stand of pines.

"Nothing but wide open spaces and hillbillies out here." Lester shivered, rubbing his forearms. "It's freaky—no sounds, nothing. One of these hillbillies could run you through with a pitchfork and nobody'd ever know. But I'll be okay." He patted the side of his sports jacket.

I glanced at him. "What've you got there?"

He pulled aside the jacket and slipped a pistol from the waistband of his slacks.

"Holy shit!" I skidded onto the shoulder, just missing some posts. The gun barrel poked out of Lester's hand like a ferret's nose. "Listen, you can't bring that inside with us!"

"Just protection, man. I never hurt nobody. I'm a good citizen, word is bond." He slipped the pistol into his pants again. "We almost there yet?"

We were. Silhouettes of trailers appeared up ahead: Meadowlands Court. I pulled over onto the frozen grass, sweat beading the back of my neck. "You leave that thing in the car, or we don't go in," I said. "When I tell Ollie tomorrow why we didn't keep this appointment, you're out of a job. You want that?"

Lester sat straight, his leg jiggling. Up ahead, the headlight beams glittered on slivers of ice along a wire fence. "All right, all right." In a movement too fast for me to see clearly, one of his hands yanked opened the glove compartment, the other hand dove in and out of it. He slammed it shut. "Let's go!"

In the trailer park, shutters clanked against metal sidings, protesting the biting wind. I rang the buzzer at #9, and the customer, Mrs. Everett—I was into the E's by now—opened the door. A wave of heated air and cinnamon scent rushed at me. The woman wore a house coat over blue jeans. Her heavy glasses seemed to make her lean forward. I introduced myself but she didn't step back to let me in.

"My husband's asleep. I can't sign no papers without his say-so."

"That's okay, Mrs. Everett." It wasn't, really, but I wanted to get inside "Would you mind if I brought along my associate, Mr., uh, Lester?"

Lester stood at attention, the padded shoulders of his sports jacket making him look like a green action-figure toy. "I'm glad to make your acquaintance, ma'am," he said, and stuck out his hand.

A smile crossed Mrs. Everett's face. She shook Lester's hand and let us in. Two teenage girls were draped over an armchair staring at a huge television screen where kids in gold outfits were tormenting screams out of electric guitars. I knew I wasn't going to sell a single pork chop—Ollie had warned me about this—if I couldn't get that TV turned down. Mrs. Everett brought us to a small, worn couch next to the set. Lester and I squeezed in. I felt his leg jiggling beside me.

"You boys like some coffee?" Mrs. Everett asked.

"Thank you, that'd be great," I said.

"Yeah, me, too." Lester glanced around the room without moving his head.

One of the girls squinted up at her mother. "Who're these dudes?"

"Salesmen," Mrs. Everett said.

"They come to the wrong place," the other girl said. "We're broke."

"You're rude, is what you are," their mother said. "Now move your butts on out of here and get your homework done!"

With surprisingly little argument, the kids disappeared down a corridor beside the kitchen area. Lester jumped up and sat down hard in the vacated chair. A deer-shaped china lamp rocked on the end table beside him. Mrs. Everett brought in two steaming mugs of coffee for us. I told her I was having some trouble with my hearing, and she silenced the set. She liked the frozen meat deal but had questions. I'd learned that the quickest way to ruin a customer's confidence in me was to say, "I don't know." So if she asked something I didn't have an answer for—"Where do the turkeys come from?"—I reassured her with a creative answer—"A big farm up near Syracuse. Beautiful country up there for raising poultry."

Mrs. Everett was especially eager to hear about the Master Card I would help her apply for. "Sometimes at stores," she said, "when the clerks ask if it'll be charge or cash? They look down their long noses at us when we pull out cash."

"It ain't right, people doing you that way." Lester suddenly leaned forward in his chair.

I could see she was startled, but she nodded. "That's true, mister."

I said, "Lester, let me tell Mrs. Everett about how we back up card applications for our customers."

"Heck, you don't got to get snooty with me—" Lester leaned back in the chair. His elbow struck the spotted Bambi lamp. Its face looked shocked as it toppled backwards off the table, smashing to the floor. "I'm *sorry!*" he fell to his knees, gathering up the pieces of china. His face was contorted into a grimace, the points of the sideburns sucked into his cheeks. When Mrs. Everett brought a dustpan and broom, he tried to push some dollar bills into her hand.

She backed away. "For Heaven's sake—don't worry!"

I heard a deep laugh from the kitchen. "That was th'ugliest damn lamp we ever had!"

We all turned. A mountain of a man in bib overalls stood there. Lester slapped his hand to his side. Suddenly I knew that he hadn't left his pistol in the glove compartment of my car.

"How do you do, Mr. Everett?" I stepped between Lester and the husband, my hand out. "I'm Edward, from All-American Meat and Poultry. Your wife probably told you we'd be dropping by—"

"She didn't tell me nothing!" Mr. Everett shook my hand, his flesh hard against mine. "We don't need to buy whatever it is you got."

His family was suddenly shouting about credit cards. Without them, Mrs. Everett insisted, they'd have to keep buying things at garage sales. The stuff was dusty. There'd been bugs in a mattress they'd had to spray a dozen times. The two kids chimed in: if the family had a credit card like everybody else in the whole country, they could go into K-Mart, they could pick out a nice living room set. And a TV that got more than two channels. Finally Mr. Everett sank onto the couch with his hands over his ears. His wife dropped the contract into his lap.

"You better sign this, Randy," she said, "if you ever want any of that cake I just made."

Suddenly everything smelled like cinnamon. Randy turned to me. "Where do I put the signature?"

On the ride back, Lester sat rigid. "You're just mad because of the gun," he said finally. "Okay, so I didn't leave it in the car."

"You lied."

"So who doesn't? Turkeys in Syracuse, beautiful poultry country?" He waved his hand in front of his face as if he'd just smelled a fart.

"If you can't tell the difference between lying and creative..." Never mind—I was sure Ollie would fire Lester as soon as I told him what had happened, so there was no point in arguing with this jerk. We passed a school where kids were playing basketball in a flood-lit playground. Out of the corner of my eye, I spotted Lester slipping the pistol from his waist band.

"I'll let you in on something," he said as he cranked down the window. "It ain't even loaded. Look here—" He sighted along the top of the gun barrel at the kids on the court.

"Hey!—" I rammed my foot down hard on the accelerator.

Click!—click!—click! went the gun. "I told you." Lester sat back in the seat, smiling.

"Will you put that fucking thing away!" I pictured the kids screaming to their coach about the man in the car with a pistol—a description of my car going out on police radios—roadblocks, flashing red lights ahead.... I swerved down a side street; the tires screeched against the asphalt.

"Slow down, man—you don't want to get a ticket!" Lester said. "And watch your language, will you?"

When I phoned Ollie he said he'd have a serious talk with Lester. "Ollie, you're not going to keep him on, are you?" I asked. I wanted to tell him: If you keep Lester, I go. But I didn't have anywhere to go.

"Trust me, pal, I'll take care of things. But hey—" Ollie's voice had that familiar happy boom again. "Congratulations—what a terrific closing!"

The next afternoon, the usual gang of salesmen—minus Lester—were eating Ollie's doughnuts and filling his office with guffaws and cigarette smoke. I went straight to my cinderblock cube to make calls. Then I heard the word "Everett" from Ollie's office. "N.G.—*again?*" he said into the phone.

I rang him to ask what this meant. He came over and stood in my doorway, his belly sagging in the purple sweater. "N.G., they're the hardest letters in the alphabet a salesman can hear," he said. "They mean No Good—the client's got a bad credit rating."

"So if the Everetts don't qualify for the credit card, the meat sale's cancelled?" I asked.

Ollie sighed. "I haven't wanted to tell you these things when you were just starting out."

"So this isn't the first time one of my sales didn't go through?" He shook his head slowly. He had dark bags under his eyes today. "But you've been paying me my commissions," I said.

"Got to keep up sales force morale."

I slouched farther down in my chair. Six of the eleven closings I'd made, Ollie confessed, had come back N.G. This was happening to the other fellows, too. Something had to be done.

I phoned Mrs. Everett to tell her that she didn't qualify for a credit card, apologizing over and over again. In a flat voice she told me not to worry, it wasn't the first time. I started to thank her again for her coffee and cake, but she'd soundlessly put down the receiver.

Only one of the next six families I signed up in Meadowlands Court came back N.G. Ollie peeled off bills for my commission. "Big changes coming up around here!" he said, his cheeks puffing out in a smile.

He called a "Sales Motivation Meeting" in his office. I was surprised to see Lester there. None of the associates looked any more like winners than he did. Many were overweight—not mountainous and jolly like Ollie, but squashy-faced, with close-set eyes like marbles pushed into dough. There were shiny suits and stained neckties, vein-mapped boozers' noses and comb-overs. Ollie was talking to a new man who had the office next to his; I saw framed photos on the desk. He was the smallest person in the room. Also the best dressed: a three piece maroon suit, off-white tie with white shirt, and half-boots with pointy toes. He stepped into the center of the semi-circle of chairs. All conversations stopped.

"Hello, men," he said, "I'm Jefferson Allen Farly—Jeff, to you—and I'm your new sales manager. From now on, I'm the one who keeps track of your work." He pointed a short, varnished stick at a white board where *Sales Associates of the Month* was written in blue marker. "I'm also the man who pays your commissions and..." He paused. "...writes your salary checks."

The salesmen all smiled. We must be doing great if we offered salaries now, someone whispered.

Slipping his pointer under his arm like a swagger stick, he lit a thin cigar. "From now on, you're going to be earning like you never did before!" He passed around a new list of meat prices.

I could see that all our products now cost significantly more. Nobody else seemed to notice. "These prices are going to make selling a lot harder," I said.

"I doubt it, Edward. They're still below what a lot of supermarkets charge." Hearing Jeff speak my name made me grit my teeth. I glanced at Ollie in the doorway. He was watching Jeff and nodding.

The sales manager had a surprisingly deep voice for his size; it sounded as if it came out of an expensive speaker system. He knew, he said, what a pain in the ass it was making cold calls to set up appointments. So from now on, those calls here were history. "We're too professional an outfit for that Mickey-Mouse shit—right?" The salesman burst into clapping. Jeff said he'd hired a firm of "solid professionals" to make calls for us. We'd pay a small amount—to be determined—out of our salaries for them. "Each time a call leads to a sale, the call's a freebie for you. But let's be up front. Anyone who don't like the new arrangements, he's free to drive away right now!" Jeff shoved the office door open wide. Cold air rushed in. No one moved.

He shut the door shut and used both palms to smooth down his hair; the sides had been blow-dried and looked like bantam rooster wings. His voice lost its edginess; he was our friend now. He knew how hard our jobs could be, he said, but how rewarding, too—once we learned to really believe in ourselves. He moved around the desk and sat in Ollie's chair. The springs gave off a rippling chord.

"I'm thirty-four years old," he said. "And I been selling since I was seventeen. Now I'm earning a good living for me and my family. I got three kids, and they'll never want for nothing the way I did coming up—never! You know how I know that?" He rocked forward. "It's because I believe...in my ability...to understand what people need!" He paused. "And you know what people need more than anything?"

Jeff tried to let a silence hang, but Lester jumped in. "Prime ribs!" he said, grinning.

"Hell, yes—but more than that. Something much bigger." Jeff stared at Lester, who seemed to be holding his breath. "Hope, my friend!"

The men nodded.

"How many of you've spent time in New York City?" Jeff asked. Everyone but me looked as if he'd asked if they'd visited Saturn. "Well, I'm telling you, there's no place that's harder to sell in than New York City!"

He took out an ironed handkerchief and wiped his forehead. "Okay, here's a story, men. I was twenty years old, and the territory assigned me was called Spanish Harlem. As you can picture, there weren't a lot of people on those streets that looked like me." He touched his white cheek. "But I banged on doors all along those dark and dingy tenement hallways. I stuck my feet in those doors—" He pushed out one of his boots—"and by God, I got orders. Week after week! Now how did I manage that?" Jeff focused on the red ember at the end of his cigar. "Okay, I'll tell you. I remember one day a lady called Mrs. Rodriguez opened her door a crack. Behind her I could see a bunch of other Puerto Ricans sitting on a long couch. I kept looking until I saw the right person—the one I wanted to sell. Her name was Maria. Eighteen years old. She had long black hair and big eyes and a smooth, sweet face. I had something very special for Maria, and I was determined she was going to have it!" Jeff pressed his lips together and nodded.

"I was representing a school that trained air hostesses," he went on. "That outfit guaranteed its graduates interviews with the best airlines in the United States of America. When I said that to all those Rodriguezes, I saw Maria's face light up like a sunrise. But her mama kept telling me, 'We got no money, mister!'" Jeff smiled. "Did I let that stop me? *Hell*, no! My pitch rolled on. It spun round and round. I'm telling you, men, it was like a carousel glittering with colored lights and singing like a calliope. But my song wasn't about spinning, it was about flying. It told Maria and her Mama all about the amazing future the girl would have high up above the clouds!

"'Maria, can you picture one of those big planes taking off?' I asked her. 'And can you picture the women in charge of the passengers on that plane, those women in their dignified blue uniforms with the silver wings right there on the lapels?'" Jeff squeezed his own lapel between his thumb and forefinger. "'Now, Maria, those women are going places—important places! San Juan, Caracas, Buenos Aires!'" I could already see the bright lights of the cities shining in her eyes. 'That's you, Maria—flying off in that sleek silver plane into the sky-blue heavens!'" Every man in the room watched Jeff's hand swoop up, up, up.

"'But mister, we got no money!' Mama said. I just smiled at her and kept talking about that training course—learning to help mothers change their little babies, even learning how save a passenger's life if one of them got a heart attack. 'Do you think you could save a person's life, Maria? Do you think you could wear that uniform?'" Maria gripped the school brochure tight. Everyone crowded around her to look at the pictures of proud women in their beautiful blue skirts and blazers.

"I gave them all a brochure—grand-dad in his undershirt and granny in her black dress and even the kids. I'm telling you, I *smelled* the excitement in that room! I knew I had what that family needed to get out of that dingy tenement! I had hope for them! And Maria had hope, now, too. She *was* that family's hope! She was going to fly them to a whole new life!" Jeff whacked his fist into his palm. "And men, *hope* is the most powerful thing in the world you are selling. Once people glimpse it, they have to *have* it!"

He took a deep breath. "Well, you know what happened? Mama and grand-dad and granny and all those Rodriguezes shoved their couch away from the wall. And right behind it...." Jeff squinted sideways, and the salesmen did, too. "...hidden in that bare plaster wall—was a hole! Mama reached in...and out came a nylon stocking that was stuffed with money! There were twenties and fifties and even hundreds. Maria gazed up at me and said, 'That's Mama's whole life savings, mister.' I looked her straight in the eye, and you know what I told her?" The corners of Jeff's mouth rose. *"'You're worth every cent, honey!'"*

Soon the phoning service in Omaha, Nebraska, started setting up appointments for me, but I still didn't know how much I was paying for them. When I went to the office, Ollie was often out and Jeff was busy interviewing new salesmen. Once, I looked through the window and saw him sitting beside an elfin blonde child—his daughter, I assumed. She wore a neat jacket and vest, like his, with a plaid skirt and patent leather shoes. He held her hand steady as she reached out to deal him a card from a deck on his desk.

I hit a string of No-Sales. At my appointments, people were stubborn, distrustful, rude. On the first of the month, no paycheck was in my drawer. When I phoned Ollie's house, his wife, Fiona, said he'd delegated the book-keeping part of the job to Jeff. Ollie was out on appointments just now.

"What's going on?" I asked. "He's supposed to be running the place."

"Oh, you know how he loves selling!" Fiona laughed.

On my next trip to the office I found it empty. On the *Associates of the Month* wall-board, the thirteen salesmen's names were written in grease pencil, eight more since Jeff had become sales manager. #1 was awarded a rib roast bonus, #2 a pork roast, and #3—me—a frozen chicken. A damned chicken! I remember all the times Ollie had cooked me big steaks. Now I had to *compete* for these bonuses? What bothered me more, though I didn't want to admit it, was that I'd slipped to #3. Lester was #13. Lester? I phoned Ollie's house again. Fiona said he was laid up with a migraine. As soon as he was better, he'd be in touch, for sure.

Two days later, I found a check and a statement in my drawer. I'd been charged $25 each for eleven appointments, only two of which I'd closed on. This meant nine calls were deducted from my monthly salary, bringing it down to $12.28. Through a window in Jeff's office door I saw him sitting back in a black leather chair. I knocked hard and pushed open his door. He scrambled to his feet.

"You don't walk into my office like that, Edward," he said, quickly hanging up his phone.

"I don't like the way you did my check, *Jeff*. The $25 you charged me per appointment call."

"I didn't charge you. The company we use charges everybody."

"I don't want to use that company's set-ups. I'll make my own."

"Not any more. It's our policy now—the sales force is out selling, not hanging around the office making phone calls and eating doughnuts." He narrowed his eyes at me, as if spotting crumbs on my jacket. "Changes have to be made if an outfit's going to keep operating. You went to college, you ought to know that." Jeff picked up the phone. "You got an appointment in twenty minutes. Good luck with it, Edward."

I didn't like that he knew my schedule, but I did have to leave. Turning on my heels, I headed for the parking lot. I called Ollie's house again later. Fiona told me he was down with another migraine, his fourth that month, but he'd be going into the office very soon. When I drove in the next day, only Lester's weird vehicle and Jeff's Cadillac were in the lot. From my front seat I saw Lester step outside and slam the office door. His face was drained, his teeth clenched hard. I noticed his bare arms in his short-sleeved shirt; they were tattooed with filigreed, homemade crosses, the kind that men in prison take months to make. He walked over to my car.

"I worked my tail off for this outfit! Ollie'd never of canned me!" Lester heaved a sigh. "Hey listen, man, I want to thank you for not saying nothing to Ollie about, you know, the pistol." He leaned forward to talk softly through my window. "I ain't supposed to even own one."

Shit! After what I'd told Ollie about the gun, he'd not only kept the guy on, but had never even spoken to him about it! "That's okay, Lester," I managed to say. "But why don't you ditch the pistol now?"

"Because what if I need it?"

I couldn't answer that.

He squared his shoulders. "I'll tell you something, maybe help you out, too," he said. "You remember the story Jeff told—about selling that training course to the Puerto Rican girl?"

Something like a toad jumped in my chest. "It wasn't true?"

"Jeff made the sale to her, all right. But one time when Ollie wasn't around, I heard Jeff telling the guys—that stewardess school never got a single interview with an airlines for its girls, including Maria."

I dropped my forehead hard against the steering wheel.

"I told Jeff I didn't think much of this. He says to me, 'But the point is, you got to believe in yourself—even if what you're selling don't even exist! You'll never be a salesman if you can't understand that.'" Lester shook his head. "I guess he could tell I couldn't understand it. 'Cause here I am—outa work again." He reached out his hand. "Well, anyway—good luck, man."

"Lester, same to you." I reached up and shook his hand.

He got into his huge vehicle. It careened off toward the big movie screen, tires skidding. The bumper mowed down half a dozen rusted speaker-poles with loud clangs that made me grin. Then Lester peeled off toward the road.

On the phone, Fiona told me that Ollie had gone to bed right after dinner. He'd be in the office first thing tomorrow. In my apartment, I scribbled away all night taking notes for sketches of Ollie, Jeff, Lester, Mrs. Everett. This was the best work I'd done in a very long time. One person was still missing, though. I wanted to keep writing my way toward him, but as light flooded my window, I sensed I still didn't have what I needed to make him appear on paper. Finally I put down my pen and drove to the office as fast as my clattering car would go.

Snow was melting all along the fields, leaving stripes of damp earth beside the road. In the strange quiet I heard a sound I'd almost forgotten existed—the chittering of birds. Several were perched like spectators on the remaining speaker-poles. Ollie's Camaro was parked at a strange angle. I stared at a boxy police cruiser beyond it.

Ollie slumped at his desk when I walked in. Then he dropped his head into his hands. Two state troopers in gray uniforms faced him in folding chairs munching doughnuts, wide-brimmed hats resting on their knees. At first, Ollie's office looked the same as always. Then I saw the bright new safe. Its door gaped open.

"Ollie?" I asked. "Did Jeff….?"

"He took it all." Ollie's fingers slid away from his eyes. They were shiny wet. "The funny thing is, I don't know how much was in the safe. I keep telling these fellows"—He nodded at the troopers "—I hadn't been keeping real good track of the books. I know we had a lot of checks from the credit card company to pay for meat the new customers ordered."

"Farly cashed all the checks this morning, in Syracuse," one of the policemen said. ("Beautiful poultry country," I recalled.) "You'd signed a form authorizing him to do that, Mr. O'Flanagan."

"I guess I did." Ollie nodded slowly. His purple sweater stretched up his belly.

"Doesn't Master Card know what they sent us?" I wanted to smash his desk-top to get his attention.

"They said they're missing about $11,000, so far." Ollie's voice was wobbly. "We'd been doing terrific sales since Jeff came on." He shut his eyes tight. "Oh, Jesus—none of my men are going to get paid, now! You, either, Edward. I'm so damn sorry!"

A groan caught in my throat. It was his face I felt like smashing, but the way his eyelids were quivering made me shove my fists deep into my pockets. "I've got a little money saved," I said.

"The people you sold to won't get their food orders," he said. "The company still owns most of them, what we haven't got stored in our lockers—"

"Aw, *shit!*" I slumped down in a chair. "Can't we make it up to them—after future sales?"

"Our franchise's credit's N.G., big time." Ollie sighed. "That's why I hired Jeff. He was sort of a specialist in rescuing businesses."

"I bet he was."

"This wasn't Farley's first job," one of the troopers said. "We pulled up his record."

"Oh, God!" Ollie dug his fingers into his scalp, his black curls writhing.

"Never mind," I said. "Try and take it easy now."

I answered the troopers' questions, then got my things from my office. Outside the window, the huge blank screen stared back at me from the hillside. I could see tufts of grass poking up around the base.

The police cruiser drove off. Ollie climbed slowly into his Camaro. I walked over to the driver's side and gave his shoulder a squeeze. He turned to stare up at me.

"I got to tell Fiona." His voice croaked with fatigue. "I guess she won't be too surprised. I've been awful tense lately. It's been hard on her."

"She told me about your headaches."

"I had some bad ones. Throwing up, flashing lights. But you know what?" He rested his palm down carefully on top of his curls. "The migraine—it's completely gone!"

"Maybe its name was Jeff."

"Hey, that could be!" He smiled. "I think I'll get Fiona some flowers." He started the engine with a roar. "We'll stay in touch, pal. For sure."

"For sure, Ollie."

And then—I don't know how he managed it, squashed as tight as he was into the seat—he gave me one of his great shrugs: head bonked to one side, both palms rising into the air.

As I listened to the Camaro's engine fade, the fresh smell of damp earth blew in across the fields. I backed my car around the storage building. On the meat lockers' shelves were frozen paper-wrapped packages of beef and pork loins. They banged like rocks as I tossed them into my trunk, knocking rust-flakes loose. I filled most of my front seat with turkeys, leaving just enough room for me behind the wheel.

At Meadowlands Court, I stacked meat and poultry on my customers' doorsteps. What I left would last the families a few weeks. After their full orders failed to appear and nobody answered their phone calls to the office, they'd probably forget the whole deal.

I never did. I still remember the feel of thawing paper in my fingers as I piled up the parcels.

ECHOES

When I first performed on the opera stage, strumming a faux-mandolin with painted strings, the palatial new homes of the Met and the New York City Opera had just opened to blaring media fanfare, glaring at one other across a corner of Lincoln Center's plaza. The Met had Chagall murals two stories tall and acres of red velvet on its swooping staircases; the New York State Theater, NYCO's site where I appeared, was a glittery glass and cement box whose lobby was guarded by a two white marble giantesses melting into one another like vanilla ice cream cones. But the Met had a colossal flop on its opening night, and we had Beverly Sills, whose Cleopatra in Handel's *Julius Caesar* was making her, at 37, an overnight sensation.

Arriving for my first rehearsal, I explored the theater's subterranean maze of corridors. They reverberated with the sounds of pianos plinking, carpenters hammering, and most thrillingly, singers vocalizing in scales that leapt and fell like the plumes of water in the fountain outside in the plaza. Passing one studio, I watched a slim, white-haired woman rehearse a row of dancers prancing in slow motion like beautiful greyhounds. In a warehouse-sized room, painters in overalls transformed plywood frames into an oriental temple.

When I spotted a door marked "Auditorium: Do Not Enter," I had to slip through it. Inside, only a few dim lights were on; I groped my way toward a seat and stared up at the walls of a shadowy canyon, tiers of boxes rising in what looked like layers of crimson shale. The curtain, rippling up to a flat sky, gave off a golden glow as if the sun were rising behind it. The scents of perfume and plush upholstery hovered. The amphitheater was not so much empty as resonating with a prolonged hush; I was sure I could hear the echoes of voices floating out over the seats. And of the footsteps of singers and dancers and supernumeraries—"supers" like me—moving like spirits up there on the stage.

My performing career had begun when I'd sung in Greenwich Village coffee houses; it later soared with my appearances on Voice of Kenya Television's "Sunday Star Time" shows. But recently it had gone into a tailspin, along with the rest of my life. Like a lot of former Peace Corps volunteers, I'd come back to America with no idea what to do with myself. In a Lower East Side tenement, I lived in a fourth floor walkup across the hall from an actor couple and a rock drummer who headed a local Communist Party branch and his girlfriend who illustrated underground magazines—sort of like *La Bohème* with sizzling radiators. During my three years teaching in Africa, performing had been a welcome sideline, an inspiration as I happily struggled to write a novel. The finished book became my life's proudest accomplishment—until it was rejected by every publisher I approached in New York.

Now all my characters, including my flamboyant heroine, wailed at me night and day to save them from premature burial. My family pressured me to get a real job and earn decent money. But I held out, living on part-time tutoring work and agonizing over how I might rewrite my novel. After midnight, I obsessively practiced my guitar—but for what? While I'd been overseas, most of the performers I'd hung around the Village with, like Bob Dylan, had either moved up to bigger venues, or had vanished into what I dreaded was real life.

My actor neighbors, recently stars in an Iowa Shakespeare troupe, were also in crisis, waiting tables in a dive called The Fat Pussycat while they hoped, mostly in vain, for audition call-backs.

Roger got so desperate to walk onto a floodlit stage that he signed up for a non-singing role at the NYCO. The next day, though, he found work playing a troll in a New Jersey children's theater, and asked me if I'd mind taking his spot.

I'd been an opera aficionado from the age of 16 when my favorite uncle—the family black sheep who played piano at cocktail parties and had a "roommate"—took me to the old Met on 39th Street. During college, I'd waited in snowstorms for standing-room tickets. In rural Kenya, I'd once climbed steep mountain paths to a village where another teacher owned Beverly Sill's first album, which we played over and over on a plastic phonograph until the batteries ran down. Would I *mind* performing in an *opera?* I was at Lincoln Center early the next afternoon.

The other supers, I soon noticed, referred to singers by their last names, except for "our" star whom everyone called Beverly. On records, her light, soaring voice had an endearing quality that made me feel close to her before I'd even seen her. The moment her laughter rippled outside the rehearsal room, the waiting cast and crew stopped talking in mid-sentence. I understood why the press had nicknamed her Bubbles; her laughter created a champagne-tinted mist that transformed that cavernous space into an intimate salon where she was about to take over as hostess, belle-of-the-ball, den mother—who could tell? But we were sure it was going to be fun.

She walked in holding sheet music in one hand and a cardboard coffee cup in the other. Unable to see her face at first, I gazed into her incandescent hair, a red-blonde aura that rippled like soft feathers. When she turned to greet the supers and chorus, her features lit up, her round cheeks glowed.

"Hi, everyone! Thanks for coming!"

A few people started to applaud, but she flapped her sheet music in the air to shush them, her smile widening.

"Look," someone whispered in my ear—a man called Horace. He seemed much older than the other supers in a threadbare suit jacket and silk cravat; the rest of us wore jeans and open-neck shirts. "It's all put on!"

I whispered back, "What is?"

"Beverly's constant cheeriness. Don't you see?"

No, I didn't. I was as smitten as everyone else and had no idea why this stranger was confiding his weird opinion to me. He slipped away, shooting me a glance that caught in my eye like a gnat.

I concentrated on the director, who sketched out the opera for us. *Abduction from the Seraglio* was one of Mozart's less frequently performed works, he intoned, but nonetheless contained some of his loveliest melodies, especially the famous aria, *Martern aller Arten*. At the drama's opening, Belmonte, a Spanish nobleman—he pointed to the lead tenor, who clapped one fist nobly to his shoulder—is searching for his lost fiancée Constanze—here Beverly clasped both hands to her breast, rolling her eyes toward the heavens—who has been kidnapped by pirates and sold into slavery to a Turkish pasha, Selim. The pasha was played by a tall, bald man who stared grumpily over everyone's heads, refusing to smile even when a few people started a stage-hiss. Beverly gave him a quizzical look and shrugged.

"*Oy!*"

This broke the tension. From then on, the rehearsal moved along quickly. Singers, chorus members, and supers were shown their positions along taped lines on the floor. The lead tenor and Beverly *da-da-da*'d their parts quietly to save their voices. But in the final act, Pedrillo, Belmonte's manservant, tried out his complete love-song beneath the window of Constanze's maid, Blondchen (called Blonde in this English-language production; Beverly pronounced it "Blondie" in the Brooklyn accent she lapsed into occasionally.) I joined the cast's applause as the young singers bowed.

On the evening of the first production, I stepped into a big, busy dressing room: metal lockers, shower stalls, rows of dressing tables with oval mirrors topped by horseshoes of carnival-like light bulbs. The supers rushed around, some pulling off neckties, some stepping toweled out of showers. Amid all the steam, the place echoed like a tropical rainforest, everyone humming opera tunes in twittery falsettos or frog-like *basso profundos*. I tapped the shoulder of a man in what looked like tuxedo pants. He turned sharply: Horace again. His hair was grey at the temples; his craggy face might have appeared distinguished except for a red-pocked drinker's nose. I told him I was subbing for Roger and asked if he knew where I was supposed to go.

He squinted at me, evidently not recalling we'd spoken before. "Christ! Why aren't you *shorter?*" His baritone resonated across the room. "You'll have to be re-measured for a robe!"

"Not your *prob*lem, Horace!" sang a guy from the showers. "You were de*mo*ted!"

"*Dem-ohh-ted!*" chorused several men shaving at the sinks.

"Fuck you, one and all," Horace muttered, and pointed me toward a corner locker. "Over there, whoever you are," he said, and walked off.

A curly-haired man stepped up to introduce himself as Rudy; he had my locker combination. Like my neighbor, Roger, he was a sporadically-employed actor. I asked him if the other supers were actors, too. "A few are. Most of them are dedicated opera lifers." They clerked in music stores, he said, and arranged their hours so they could rush over to Lincoln Center for rehearsals and performances. "Since my boyfriend started here, he's in such a daze he's forgotten how to ring up a cash register."

I nodded, but—in these days before gay acceptance—I had to hide my surprise at hearing a man talk openly about "my boyfriend." I realized that, for the first time in my life, I was probably the only straight guy in the place. It was a little like the feeling I'd had on my first day in an African schoolroom, an uneasiness that had vaporized quickly—as I had a feeling it would here—when I became too involved in my new work to think about it.

What Can You Do

"Don't mind Horace, by the way." Rudy twirled his finger beside his head. "He used to be in charge of the supers. Strutted around this place barking at everybody. Then he missed some rehearsals, and I got his slot. Which is mostly just doing roll calls and handing out pay envelopes at the end of the run."

"So why does he think the position's such a big deal?"

"I heard he was a Broadway star years ago, but he hit the skids. This gig is all he's got left."

Roger had lent me a stage make-up kit, but I had no idea what to do with the creams and powders I found inside. Rudy showed me how to put on a mud-colored foundation, terra-cotta blush, then dark eye-liner. "Don't worry, no one's really going to notice us on stage. All this—" his powder brush traced a flourish in the air. "is just part of the fantasy, a perk of the job."

"It doesn't feel like a job," I said.

"That's the point." He got my robe—which fit—and turban, and helped me put them on.

"*Wow!*" I grinned at the beige troubadour admiring himself in the mirror. It felt terrific becoming someone new—just as when I'd fled my family to go to Africa years before. I'd left behind an insecure kid to become not only a professional singer/musician but a novelist, as well as a high-school teacher who'd been called *Mwalimu*—a Swahili term of respect—helping to educate the first generation of post-colonial Kenyans. Back in the US, though, I was a tiny frog whom nobody noticed, let alone respected, in a huge, impersonal pond. But look at me now: this exotic character—*his flashing eyes, his floating hair*—on his way to Xanadu!

I rode upstairs with an elevator-load of humming fellow-Turks and some cartoonishly sexy harem-girls in pantaloons and pointy hats trailing clouds of gauze. Everyone was smiling with expectation, women bouncing silky bodices in rhythm to the music. We burst out in a happy scrum and dispersed into the backstage world of canvas palaces. Costumed villagers and stagehands, singers and lights-men milled around. Hoisted on cables, metal banks of lights clanked into place overhead; yellow, blue, and scarlet beams blazed down through the jells and blended into an iridescence swirling with firefly-like dust-motes. The air smelled of sweat, make-up, fresh paint. From beyond the curtain I heard violins squeak, oboes honk: the orchestra warming up.

"*Ah-ah-ah-AH!-ah-ah ahh—*" someone sang scales from a little room offstage. Then a trill, two high-notes rippling together like fluttering bird wings. A woman stood in the doorway in a long skirt and puffy blue blouse. There was that conflagration of red-gold hair—Beverly. Previously I'd been positioned a few feet from her in rehearsals, but hadn't wanted to spoil her concentration by speaking to her. Did I dare, now? I waited. Finally I strolled in front of her door.

"*Sorrow had become my lot....*" she sang. Her voice faded out.

"You sound wonderful," I said, pausing as I walked past.

She gave a slight bow of her head, her gaze far away, but for a split second, her lips parted just enough for her white overbite to shine out, a sliver of a smile.

Tripping over my robe, I continued on to the props table. When the man handed me my mandolin, I nearly dropped the thing, it was so light. Once I'd wielded a gleaming dreadnaught of an instrument, the only 12-string guitar in the Republic of Kenya; the TV studio musicians used to examine it in wonder. This mandolin felt like a papier-mâché melon. Never mind—like my costume, the instrument made me a *bona fide* cast member, and if it hadn't been so fragile, I'd have hugged it.

The standby signal was given; a hush fell over the backstage area. The overture leapt up. I stepped into my spot on stage, raised my ax into strumming position. Applause broke out as the curtains parted; a fog-bank of blinding light appeared between me and the audience. Mozart's music swelled around me. The pasha glided onstage in a wheeled boat pulled by concealed cables. Accompanying him was his prisoner, Constanze—Beverly—who stepped on shore to sing her lament to her lost love.

Off to one side, I strummed the painted-on strings of my mandolin along with the orchestra. Magically, they gave off a rhythm I could feel in my fingers—because Beverly, glancing my way, was actually keeping my beat.

In rehearsals, sung quietly, her aria had just been a pretty tune, but now its swelling notes flew into my ears and unnerved me. I'd lost a love, myself—my failed novel's heroine, no less real to me for being fictitious than Constanze's fiancé was to Beverly. Until now, operas had been sublime entertainment: outdated spectacles as the occasions for glorious music. Suddenly the soprano's clear, plaintive voice exposed my own aching sorrow. Yet the music illuminated it with such an intensity that the pain was not only bearable but something to value, even to treasure. Love's power expressed through art was never lost; it might still sustain me.

This didn't come to me whole, in a flash. All I knew was that I was overwhelmed by something important and felt an enormous gratitude for it. As the audience applauded, Beverly's lips preserved her character's sadness but her sparkling eyes revealed—to us in the cast—the joy she'd felt at expressing it so eloquently. Only when the pasha began complaining about Constanze's refusal to yield to his advances did I remember that this was a comedy, one of Mozart's lighter dramas. Some comedian, Mozart.

During an intermission, I saw Beverly chatting with the lights man at stage right. Holding her hand was a curly-haired little girl. Beverly lifted the child's chin so she could watch the banks of colored lights move high above the stage. A look of wonder broke out on the girl's face as three bright orange suns shone down from the flies.

"That's Beverly's daughter," Rudy whispered, standing behind me.

"She must love listening to her mother."

Rudy sighed. "She's never heard a note Beverly sings. The kid's deaf."

"Oh, no...." I sucked in my breath, following the child's upward gaze.

Beverly stooped beside her, face pushed into her curls as if to inhale them. Then the curtains parted. Violins plinked; in the spotlight, Belmonte and Pedrillo snuck up to the seraglio. Beverly paid no attention to them; she was miming speech to her daughter, her brow furrowed in concentration, lips stretching wide.

"She must be teaching the girl to lip-read," I said, and Rudy nodded.

Then, as Beverly straightened up, she quickly rearranged her mouth and eyebrows. Her whole face suddenly shone with her famous smile. In a single beat she stepped onto the set and broke into a lilting coloratura. Her daughter bounced on her toes as she watched her mother sweep across the stage.

More productions followed in the weeks ahead. During Act Two, when I didn't appear, I always stood in one of the wings to listen. None of us wanted to miss the great *Martern aller Arten*. As the orchestra swelled, I watched Beverly glare defiantly at the pasha, about to accept a sentence of death rather than sacrifice her integrity. The aria began. The music soared through me. Along the wings, the heads of the backstage listeners nodded as if in a trance. All eyes were half-closed, as if the sight of Beverly, her arms rising into the beam of light from above, was burning almost too brightly for us to watch as she concluded: *in death I shall...—be free!*

I heard shouts, screams, the stomping of feet amid the thunder of thousands of palms being smacked together—from the front seats to the highest boxes. It was the sound of catharsis, a release of an ecstatic tension. But the audience wasn't only bursting with admiration for Beverly's voice; nor were they just cheering for a Brooklyn girl who had, from the age of twelve as a warbler of radio commercials, finally sung her way to the very top of the musical world. They were releasing a roar of triumph for the victory of courage over tyranny. Or so I was utterly convinced. I wasn't the only one; the applause created a tremor in the house I could feel rising through me.

In the opera's finale, the pasha—played by the bad-tempered, bald man whom I'd heard arguing off-stage with Beverly—suddenly decided to release his prisoners, including Constanze and her maid, Blonde. With their lovers, the two women glided off-stage to freedom in the boat while the supers stood rigid and the chorus sang hosannas to the beneficent ruler. On the last night of *Abduction's* run, the curtain closed as Beverly was still waving in gratitude. Suddenly her tongue stuck out. She raised her middle finger to the pasha. The curtain parted again. She didn't have time to hide her gesture from the audience; I heard laughter amid the cheers. Us Turks, supposed to be staring dourly straight ahead, were breaking up. I quickly stood at attention again, looking blank. I was a pro now.

That night I went home hoping my ebullient mood would fend off the gloom of staring at my wounded novel. And it did, for a while; I even managed to re-write the first few pages. I thought my opera career was over, but early one evening, before the final, now-famous production of Handel's *Julius Caesar*, Rudy phoned. He was out of town and couldn't get back until around ten o'clock.

"I'll be there in time to hand out the payroll," he said. "But can you go on for me?"

"I haven't rehearsed it! I don't know when to make my entrances, where to go—"

"Ask the stage manager what to do. It'll be easy. And hey, there's the big cast party!"

With just an hour to get to Lincoln Center, I dashed to the subway station. The dressing room was in a state of season-finale flurry. Aisles were gridlocked with Roman soldiers in shiny breastplates. As soon as I'd stashed my clothes in my locker, I was yanked off to have my face, hands, and shins slathered with make-up. Then two wardrobe men frog-marched me into a room where I was stuffed into a leather tunic that weighed at least thirty pounds. A helmet was clamped down over my forehead, cutting off my vision just below eyebrow level.

"You're the general of Cleopatra's army," a dresser said. "And you're on in nine minutes!"

Oh, shit! As I rode the elevator up to the stage level, sweat dribbled down my legs into my clunky, silver-coated boots. Stumbling into the wings, I searched for a familiar face. There was Horace, in Egyptian military garb.

"Hey—where do I go?"

"*You're* in charge!" His voice was thick. "Wha' kind of leader of men are *you?*" He strode off.

"I've never seen Horace so pissed," one of my warriors whispered to another.

"He thought he was going to be asked to take Rudy's place tonight."

"Rudy's not here? Bad news for our side. Ptolemy's soldiers are really butch!"

I finally found the stage manager, who grabbed my arm. "Okay, pay attention. Your life depends on it!" I dashed behind him across the stage, stopping at the foot of one of two staircases that slanted down from a narrow wooden balcony. Beverly rushed by, her feet invisible in a flurry of ruffles. She'd once said in an interview that her Cleopatra costume, cinched tight at the waist and spreading in long, creamy pleats, made her look like a Victorian lampshade, and she hadn't exaggerated. Her head-gear hid her hair and was topped by two high white plumes that a performing circus pony might have worn. But reportedly she looked terrific from the house.

I managed to follow my marching orders until, after a battle scene opening Act Three, I led my troops away in retreat and found myself approaching a staircase. Was I supposed to walk around it and into the wings, or march up the steps and exit offstage left from the platform? I'd forgotten completely. My eyes stung with sweat; the scene blurred.

Up the staircase, or around it? Music and blinding lights swelled. I placed my right foot on the first step, then my left. With sinking heart, I sensed a hesitation in the soldiers behind me.

On the top step was a woman in a plumed headdress, and she seemed to be poised to descend toward my platoon. She was Cleopatra—Beverly Sills—and she was glaring straight at me. She took a step downward. Then another. Her mouth opened. And she sang—a series of high notes which pierced my leather tunic like tiny, flaming arrows.

My helmet dug into my eyebrows. I was tilting backwards, my arm rising at my side. Suddenly something stopped me—a hand gripping my shoulder. A whisper—*"About face!"* Horace.

I caught my balance. Turning very carefully, I managed to step down...and marched slowly offstage into the welcoming darkness. As the troops broke formation behind me, I stood trembling until the curtain finally closed. Then I slunk deep into the wings.

My men and I were onstage once more, standing with spears behind the chorus. I'd never heard Beverly sing as ecstatically as she did in the finale. Wild applause broke out, buffeting the scenery like a gale; I was sure I could see the side-curtains flutter and swell. On this last night, the audience didn't want to stop cheering. Bouquets of flowers flew from the boxes. Beverly gathered one armful, then another, bowing, rising, bowing. The entire cast, even chorus and supers, joined hands to pump their arms in the air.

The crew didn't want to leave. Like the others, I stayed backstage to soak up the triumphal atmosphere, breathe in the heady smells, memorize all the color and lavish costumes. I also hoped to thank Horace, but I couldn't spot him anywhere. Finally I crowded into the elevator with the other supers and we descended, all of us raucously humming snatches of arias. The metal music box plummeted through space. The doors slid open. We spilled out, still humming, and headed for the locker rooms.

Several supers mentioned that it was payday. The wages were small but they'd add up to a lot of grocery money. The first person I saw downstairs was Rudy, sitting on a bench in street clothes that made him look strange among the armored soldiers. Then I noticed that he was slumped over, head down. In front of him, his locker door gaped open, its hasp wrenched off.

"I'm sorry," he whispered, pointing to the empty locker. "I just got here a few minutes ago." "What happened?" someone asked.

"Has something been stolen?"

"The payroll." Rudy's head rose, eyes burning. "The manager put the envelopes in here before the performance."

"Damn! Someone must have used a tire-iron on that door!"

"Who?" I asked.

Everybody looked around. We were all here, weren't we? No, we weren't. I heard a name whispered—a kind of shudder: *"Horace!"* Someone said they'd seen him step into the elevator the minute we'd come off-stage. He'd been the only super who hadn't been upstairs milling around in the wings.

"God*damn* his ass!" I kicked the nearest locker. Spangles sprayed off the toe of my boot.

Someone threw a helmet; it cracked against the wall, a hollow half-sphere of cheap shiny tin. Everything looked phony now—my heavy tunic with its scruffy lining, my boots with their plastic silver trim. The Roman soldiers' armor plates made clinky noises as they dropped to the floor. The place smelled dank; the steam that billowed from the shower room felt like a heavy, hissing fog.

"Did Horace get *your* money?" a blond super asked me. "I thought you two got on okay."

In my rage I wanted to deny it. I couldn't help remembering his hand on my shoulder, though. "I guess we did," I said, finally. "But I hardly knew the poor bastard."

Silence. Supers shuffled around. The blond guy muttered, "He fucked up everything!"

"He *can't* have!" I stood up. "Hey, what about the cast party? It's still on, right?"

Faces turned toward Rudy.

"Do supers get to go?" someone asked.

"*Yeah!*" Grinning, Rudy jumped to his feet. "Damn right we do! We can still go!"

Costume-shedding instantly sped up. Bathroom mirrors crowded with faces being cold-creamed free of make-up. I inhaled blasts of cologne. Suit jackets were briskly brushed down. On my way out of my apartment I'd grabbed a sports jacket, and now gave my lapels a last-minute brush.

Outside our locker room door, the women supers waited, elaborately coiffed as if they were nominees on Academy Awards night. Rudy led us up the long hall. When the story of the locker break-in was repeated, the women sympathized but were quickly shushed. As we turned one corner after another, snatches of Mozart and Handel rippled through the air. Our reverberating hum filled the corridor like an anthem.

Hushed, we filed into an enormous grotto lit with chandeliers and glittering mirrors. The cast party was a blur of balloons and tinsel, echoing laugher, congratulations, hugs, chatter and squeals. Singers and musicians and crew members mingled, drunk with bubbly mirth. Champagne glasses clinked and overflowed. Beverly rushed from friend to friend, embracing everyone, looking somehow both sleek and zaftig in a leopard-skin print outfit. Her hair, no longer hidden under a carnival headdress, rippled in its red-golden cascades of curls. I kept standing on tiptoe in the crowd to catch glimpses of her, wanting badly to apologize for my stage gaffe. But this sure wasn't the time; besides, I couldn't get near her. She was gone out the door in explosions of flashbulbs.

Years later, living in Los Angeles, I saw Beverly Sills again when she performed at a big outdoor theater. Her fame would peak soon: the television talk-show appearances, her long-overdue Met debut, a Presidential Medal of Freedom. That night, I could hear in her voice—a little strained, and of course with none of the thrilling intimacy I remembered—that her singing career was winding down. The audience still loved her, though, and showered her with cheers.

A month earlier, I had decided to return to Kenya, where, with a grant I'd received for some short stories, I planned to live—not teaching or singing this time, but finally re-starting the novel I'd nearly abandoned. After Beverly's concert, I realized, my season at the opera had helped show me that a life in art was not only possible for me, but necessary.

As the audience left, I was feeling exuberant but disoriented, and wandered away from the seats toward some fans gathering at the end of a tunnel leading to the stage door. A policeman asked me who I was. On impulse, I said with straight face that I was "a former colleague of Miss Sills from New York." For some reason he believed me, and let me into the corridor. The old magic of walking through a subterranean theatrical maze rushed over me again.

Beverly was just coming out of her dressing room, no longer in her performance gown but looking great in slacks and a blazer, her hair as bright and feathery as ever.

I stepped forward. "You won't remember me, but…."

She stopped. "Of *course* I remember you!"

Of course she didn't; I could see that in her patient expression. Why bring up our last near-encounter, after all this time? Because I couldn't stop myself. I blurted it out: about playing the general in her—Cleopatra's—army in *Julius Caesar* and nearly leading my troops up a staircase into one of her arias.

"*That* would have been fun." She rolled her eyes. "So tell me, what happened?"

"Someone stopped me. I did an about-face…and took another route."

"Good move, *mon général.*"

I nodded, catching my breath. "Anyway—you sounded wonderful tonight."

"Well, thanks so much!" She gave me a plump-cheeked smile, her teeth flashing white. Then she raised her fingertips to her right eyebrow—was that a salute?—and walked off down the corridor.

In a moment, I left, too, listening for the echo of a hum to follow us out.

GRATITUDE

I rub the back of my finger where the loss of my ring aches like a phantom limb. The ring was embossed with a gleaming silver quetzal, the national bird of Guatemala, and over the years I turned it round and round so many times that the bird was worn down to a ghost of itself. Now that it's gone, though, I long to feel the tiny beak and stroke the curl of its feathery tail.

When I was twelve, my parents took me to Guatemala where, after a week in the north, I developed a raw throat and broiling fever. Lying in my hotel bed in the capital, I heard my father shouting at the manager, Please—get my son a doctor! The manager, a chubby man in a tight suit, said he regretted my illness very much but the hotel physician, whose office was many blocks away, could not come because the army had ordered a curfew in the city. He added that the curtains to our tiny balcony must please remain closed; its glass door looked out on a street close to the National Palace which had been targeted by rebel planes.

When he left, my father said, Does that jerk think drapes can keep out stay bullets? Not that any're going to come buzzing our way! My mother begged him to phone the American Embassy to find me medical help. He dialed the number over and over, but each time the line crackled for a while and went dead.

She pressed her knuckles to her lips, staring at the closed curtains. As groggy as I was, I knew she was on the verge of tears not just because she was worried about my fever and the possibility of gunfire outside, but because she badly needed a drink. Earlier that afternoon, after green-uniformed soldiers had told the manager to lock the hotel's front door, I'd heard her plead with him to open the bar. The keys are right there! she insisted, pointing to a rack behind his desk. She winced as if jets of gritty wind were blowing against her eyelids.

The manager—SR. FERDINANDO, according to the brass plate on the counter—didn't reach for the keys. The barman is not able to come in, he said, and I must stay at my post—I am obliged to think of the safety of my guests! He kept mopping his face with a handkerchief. Madame, I can not even learn if my own family is safe!

My mother started to complain again, and I expected my father to yell at her to shut up, but he just gripped her elbow and guided her upstairs to our rooms. At home I'd sometimes told her to shut up, myself, when she tried to cajole me out of my sullenness. But after she put me to bed here, I was aware of her hand trembling as she stroked my forehead, and for the first time ever, I felt very sad for her.

Then the moment passed. I was aware mostly of hot coals blistering my throat. The rumbling of heavy vehicles in the street reminded me of faraway thunder, as if I were lying on an island in the eye of a storm. I did know something unusual was going on outside this overheated space I shared with my parents; whatever it was intensified their urgent voices and shadowy movements around me. My father's shouts into the phone—The boy's running a temperature of 104 degrees! *Can you hear me?*—were both alarming and reassuring. He was ordinarily a severe, distant man; I hadn't heard him sound so upset about me before.

I'd never known him or my mother very well. They lived in the main part of our sprawling country house while I occupied the wing off the kitchen with my nanny-cum-housekeeper, whom I called Miss G. From our two rooms there, the old servants' quarters, we often heard my parents shouting and slamming doors late into the night. Miss G complained that our "cells" were cramped and dreary, but to me they were safe, cozy caves.

One day, when I was eleven, I came home from school to find our doors locked. My parents had dismissed the woman who had loved and raised me. Afterwards, they let me phone her every Sunday, but we both cried so hard we could hardly speak to each other.

For over a year, as they tried to take over my upbringing, I did my best to make sure they'd fail at the job as disastrously as Miss G had warned me they would. My father took me to the country club; I refused to jump into the pool with him. My mother bought me books and toys; I flung them into the back of the closet. Now I had to eat meals in the dining room with my parents and sleep in a new bedroom upstairs from which I could hear them arguing about what on earth they'd do with me.

Once at the top of my class in school, I started getting F's—except on one paper about the ancient Mayan Empires. My father asked me if I'd like to visit Guatemala to see the actual Indians. I said *No!* and started tearing up the paper he'd barged into my room to read. He slapped my face so hard I bounced off the wall. I was too surprised to cry; the tingling in my cheek almost made me laugh with relief. My father helped me pick up the scraps of paper, both of us out of breath.

My mother worried about whether going to a place like Guatemala could be safe. My father assured her that, though its government was communist-leaning, President Eisenhower, who'd won the war in Europe, wasn't going to let any troublemakers bother Americans in some tiny Latin American country. And if we were careful about what we ate and drank, we'd stay perfectly healthy. My mother relented. When I refused to pack, she stuffed my new suitcase with clothes, including mismatched socks and long-outgrown shirts.

Having learned from Miss G to be sly around my parents, I kept up a silent defiance in northern Guatemala by sneaking away from our hotel to gulp down the strictly forbidden syrupy drinks that local people sold from roadside carts. Eventually, though, I grew fascinated by the old temples and the villages where Indians in brightly dyed cotton clothes came out to greet us. My father and I had something to talk about other than the problems I was causing at home. In one town's market, I admired a ring with a silver bird on it; my mother offered to buy it for me. I shook my head. But the old man who'd made it said the bird, a quetzal, was a powerful Mayan spirit; when he reached out to slip the ring on my finger, I raised my hand toward it.

Crack! Crack! I sat up in bed, rubbing my eyes. *Crack!* The noises reverberated from the street below the balcony. Are those guns? I croaked.

My father lowered the phone receiver and turned to me. No, no—store owners here slam big metal blinds down over their windows when they close for the day, he explained. That's all you hear.

But it's too *early* for them to close! my mother said.

The merchants are probably just worried about some…rumors or something. My father's eyes weren't shiny like the manager's, but they had a similar worried glint. Señor Ferdinando had almost no hair; my father's was thick and gray. I've never seen it uncombed before. He stared down at the phone receiver in his hand as if it were a useless dog's bone. It's outrageous! I can't get through to our own embassy!

More heavy blinds hit the sidewalks. I felt like whimpering with each crash but that would have hurt. Turning my ring round and round on my finger, I waited until the street outside was quiet again. The raw swelling in my throat made my breaths come out in scratchy moans.

My mother leaned over me, a thin-faced woman with frizzed grey hair, her forehead deeply lined. Can you open your mouth? She asked me, and I did. She dribbled some liquid down my throat from a tilted cup. It jiggled as her hand shook, splashing my lips. Later I learned that it contained water mixed with some crushed morphine tablets Señor Ferdinando had given her. All I knew then was that my pain was drifting away and my bed had turned to a soft raft floating on a sea whose warmth I could feel rising through me.

My parents and I had adjacent rooms containing two beds each; now my mother and father took turns watching me from the extra bed in my room. My mother lay on her side, staring blankly at the closed curtains the way she sometimes did at home when she spent days in the chaise longue in her room refusing to come out. When my father took her place, he sat up against the bed's headboard with his stocking feet resting on the blanket. I'd never seen his feet in anything but black shoes or tennis sneakers. Changing shifts again, my mother and father spoke in phrases that hovered in the air like streaky little clouds.

told you we shouldn't have risked bringing him here, Ralph. Now look what

but things were going so well in the north. You said so yourself, he

I kept hoping and hoping. Oh, why do things always have to go so wrong

dammit, he was finally *talking* to us, Marion! He was smiling, eating and

A grinding sound cancelled out their words—the big fan on the bureau clunked to a halt. A whirling circle of wind had become the petals of a caged, steel daisy.

all we need! Can't you *do* something, Ralph, my God it's too hot to

My father sucked in his breath and strode out of the room. I waited to hear the door slam but it hung somewhere between wide open and closed.

The morphine freed my mind from being continually scorched by pain, and my thoughts seemed to come from somewhere outside my body instead of from inside my throat. Ever since we'd arrived in Guatemala, I reflected, my parents had fought less and less. In the north, I'd watched them walk around the hotel patio together, leaning over to touch the flowering bushes whose eager colors splashed over the walls. Here in the capital, they agreed that the park was a pretty place to walk in, that our hotel was charming.

I'd liked the hotel, too, before I got sick, especially its wood-paneled library full of big, dusty books in Spanish with drawings of armored conquistadores fighting feathered savages. Just at five o'clock my mother carried in her drink from the bar and, with the ice cubes clinking softly in my ear, looked at the pictures over my shoulder as I turned the pages. Then she sat in one of the overstuffed chairs facing me, smiling faintly. The piney scent of gin and the room's beige warmth lulled us into a peaceable silence.

Following my father, Señor Ferdinando came back to our room to see about the fan. Beads of sweat trickled down his plump cheeks like tears. I'd once read a book about a Spanish bull named Ferdinand who preferred smelling flowers to fighting, and now I

pictured the manager as a hornless bull in a tight suit. But I liked him; he always smiled at me in the lobby, even after my mother had screamed at him.

Electricity is not functioning in the hotel at present, he said.

My father clenched his fists. But you must have an emergency generator!

I hoped not. Years before, one winter while Miss G was away on her vacation, a storm had knocked out the house's electricity and I'd slept wrapped in blankets in front of the living room fireplace beside my parents. For several days and nights, they didn't shout or slam doors. My mother cooked on a grate over the flickery logs while the wind howled outside the windows. My father whittled a piece of kindling into a long fork so I could turn bread into toast above the low flames. It was an adventure, like being marooned on the Swiss Family Robinson's island.

There is no generator, Señor Ferdinando said to my father.

It's too goddamn hot in here to keep those curtains shut.

My mother patted the air with her palms. We know this is difficult for everyone—

Right—let's just try to stay calm, my father said. This whole thing's going to blow over in a day or two and everybody'll forget it ever happened.

Isn't there a doctor.... My mother spoke very slowly to Señor Ferdinando to make him understand. ...close to the hotel?

The manager frowned. There is one certain doctor. But we do not like to call him.

Why *not?* My father demanded.

For heaven's sake.... My mother's voice trailed off as she stared at the manager's face.

I understood only a little of what he and my parents said next, but the tone of their voices alarmed me.

The doctor lives across the street from the hotel. Señor Ferdinando's voice was almost a whisper. That man...he came to this country from Germany years ago, after the war. It is known...that he worked in the extermination camps.

The rumbling sounds from the street grew louder. My mother pressed her knuckles against her lips. My father shook his head over and over.

Among the few things I knew about my parents were what they'd done in the wars. In the first one, my father's bi-plane had been shot down on the German border and he'd been dragged away from the wreck with a smashed leg. During the second war, he worked for the government in Washington, and my mother, wearing the uniform of the Red Cross Motor Corps, drove sick soldiers from troop ships to hospitals near our home in Connecticut. I still remembered a summer afternoon when she'd stopped to rest for a few minutes at our house; I'd climbed onto the running board of her brown station wagon to peer through the window. Two shirtless men were lying on cots in back; I could see their chest-bones almost poking through their skin, their eyes bulging out of deep hollows. I screamed until Miss G grabbed me away. She told me years later that the Germans had shut the two men up in camps just like Jews and forced them dig huge tunnels, day and night, with hardly anything to eat. I had no idea what Jews were but the thought of working in dark tunnels gave me nightmares.

I don't know...what to do, my father said. I'd never heard his voice sound so shaky.

I don't, either. My mother wiped her eyes.

Is he a good doctor? My father asked Señor Ferdinando. I don't mean *good*, I mean....

Patients come to his office. This is all I know.

My mother sat down hard on the side of my bed. Maybe we'll have to a take a chance.

My father leaned over me. But listen to how much better his breathing is.

That's probably the morphine. My mother's fingers rested on my forehead. Are you awake? How do you feel?

I feel.... I was still floating on the raft. All I knew for sure was that I was terrified of seeing a German. I feel...okay. Honest, I.... My throbbing throat blocked my voice.

His forehead's burning, my mother said. We can't wait any longer—

A rattling sound crashed into the room—stopped—started again even louder. I heard rapid clatters—faster and faster—like an enormous swooping can of nails shaking furiously overhead. The walls vibrated, the air rippled. A copper lamp crashed to the floor, rolled over and over, slammed against a bureau.

I must have blacked out. When my eyes blinked open, my mother was wrapping gauze around Señor Ferdinando's wrist. A bullet had flown through the glass balcony door and the curtain, grazing his skin. On the bureau a small metal box was open: my mother's Red Cross first aid kit that my father had laughed at her for bringing. Now he had a dazed look on his face as he watched her bandage Señor Ferdinando. I'd never seen her do anything like this, and perhaps he hadn't either.

When she'd finished, the manager stepped back shakily. Pebbly pieces of glass sparkled at his feet, and a lot more lay like tiny ice chinks beneath the curtains. The heavy cloth had kept the glass from spraying all over us.

My father took Señor Ferdinando's arm. They stepped toward the door, speaking in low voices.

It's night. A hush has dropped over the room. My throat burns again. The room is very dark. Then candle flames flicker close to my bed. A piney gin scent blows softly over my face, my mother's breath. She's trying to smile, though her lips are tight at the corners. Beside her, my father's face glows in the amber light. At the edge of the darkness the bald dome of Señor Ferdinando hovers like a planet.

Between my parents, a stranger's face comes into partial focus. He has veiny cheeks and white eyebrows that sometimes give little jumps as if they're alive. Below them I can't see the eyes but I feel the man's gaze. Around his neck hangs a stethoscope whose twin tentacles glitter.

Do not be frightened, my boy. His tone is jovial.

I see a shiny hypodermic needle approach out of the darkness. It pierces my skin and shoots some heavy fluid deep into my arm. I shudder as an ache begins to spread through my muscle. Then the feeling fades because the red-hot coals deep in my throat seem to be screaming.

My mother grips my wrist. It's all right, it's all right....

Shall we give two injections? The doctor snips his words off at the ends as if with scissors. I think so. The swelling of the throat must be reduced immediately.

Is it safe to give him so much? My mother's voice is a whisper in the darkness.

What's that drug you're giving him? My father asks.

This is a new medication. Penicillin. The doctor's eyebrows jump. It is being called a miracle drug—invented in America. Without it, your son—

Yes, give it to him!

Yes!

Another prick, this time in the other arm, and the ache spreading.

The doctor nods at me. You are a brave boy.

I croak, Go away....

His face rises.

Señor Ferdinando's dome disappears. His footsteps fade across the room.

As I begin to doze off, I hear the doctor talking.

serious strep throat. The symptoms very much resemble trench mouth

soldiers in the trenches.... My father's voice is faint. Some of them even died

oh yes. But nowadays such diseases are found only in these backward countries, with sanitation of Indians so poor, contamination of water

but we were always so careful
did the boy take the sweet drinks they sell on the streets

I push my face into the pillow. My thumb presses the outline of the bird on the ring. Behind my eyelids, the candles flicker for a moment until I sink into darkness.

Sunlight stung my eyes. Near the open balcony doors, a small dark woman in a blue uniform squatted to sweep glass flakes into a dustpan, a crunchy sound. On the bed beside me, my mother was sprawled in her grey suit, one bare foot hanging over the edge, jiggling fast.

It was night when I next looked around. My father sat up on the bed where my mother had been, his socks pushed into the blanket. The fan whirred again, the bedside lamp blazed. My parents whispered. I heard my mother crying. My father stood close to her with his hand on her shoulder. Palms pressed my forehead again and again. My mother lifted my arm, my father slid a thermometer into my armpit.

What does it say?

My father paced. The ice in my mother's glass clinked close to my ears as if she were trying to cool me off.

It was morning. I sat up, blinking. The pain had gone from my throat. I could swallow again! My father took my temperature and held the little rod up to the light. Ninety nine! *Look at that!*

My mother grabbed his arm. My God, it really was a miracle drug!

Can I get up? I asked her, my voice still scratchy but loud. I want to get up now!

That evening I was able to dress myself and walk down to the dining room with my parents. The floor was wobbly under my feet. I looked for Señor Ferdinando at his post behind his desk, but he'd disappeared.

At breakfast-time the next morning, he was still missing. I felt bad that I'd pictured him as a timid bull. At lunch, he wasn't behind his desk, either, and I was afraid I might not see him before we checked out. The idea of going home depressed me, and I wanted to hide in the library looking at picture books. My parents decided I could stay there while they packed, if I promised not to go anywhere else.

As I flipped pages, the air felt heavy. I grew terribly restless. The drawings, mostly of old battles, scared me now. Dizzy as I was, I tiptoed across the lobby and stepped out the hotel's door onto the sidewalk, taking big breaths of fresh air. The city seemed almost deserted. Buildings looked scorched in the sunlight's glare.

I found myself in the small park where I'd seen Indian men and women sitting with their children on the grass and selling things from carts. They were all gone. Traffic noises were faint. Two gray-uniformed soldiers with rifles passed me, their boots thunking on the path. I held my breath; they didn't notice me. I approached a fountain: a statue of a robed woman pouring a continuous stream of water from a white pitcher into a tiled pool. I reached out to feel it splatter into my palms.

Wandering away from the park, I walked across an expanse of asphalt in front of the National Palace, a huge building with columns embedded in the façade and high, dull windows. I didn't notice that all of them were broken until I felt glass crunching underfoot. Shards of it were everywhere, glittering sharp as smashed ice. I felt precarious, as if I were crossing a frozen surface that was about to crack open beneath me.

Looking up, I saw my parents hurrying in my direction, and glanced around for somewhere to hide. Then, suddenly, I started waving to them with both hands. They had trouble walking on the glass, too, my mother gripping my father's arm. But they kept coming. They tottered on either side of me, my father steering me back to the solid ground of the park. I felt my mother trembling, though not the same way as she had days before. It occurred to me that she was frightened, and I stood straighter so that she could steady herself against my shoulder as she walked. In the park, we sat on a wooden bench beside a path.

Why did you leave the hotel? my mother asked.

I just needed to leave that room, I said, meaning the library. I wanted to see what had happened outside.

It's all right, Marion, my father said. The boy was curious.

It would have been cleverer to say I was sorry, but I wasn't. Are you mad at me, I asked them.

They glanced at each other and at me. Then, amazingly, they shook their heads.

I wish I could say that after we returned home, we stopped fighting and became a close, happy family. We didn't, but we did try, and I recall a period of détente—an island in time—when we talked calmly at the dinner table nearly every night. Occasionally we spoke about our escape from the revolution in Guatemala; my father assured us that shoot-ups like that were always going on in little banana republics. We never mentioned the doctor who'd come to my room. Soon I went away to boarding school, and then to college and jobs overseas. I saw my parents seldom, avoiding political discussions whenever I visited. We stayed in touch over the years until they died.

After the loss of my ring, I suddenly need to look up information about Guatemala on my laptop. With a few clicks, I find documents that weren't released for many years after the revolt. They report that the aerial machine-gun strafing I heard that afternoon in the capital was the start of an American-orchestrated coup that deposed the country's last democratically elected government and installed a series of dictatorships that secretly carried out what became known as "the silent holocaust." Over 40,000 people were caused to disappear. Had our hotel manager been among the first? Over three decades, regime after American-backed regime carried out the extermination of at least 200,000 Mayan Indians.

Is there any way for me to fit into this history the night when my parents saved my life by calling in a Nazi doctor who had been part of an even more widespread genocide?

All this time later, I still recall the ache of the miracle drug spreading under my skin. Instinctually I reach for my ring finger to calm myself. Then I have an angry impulse to phone the front desk and report the quetzal ring missing from my room. But I don't, because I'm staying in an Asian country in which any hotel employee accused of stealing from a United States citizen will be beaten senseless in a police dungeon, perhaps never to be seen again. Even in my silence—especially in my silence—I feel I am implicated in such scenes that occur in police facilities all over the world, everywhere that my country's influence is as powerful as it was on the evening when American-trained pilots opened fire on Guatemala's National Palace.

I think the best that I can do is clarify my own memories of the country, where the people are finally struggling to bring to light what happened in their cities and villages years ago.

Most of all, now, I want to picture the day when the three of us—my father and mother and I—are resting on a bench in the capital's park. Tree branches make a patch of shade for us. The air is hushed, warm. I smell wet grass around the fountain's overflowing pool. Up a path comes a clanking sound. Some men, followed by women and children in brightly-dyed cotton clothes, push wooden carts on which candies, cigarettes, and bottled drinks are arranged. I watch them go by, the carts' metal wheels bumping on the hard-packed dirt. Leaning back, I sit between my parents and listen to their quiet voices rise and fall as the water splashes in the fountain.

WRITING DANGEROUSLY

Picture a box of dark, stagnant air five stories high with walls of stone and windows glowing dimly like pillars of ice. The floor is puddled pavement; the lid is the frozen night sky which presses down overhead, making you feel very small as you walk the hundred or so yards from one end to the other. Behind the heavy glass you glimpse the guts of the place: the cellblocks with their rows of barred cages that seem to stretch into infinity. Muffled shouts from behind the windows seem aimed at you—in jagged tones of longing, hilarity, and who-knows-what anguish. Hundreds of men you can't see are in there, watching your every step.

When at last you reach the classroom area indoors, the empty prison yard's chill fades from your bones. The radiators hiss softly, and these fogged windows hide all views of walls and bars; you could be in a school in a poor neighborhood in the 1950s, with its exhausted blackboards and porcelain water fountains in the corridors. Warmth radiates from the students. They file in with grins on their faces, shaking your hand and joking—but politely, politely—with your beautiful 19-year-old teaching assistant for whom they've spent the week rehearsing their greetings. She's the only civilian woman some of the men have spoken to in years, and you're the first teacher many have known whom they didn't hate for making them feel stupid and ashamed.

Welcome to Auburn Correctional Facility in upstate New York, the nation's oldest operating prison, built in 1816, and now visited on weekdays by volunteer teachers from Cornell University. I've been giving Fiction- and Personal Essay-writing classes here for three years. Auburn, a maximum security institution, has broken my heart repeatedly, but it's also given me the most exhilarating teaching experiences I've had anywhere.

The Cornell students are the brightest of the prison's 1700 inmates; all of them have high-school diplomas or GEDs and have spent a great many hours with books as their favorite companions. Some have read more Russian classics than I have; they've inhaled Shakespeare, Plato, Charlotte Brontë, also tons of paperback Westerns, crime thrillers, and plenty of porn. Black, White, Latino, Indian, young and old, they're wildly eclectic in their interests and constantly hungry for activities that challenge their minds. No wonder I like them. Aside from the chaotic lives they've led and the brutal crimes most of them have committed, they're a lot like me and my writer friends.

I've learned what their offences were by going to the Department of Correction's web site and Google News, but soon I'm so busy I nearly forget their backgrounds. Occasionally, I'll find myself marveling at a student's deep sensitivity and suddenly remember that he'll be making license plates in here forever because he emptied his pistol into a 7-11 clerk during a robbery. That's when I feel awful— what a horrific waste of lives, both my student's and the clerk's! And for *what? Why?* It drives me crazy. Then I get back to work on the man's writing project.

These questions are much more burning for my students than for me. Some grapple with them in their essays and stories, but indirectly and cautiously. I usually don't encourage them to write about their criminal activities, which are depressing to for them to dwell on. I give them class exercises that challenge them to examine the parts of their lives that have given them some insights, some pride, maybe even some laughs. Like getting a crush on a neighborhood girl, dealing with bullies, handling a family member's problems.

The stories I get at the prison aren't much like the ones I see in other classes. One first girl an Auburn student loved became a teenage prostitute, a bully was a rival gang member who left him for dead with stab wounds, and one family problem resulted in a mother's death from a heroin overdose. The students know, though, that spilling their pain onto paper isn't enough. They want to use their new writing skills to transform their material—to create essays and stories that allow them to find some meaning and dignity in their lives.

After reading James Baldwin's "Sonny's Blues," a story about a man leaving his parents' family to get off drugs and become a musician, I asked my students to write a letter that a troubled younger brother might mail to an older one about his struggles. A few students wrote angry, defiant letters justifying their reckless adventures. Most wrote more introspective ones, explaining how bad breaks and worse judgment had led them astray; they hoped that they could still be valued as human beings.

When the men read aloud, I heard some voices crack—in a place where, normally, showing emotion can brand you as a pussy and put you in grave danger for your life. But my classroom wasn't a normal place in the prison, as my students often told me. Here they could show feelings without being scared or ashamed; they trusted me and their fellow students to keep it a safe place for them. Though most of them are black and/or Latino—as are about 90% of Auburn's inmates—members of different groups were unusually supportive of each other, too.

The students wanted to dig into the meanings of their letter-writing exercise. After reading his paper full of bad-ass bravado, a man called Harry listened to the critical discussion he'd inspired and suddenly asked, "Hey, do you think the criminal life-style—all the danger and excitement—is as addicting as the heroin the brother uses in Baldwin's story?" Many of the students nodded gravely at him. Now he understood "Sonny's Blues" in new ways, and so did I. It wasn't a grim realization; the jolt we all got from having that insight was powerful, and empowering. Sonny could keep working at playing the piano, despite carrying the burden of his past troubles, and we could find the courage to keep writing stories ourselves.

I gave the men an exercise in which they were to describe a toy they'd treasured as a child and then to use it as the object of a conflict in a made-up story. Several wrote about super-hero action-figures who, in their daydreams, had helped them vanquish childhood enemies and rescue girlfriends in distress. "Does writing give you super-powers?" I asked. "Hell, yes—that's why I'm taking this class!" one student answered. And so it does, I'm convinced—the most powerless people in the world get to fly through space (and through prison gates), right the wrongs done to them (or atone for the ones they've done), and experience the elation that comes from successfully imagining a character into life on the page.

Inevitably, one guy wrote about a teddy bear. I told the class that I'd assigned this exercise in workshops in several states and overseas, and in every single one somebody had written about a stuffed bear. I was just marveling out loud, but one student asked me if I was trying to show them that they were part of an international community of writers. I hadn't thought of this but of course it was true—they *had* joined this community, and I could tell that the stone walls that surrounded them had just gotten a little bit more porous.

I invited guest writers to come to the class and talk about their work. Jeanne Mackin read the students a ghost story, then asked the students to write about strange happenings that they'd heard about. Some reported on spirits that had been spotted in cells near the storage room where "Old Sparky"—the first electric chair used in the US, in 1890—was reputed to be kept. One student named Jack wrote about visiting a conjure woman in the backwoods of Georgia where he'd grown up. This led to a discussion of how folklore can inspire new stories; the wonder old tales evoke is similar to the way people still feel when reading good fiction.

Novelist and English professor Helena Viramontes discussed her first-person story about a mother's anguish at holding her dying baby. A somber subject, and several students offered her commiseration. "No, no," she said, "this didn't happen to me! I just got the idea from a photo I saw in a magazine." The students were amazed, and asked if all writers could put themselves in the place of anyone they saw. "Pretty much, " she said, "But I couldn't have written about that character if something in the woman's picture hadn't woken up my compassion—the way it did you guys when you read it."

The men liked the idea of becoming another person for a while—something every writer enjoys doing. Next week, I brought in Xeroxed photos from the Robert Frank book, "The Americans." Each student picked out one that interested him to write about. A picture of a man staring out at the Mississippi River captivated Benny, a lifer who'd spent time in the South as a boy. He read aloud from his narrative about an old man who believes his life is ruined when his home is destroyed in a flood until he comes upon a woman and her child, whom he's able to pull to higher ground. This was one of many redemption-themed essays the assignment inspired.

"Great photo," the author said.

Poet, essayist, and professor Kenneth McClane discussed his article about Martin Luther King, Jr., whom he'd met as a child with his father, a prominent Harlem doctor. The students, who'd been reading Barak Obama's memoir, were enthralled by the idea of meeting such an important historical figure. "You guys have known people who were important to you, too—in your families, your neighborhoods," Ken said. "Think about it." They did, and came up with essays about adults who'd had powerful influences on them as kids. Some of these people had been positive role models, but others had been drug dealers and gangsters, whom a few of them still looked up to. Some said that these people had betrayed them, and now they hoped they'd do better for their own kids. I hoped so, too; at the same time I realized that many would never get a chance to influence their children at all; their families had stopped visiting them years ago. Still, I could see that all the men were beginning to view themselves as role models for other prisoners; several reported that, as students, they were getting more respect from their block-mates.

I assigned the class a chapter from *The Language of Clothes,* a book written by another visiting author, my wife, Alison Lurie, an emerita English Department professor. In it, she explored messages about inner qualities that people communicate, consciously or unconsciously, by the outfits they wear. She brought in pictures for the students to write about. Later, she said she'd heard that even people who have to wear uniforms, like nurses or soldiers or prisoners, find ways to make themselves look distinctive by creating subtle alterations in their clothing. "Is that true here?" she asked.

I'd hardly noticed the students' baggy "forest green" uniforms—drawstring pants, work shirts, hooded sweatshirts—since the first class. But now I did, as they wrote about the ways some men tried to look laid-back by leaving their sleeves loose while prisoner leaders rolled up their sleeves to show they were ready to defend turf. Gay prisoners wore their pants higher than gang members, who wore them far down on the hips, despite a poster on the corridor walls outlawing this fashion. Physical descriptions of characters in the students' stories improved dramatically after Alison's visit.

I gave the men a chapter from one of my own novels to read; in it, one old man in a mental hospital did such credible impressions of a preacher that the other patients, and even the staff, came to listen to his sermons. "Was he just crazy, or was he onto something?" I asked. As they debated this, I heard rhythmic drumming from a room up the hall where Native American prisoners were having a service with their visiting chaplain. In a moment of synchronicity, a student recalled a character in a Sherman Alexie story I'd assigned—a misfit whom other members of his Indian tribe considered both a madman and a wise prophet. Many students had known neighborhood eccentrics, whose behavior they wrote about with fresh insights.

"Hey, look—she's at it again!" a student named Jackson said, pointing through the window to a room across the hall where Clarice, the official Pagan Chaplain of the Auburn Correctional Facility, was sweeping the air with her broom and wafting the scent of burning sage toward our classroom. The men liked her, a woman with waist-length gray hair who wore "witch shoes" and dresses decorated with arcane symbols. They decided that she resembled the Holy Fool in Native American and European traditions, and also the conjure women and Santeria priestesses in African-based lore. Often preferring to stick with realistic fiction, the students' imaginations roamed further into fantasy in their next assignment.

James McConkey, another visiting writer and retired English professor, discussed one of his autobiographical stories about spending parts of his youth in Arkansas and rural Ohio. His shame at being poor and homeless, he said, had felt like a "psychological prison" to him. One student said that learning to deal with this kind of mental prison was the only way to survive inside a physical one; creative writing was the best way he'd found of doing it.

Friends have asked me what I think the point of teaching prisoners is; that man's insight is part of my answer. Another part comes from John Crutchfield, my only student so far to publish his work; a chapter of his memoir-in-progress recently appeared in *Epoch,* a top literary journal which is published at Cornell. He wrote me that "the training and criticism I got in class shaped a genuine confidence I'd never had before. Writing helped me build a new identity."

Auburn's superintendent, Harold Graham, one of his field's more enlightened administrators, welcomes educational projects like Cornell's, which is funded by a grant the from the Sunshine Lady

Foundation, a project of Doris Buffett, the sister of Warren Buffett. "The more of your programs we have," the superintendent told me, "the less these guys are going to be using their minds to get in trouble on the blocks. The place will be a lot safer for everybody." I see his point and agree with it. But I hope we can do more than tranquilize our students.

Helena Viramontes, who's also taught prison courses, has told me she hopes to "give a voice to the silenced people" in her class. Having written about Mexican-Americans in the *barrios* of East Los Angeles, she feels as if she's going home, in a sense, to help bring out messages that not only need to be spoken but to be heard.

Jim Schechter, the Cornell Prison Education Program's director, believes that prison classes help just-released prisoners to navigate their difficult re-entries into society. Professor Pete Wetherbee, who founded the program in the early 1990s along with Paul Cody and Professor Paul Sawyer, told me that inmates who won't be leaving find in the courses sanctuaries where they can keep their sanity and productiveness.

One of my students said simply, "Now I know what it means to think outside the box."

A few men, though, still give me gangbanger melodramas, full of casual shootings and rough sexual conquests. I have to tell them that frankly, I don't much like these stories. Action-adventure and porn are very limited genres; what interests me—and, most of the students, too, once they catch on—is exploring the emotions surrounding conflicts and sexuality, feelings everyone faces. Most prisoners have hardened themselves against troubling emotions, and still need to be hard outside the classroom to survive. But my students are as sick of living in a vicious, unfeeling culture as I am of reading about it. And most of them gradually become eager to explore in their writing the inner lives of law-breakers and their victims. John Crutchfield's essay wasn't engaging because of the details about drug addiction and burglaries that appeared in its early drafts, but because of the ways he learned, in later drafts, to understand the effects his illegal activates had on the relationship he was trying to sustain with his girlfriend, and the pain he felt when it ended in a prison visiting room. His story was hell to write, he told me, but he'd seldom accomplished anything that made him feel so good in the end.

When I watch my normally shut-down students enjoy becoming writers…well, I have to admit that it's a terrific high for me. Sharing the trials of creating stories with men who are discovering what a liberating process it can be encourages me to keep at my own writing, too.

When I first started coming to the prison, a student who'd been working on his autobiography for years told me that the reason he was serving a life sentence was that he'd killed another prisoner who'd tried to steal his typewriter. A true story? Doesn't matter—it illustrates a commitment to writing I've never found anywhere else.

BELIZE: BRITAIN'S LAID-BACK COLONY IN CENTRAL AMERICA

Belize gained its independence in 1981, two years after this article was published. In recent years the Delaware-sized nation has become a popular ecotourism destination and has changed in many ways. Even while I was there, the place felt like an anachronism. So now, my essay seems to me a time capsule about a slightly magical land, just on the cusp of being transformed into part of the modern world.

Arriving in Belize, the small British colony formerly known as British Honduras, on the Caribbean coast of Central America, I shared a taxi with a Colorado-born settler who was returning from a visit to the States. "Belize is like another century, another world," he said. "It'll blow your mind."

All I saw out the taxi window was mangrove swamp. I'd seen swamps before. I told him I'd been in Guatemala and the West Indies and lived in Africa for three years; I reckoned I could handle this place.

He shrugged. "Belize is different."

Within an hour after the taxi had left me off in the city, I knew he was right. The pages of my journal show how well I initially handled Belize:

"...I only feel secure walking here when I see a donkey–cart coming. I know it's going to slow down the frantic traffic for blocks. There seem to be no sidewalks in Belize City. Everyone walks in the streets. The streets would be called alleys anywhere else, but here, vast American cars squeeze through at top speed, careening and honking, and I find myself leaping for my life into the gutter. Belizeans don't leap for their lives—they sidestep traffic like toreadors. Maybe I need practice....

"...Standing ankle-deep in a gutter is not a happy experience. The gutter is part of the sewage system. Another part of the system consists of the city's canals and the Belize River, homes of ferocious catfish that froth to the surface snarling after flotillas of mango rinds and entrails thrown from the market butcher shops. Belizeans aren't afraid of catfish or sewage. They navigate the waterways in everything from dugout canoes to motorized barges. Maybe I will get used to the smell....

"Practically all the private houses here are made of wood slats and raised on wooden stilts, standing like rows of cheerful square mantises. Many are painted blue, beige, white, pink, red or orange. Closer up, I see graceful wooden balustrades and outside staircases. Other houses are sun-charred black, in various stages of collapse. Living on the second stories, Belizeans distance themselves from the floods that come with the annual hurricanes, one of which turned ¾ of the city to kindling in 1961. No wonder there are no buildings taller than four stories....

"...There's no TV in the country, but Radio Belize blares from every other house—Children singing hymns in English (the country's official language)...The Further Adventures of Sherlock Holmes...classic reggae hits...Children singing hymns in Spanish...a schedule of events celebrating Belize Mental Health Week...the next dynamite soul hit is dedicated to Esperanza and Rosalia Cruz from the boys at the Central District Forestry Station...(gong!) BBC World News...if Mr. Sammy Ahmed is listening, would you please call home immediately, your wife is ill...Johnny Horton singing 'The

Battle of New Orleans'...a talk on the Peaceful Constructive Belizean Revolution's Economic Plan...children singing hymns....

"...Five friendly teenagers have tried to sell me weed today. It comes in little bullet-shaped packets which are called "bullets"...."

"...The National Telephone Directory is 43 white pages long. If the phones aren't working (this is most of the time) when you want to make a call, just walk around to the house of whoever you want to talk to, much friendlier...."

"...Night: temperature 97 degrees, humidity 99 degrees. I want a dozen cold beers at the local Grande Hotel Tourismo but there doesn't seem to be one. So just sit here on someone's front stoop in the dark (power outage) and eat a warm orange, much healthier...

"...Where the hell are those friendly teenagers when you need them?..."

"Next morning: Here's what happens when a boat with a mast needs to get past the Swing Bridge over the Belize River in the center of town. Four men walk to the middle of the bridge, fit a T-shaped crank into a socket there and, straining mightily, turn it round and round and round. Slowly the whole bridge (and a 30-foot length of street) rotates on a metal column. Half the city's traffic comes to a halt and backs up for many blocks in both directions. Pedestrians arrive to watch the boat putt-putt out into the Caribbean. *Toot toot!* (Thank you!) says the boat. The four men turn the crank in the opposite direction, round and round and round. The street becomes contiguous again. The four men wave to the cars. The traffic surges forward...."

"...On the riverside: An elderly Maya Indian woman in a purple Wild West t-shirt and long skirt is eating an ice cream cone. A black child with blue eyes tugs at the hand of a sunbaked blonde woman in a traditional white Maya frock. A Chinese man speaks in Spanish to the driver of a Land Rover with Mexican plates. In his pirogue on the river a tall Afro'd fisherman floats by in a denim jacket with a crossed tennis rackets patch on the back. He pauses to banter with a policewoman swinging a billy club—no, just an umbrella. She smiles and glances away, strikingly beautiful with jet black skin, thin delicate features, silky hair twined under her cap. All these people, in fact, are as attractive as their city is not...."

My journal goes on for many pages about the people I saw and met. Once I began to learn about them, about the way they live and their political institutions, I began to understand why, despite the heat and the catfish and kamikaze traffic, I was beginning to love this very different place called Belize.

The only original inhabitants of the colony, I learned, were Maya Indians, most of whom still practice subsistence agriculture, keeping to their ancient traditions, language and religion. They live in the sparsely populated, jungly countryside among unexcavated ruins which they are in no hurry to have discovered and turned into tourist attractions.

A little over half the country's people are black—Creoles, descendants of the slaves who first accompanied British loggers to the mainland in the 17th century, and Black Caribs (also called Garifunas) whose ancestors—having mixed with local Indians—established settlements of escaped slaves in the Windward Islands and began emigrating to the Honduran shores in 1802. Other Belizeans are of Spanish stock, many descendants of refugees from wars in the Mexican state of Yucatan to the north. A more recent group of arrivals are Chinese, Lebanese, and East Indians, who today run many of the colony's small businesses.

According to tradition, the first British settlement was established in 1683 by a Scottish buccaneer named Peter Wallace, of whose last name Belize is said to be a Spanish corruption. Thick jungles prevented the British from setting up plantations, as they did in the rest of the Caribbean region. Instead, they cut down all the mahogany trees they could find and, over the next three centuries, shipped them out. Those who stayed intermixed openly with everyone else and established families—one reason slavery was not as oppressive in the British Honduras settlement as elsewhere.

Few Belizeans nowadays are full-blooded anything. They are as proud of this as they are of their history of rugged independence. "We have never been conquered," I was told repeatedly. In fact, British Honduras did not officially become a colony until 1862, when the people petitioned the Crown to make it one. By so doing, they hoped to bring orderly government to a territory where a confusion of cultures was loosely held together by informal frontier justice.

"Belize Town [now City] was built on mahogany chips and rum bottles," Leo Bradley, a local historian, told me. The mahogany is nearly all gone now but other remnants of a frontier culture are still in evidence.

The map of Belize is scattered with towns whose names recall the colony's hybrid backwater heritage: Crooked Tree, Dolores, Indian Church, Gallon Jug, Monkey River Town. Many Creoles born in the city like to think of themselves as rough-tough "mahogany Coloureds" who have only come to town temporarily to raise a little hell between labor contracts in the jungle. This I was told by Evan X. Hyde, a Dartmouth graduate, former member of the Nation of Islam, author of several books, a sometimes politician who has tried (without success) to start a Black Power movement, and now a newspaper editor/owner. Outside his open window, the brothers were hanging out along the street, hustling up a dice game, racing around in beat-up passengerless taxis, just waiting for the parties to begin at nightfall.

"It's bad," Evan said, shaking his head, then grinning. "But it's beautiful. This place may not look like much to some people, but man, it's alive!"

The frontier atmosphere of the colony has been perpetuated (in a much different way) by the Mennonites, a plain-living German-speaking sect who have flourished in Belize's climate of racial and religious tolerance. Maya children stare like tourists at the gray-bearded white men in straw hats and the women in ankle-length mother Hubbards and black head-cloths. Many Mennonites still refuse to use machinery. Though their horse-drawn wooden farm wagons may look like anachronisms, they are about the only vehicles running when the torrential rains turn the roads to porridge. There are only 7,000 Mennonites out of the country's population of 126,000, but they are important to the agricultural economy, producing 100% of its fresh milk and high percentages of its vegetables and animal feeds.

Other immigrants are North American couples who haven't just dreamed of living off the land but have gone into the jungle and done it, sometimes armed with little more than machetes and determination. Jeff Dodson was a carpenter and his wife a licensed masseuse in Los Angeles; now they live without electricity or running water in a cabin built of lumber they cleared on their ten-acre farm. Vegetables, sesame, and an occasional wild pig are sometimes the only things they have to eat for weeks. The nearest store is fifteen miles away, the first four miles of which is a steep path through imposing tropical foliage. They would like to make enough money to buy a tractor some day, but a three-horse plow rented from a Mennonite neighbor is the implement that their harsh—but apparently exhilarating—life depends on now.

Few tourists visit Belize except for the international fraternity of back-packers, who pass through on their way to Alaska or Tierra del Fuego or wherever it is they continually migrate to. The Cays are the only real tourist attraction—beautiful sandy islands where palm trees crackle when the breeze blows and mosquitos feast on human flesh when it's calm. The barrier reefs—the second-largest in the world—offer spectacular snorkeling, provided you can convince a fisherman to take you out. The laid-back back-packers are good at getting on with local people, and don't mind sleeping on lumpy mattresses at very inexpensive little hotels. In Belize City, many low-end visitors find their way to guest houses like the Posada Tropicana, where I stayed. It was always alive with the buzz of travelers' tales and the cries of a pet spider monkey chasing parrots around the sitting room or being pushed off guests' laps. The hotel was run by an openly gay

North American couple; the accepted-as-fact-but-who-cares rumor that the colony's much-admired prime minister is homosexual has contributed to its relaxed atmosphere toward gays.

A few British farmers have settled in Belize, too, but I had to look hard to find traces of real colonial influence. A crocodile of dark-skinned school-girls in bright blue uniforms, a Union Jack drooping over a police station, a phallic London-style red mailbox on the corner here and there…that's about it. Red, white, and blue Coca-Cola ads are plastered on everything from funeral parlors to thatch-roofed huts in the jungle. North American pop music, clothing styles, and consumer goods abound. Yet my impression was that Belizean culture is not a cheap imitation of any other. Its multi-ethnic people have their own language, Creole (or Kriol) and a unique history. Unlike many Latin Americans and Caribbean Islanders, Belizeans have never measured each others' worth, I was told, by how closely they approximate the mannerisms of powerful foreigners. Belize rejected a British proposal to join the Caribbean Community, and has few ties with the rest of Central America. Whenever I asked what sort of model the country's development was following, the reply was always "Belizean"—one which stressed non-alignment and self-reliance.

At present, however, the colony is far from self-reliant. British grants and other foreign aid account for about half the government's capital expenditure, which is a small one—about 33 million dollars—even considering the small size and population of the place. I had trouble determining exactly what shape the economy is in. Less than a third of the adult population is listed as "labor force" in the government's Development Plan. The rest of the people are presumably dependents, unemployed or marginally employed men and women, or subsistence farmers. The per-capita income is $700, which, though only one ninth of that of the US, is high for the Third

World, and probably represents a more revealing figure than those of many southern hemisphere countries where extreme wealth is averaged in with extreme poverty.

On a bus trip through Guatemala, some Peace Corps Volunteers and I once saw an Indian woman suddenly begin to cry: the baby on her lap had just died of starvation; a few miles later, some young people in sunglasses raced their sports cars past us, spraying the bus with clouds of dust. In Belize, though, I never saw such extremes of poverty and wealth.

Even the most dilapidated one-room cabins looked clean and decently furnished inside, and most houses, at least in the cities and towns, had electricity. Nearly everyone, even children, wore shoes; the clothes people wore were rarely ragged and dirty. Though sanitary conditions are far from the best—see "catfish" above—the water is drinkable everywhere. The people eat rice and beans, rice and beans, and on special occasions, rice and beans with a little meat—monotonous, perhaps, but of adequate nutritional value. Though there are only 600 hospital beds in the entire colony, I saw no children's kwashiorkor-swollen bellies or running sores which, in other tropical countries I've visited, are ubiquitous signs of malnutrition and untreated disease.

If a super-rich élite exists in Belize, I never saw any evidence of its presence. There are no opulent night-clubs or restaurants for showing off wealth; the colony's four or five small resort hotels are comfortable but by no means elegant. The only luxury cars were clunking old Cadillac taxis. The poshest homes in the city were the sort of pleasant stucco dwellings that thrifty shop foremen or accountants might own in San Diego. At the graduation exercises of the most prestigious high school in Belize, only a few teachers wore suits, and the fanciest cameras flashing for family portraits were drug-store Instamatics.

Only a third of the people live in the cities and towns. To learn more about how the country worked I had to go out into the countryside. I squashed into a converted school bus with a sign promising MEMPHIS over the windshield, and left the city for the land of steaming mangroves swamps more evocative of the Nile Delta than of Tennessee.

Scrub bush and jungle gradually took over. Only occasionally did we pass signs of human habitation—a cluster of wooden huts or a struggling garden. Then, suddenly: Belmopan— the modernistic brand-new capital city, a square of bare earth on which the austere National Assembly building and government offices are surrounded by rows of small identical houses. It's a settlement huddling in the green heat like a bewildered family of large gray beings and their children recently dropped to earth by a flying saucer. Though clean and neat and hurricane-resistant, the place is so isolated and dull, I was repeatedly told, that no one wants to live there if they can help it.

Past Belmopan, the road turned from asphalt to one-lane dirt, poetically named the Hummingbird Highway. All that indicated that we were passing a town was a small wooden church with a one-room schoolhouse attached. 170 of the colony's 185 schools are still church-run.

Near San Ignacio, a pretty farming center build on a hillside overlooking a jungle-walled river, signs of large-scale agricultural began to appear. People along the roadside looked Spanish or Indian, and occasionally a man on horseback rode past. Fat cattle grazed among rows of grapefruit trees and cocoanut palms. The land became fenced, with *No Trespassing* signs on the gates. The man sitting beside me pointed out the sights: "Timber—British owned company. Cattle ranch—North American company. Citrus and cocoa—North American farmer. Lumber Yard—Lebanese man's. Orange tree orchard—North American owned company...."

"Belizean?" I asked.

He shrugged and pointed to some wooden cabins surrounded by a vegetable patch.

"The Nationalist bourgeoisie is responsible for this situation," I was told by Mecheck-Chigayo Mawema, General Secretary of the National Trades Union Congress of Belize, who lives in Dangriga (also called Stann Creek Town), a tranquil little community about half-way down the Caribbean coast. Mecheck believes that the government offers inadequate incentives to Belizean entrepreneurs, while giving foreign investors, often absentee landlords, *carte blanche* to buy up land at low prices. According to the most recent figures available, he's right. Only 365 people in the entire country own more than 100 acres; 50 people own 10,000 or more acres; of those 50, only 3 are nationals. Recently the government has bought up 250,000 acres for land distribution, but to date, only 10% percent of Belize is in cultivation or forestry—leaving nearly 90% of the nation uninhabited and unused.

Foreign-owned citrus, sugar cane, and banana plantations do provide rural employment, but many Belizeans are reluctant to come out into the roasting countryside to work on them. "One reason," Mecheck told me, "is that people can live off money sent by relatives living in the States. Maybe five million dollars a year comes in here through the post office. Nobody knows exactly how much, but it's a hell of a lot for a place this small. Remittances are probably the biggest single source of income in the country."

Another reason people don't like working on rural plantations is the way they have to live. "Banana workers get about thirty-six cents an hour, orange workers about forty cents, cane farmers a little better. To pick fruit, people have to leave their families and stay in isolated camps cut out of the jungle," Mecheck said. "It's hot out here. People live in 'chicken coops'—raised one-room wooden cabins, twelve by sixteen feet. Eight men share a house, with no toilet, no running water, no electricity. Nothing to do but drink rot-gut rum and fight." Mecheck is concentrating much of his efforts these days in organizing the Southern Christian Union, a cooperative society of farmers, fishermen, and builders.

Mecheck, a muscular, bright-eyed man with a goatee, was exiled from his native Zimbabwe (then settler-controlled Southern Rhodesia) in 1966. After traveling through four continents working as a cane cutter, dock worker, high school teacher and journalist, he settled permanently in Belize with his Belizean-Jamaican wife and three small daughters. As we talked in his book-cluttered living room, his daughters decided that his toenails were too long and took turns trimming them, causing him to grin proudly.

According to Mecheck, the cooperative is a way out of what he calls the "Coca-Cola culture" that is starting to sweep Belize—an over-reliance on Western products and ideas. "Take Fanta," he said, referring to the orange soda made by Coke. "Tiny bits of fruit extract, mixed with 99.9 percent water and God-knows what chemicals. People could eat their own oranges for less than one percent of the cost of the soda. Instead they pay fourteen cents for the bottled stuff because it's more 'modern' and then sell their own oranges at the market so they can afford it. Much better if the local grower will sell the fruit he doesn't eat to a local fisherman, for instance. He might not get quite such a high cash price, but he'll save money in the long run because the fisherman will sell him fish much more cheaply. And they'll both save, because they don't have to compete on the inflationary Belize City market." Belize's agricultural products must compete on an overcrowded world market, as well. To Mecheck, cooperatives are the best ways of reducing the colony's reliance on foreign buyers.

We were joined by the president of the cooperative, Pablo Lambrey, a burly older man who, like many Belizeans, had once emigrated to the United States and found a relatively high-paying job. Unlike many, he had returned. I asked him why.

"To rejoin the struggle," he said. "Today we all eat grass. Maybe one day we get rice, meat. *Then* I can eat well, with my people—not before." And meanwhile? "Well, we keep hustling. Like me. Sometimes I drive a truck, sometimes I fish, sometimes I pick oranges. My wife has a little farm and we sell some vegetables. In Belize, everybody does a little of everything to get by. We survive."

From Dangriga, I took a Maya Airways twelve-seater plane south toward Punta Gorda near the Guatemalan border. We flew low above sixty-five miles of swamps and jungles and glistening snaky rivers, an all but uninhabited emerald-green landscape broken by the occasional cut-out square of a plantation. At each one, the plane's wings dipped and we bounced along a tiny, grass-covered airstrip marked by a wind-sock hanging from a bamboo pole. There the owners and their children would rush out to meet us. The pilot handed down bags of groceries and mail; the settlers gave him letters and hand-written messages to friends along his route. Then, as they stood waving good-bye, we swooped up just over the tops of the trees and on toward the South.

I'd heard rumors that oil had been discovered near Punta Gorda, and because of this, Guatemala was making renewed claims to ownership of Belize, which it has always maintained is part of its territory. I hoped to see some evidence of drilling operations, but found nothing oilier than the Spam served at the town's only restaurant. I did see a lot of British soldiers, though. Previously I had encountered them only in small road convoys, passing from one secret jungle location to another where they practiced anti-guerilla training exercises. Seen close-up, they were shy, rugged teenagers with Midlands accents. In the Mira-Mar Bar, a doorless plank-walled establishment, they crowded around the darts board in neat slacks and bright cartooned t-shirts—"The Flying 57th"—depicting an inebriated pelican careening into a palm tree. Spilling out onto the dirt street, they competed rather politely for a few local girls doing giggling imitations of fallen women. Obviously, the army has been told to keep its profile low and its lips tightly sealed about its operations in Belize. About 2,500 troops are here, I was told—a sizable force in a place whose only other means of national defense is a 200-man Home Guard that drills on weekends.

I learned what at least some Belizeans think of the British army—and something about the colony's political life—when I attended a rally one night on a wharf in Belize City. Beneath a flying tropical moon and an insect-buzzing street-lamp, a massive black man in a watch cap was shouting into a microphone at a crowd of perhaps a hundred men, women, and children. The speakers' stand appeared to have been made out of scrap boards. Slogans—"Human Rights!" "Freedom of Speech!"—were hand-painted on it in cheerful colors. A Union Jack fluttered beside the podium. The speaker warned his audience about trusting the Premier's talk of immediate independence, and especially about relying on the government's new allies, the Panamanians.

"Why the Premier he want to be friend with they?" the man demanded. "Panamanians just little people—five five, five six maybe. Only carry machete. They can't defend Belize from Guatemala no way! Everybody know British army is the best. We want to see Brits long time more here! I tell you—" He clutched the Union Jack tenderly in his huge fist and shook it at the crowd—"I thank God this flag fly here tonight!" The crowd, which had been sitting sedately along the curbside, burst into loud applause.

Not the sort of sentiment one often hears applauded in the Third World these days.

The next speaker, representing the opposition political party, was a wiry, middle-aged mestizo. He doggedly recited one insult after another at the party in power—the People's United Party, referred to everywhere, straight-facedly, as the PUP. He focused much of his wrath on George Price, the Premier, denouncing him as a snake, a thief, a lunatic, a slave of the Pope, a communist, and a traitor who intended to sell Belize to the Guatemalans as soon as his party got Belize independence from Britain.

The crowd laughed at times, murmuring both approval and disapproval. As the harangue continued, I glanced around anxiously to see what the police were doing. After all, this was Central America, a region not famous for its gentle treatment of anti-government demonstrators. I counted four city policemen, unarmed, smoking cigarettes as they sauntered among the crowd. They looked bored, as if on assignment to supervise a church outing. When the rally ended, they jumped on their bicycles and pedaled away.

None of the symbols of authoritarian rule I associate with Central America are present in Belize. There is no Presidential Palace with a high balcony from which a succession of military dictators in gold braid harangues sullen crowds. The Premier, a trim, casually-dressed mestizo named George Price, has been in power since his election 1964, the first year full internal self-government was granted to the colony. He lives alone in a one-room, nondescript house in Belize City; everyone knows where it is, though no guards or government vehicles are ever posted outside. He drives nothing grander than a banged-up Land Rover in his trips into the countryside. "His feet are dirty but his hands are clean," a former trade-union rival of Mr. Price told me, referring to his reputation for strict integrity. Among his supporters, he is something of a Belizean Moses who has been leading his people toward political self-government since 1954. [Note: when Britain finally granted Belize independence, George Cadle Price became its first Prime Minister, serving from 1981 to 1984 and again from 1989-1993. A recipient of the country's highest honor, the Order of the National Hero, he died in 2011 at the age of 92.]

The only obstacle to full independence has been the Guatemalan Claim. That county insists that it was given jurisdiction over the area that later became British Honduras by the Spanish Crown centuries ago. Any pretense of Belize being British—or worse, independent—is an insult to Guatemalan territorial integrity. An 1859 treaty settling the boundary dispute between the United Kingdom and Guatemala was later declared void by Guatemala, which claimed that Britain did not live up to all its parts of the agreement. Off and on since the mid-Nineteenth Century disputes have raged. Though the recent arrival of British troops seems to have checked the latest Guatemalan threat of invasion into Belize, the issue is still not settled, though the colony declares itself every morning, when the radio station goes on the air, as "a new nation in the heart of the Caribbean Basin."

The issue of independence now or later was being argued vigorously in the newspapers while I was there. Freedom of the press, like free speech, is rampant. The two political parties often blast each other scandalously through the newspapers, claiming credit for what good news there is and blaming the other side for the bad news. Like so much else in the colony, the newspaper business is a small-scale operation. The pro-government *Belize Times* comes out twice a week and rarely runs more than sixteen pages, most of them covered in ads and grainy photos. The other four papers are smaller weeklies. In a place that boast a 95% literacy rate, the highest in Central America and the Caribbean, there is not a lot to read.

But then, until the recent Guatemala crisis, there seemed to be little going on to fill columns of print except Mother of the Year awards, high school sports, recipes, astrological advice, labor disputes at the sugar cane refinery, and a great many letters and opinion pieces. But as the Commonwealth Conference approached this year, the government reported that it was seeking international support for Belize from other nations besides Britain. Suddenly the newspapers flared to life, reporting that General Torrijos, the dictator of Panama—labeled a Marxist by Belize's opposition party—had broken off diplomatic relations with Guatemala and declared his "friendship" for Belize. Premier Price left for the conference. One editorial suggested that that an independent Belize, guarded by Panamanian troops and a proposed Commonwealth Peace-Keeping Force, was just around the corner. Other papers cried out that (one week) the Premier was flirting with Cuba or (the next week) was plotting a secret deal to turn Belize into a Guatemalan province.

Earl Ferguson, 29, is not only the editor of the *Belize Times;* he writes every word of every issue himself. He gets an intense look on his face when he talks about the colony's independence. Nationhood is necessary not only for reasons of pride, he told me, but to allow Belize to develop faster with assistance from the World Bank, the United Nations, and other countries beside Britain. "We'd like to see more American investment, too," he said. "in tourism and other projects—but at a controlled rate, with full Belizean participation to retain its people's self-respect. We do not want to become a nation of bellhops! Nor are we trying to attract any more absentee landlords."

As for the Guatemalan Claim: "Not one centimeter of Belize will be negotiated!" Ferguson hoped that the United States would make more concrete contributions to Belize's survival by voting with the colony in the next UN referendum—rather than abstaining, as it did last time the dispute with Guatemala was discussed. "President Carter has been saying he's concerned about human rights. We're hoping that this concern is as important to him as the US's financial investments in Guatemala, and that the US will take a good look at our vulnerable situation here."

The independent *Reporter,* has a staff of seven people and about the same circulation as the rival paper, 6000 readers. Harry Lawrence, the editor, looked tired and wary when I spoke with him—he'd just been called a "traitor" in that week's *Times.* He, too, spoke of foreign investment. "It's not our colonial status that's holding up outside participation in the economy, it's the government's left-leaning stance." Like Dean Lindo, leader of the opposition United Democratic Party (UDP), he is worried about Belize's sudden friendship with Panama. Mr. Lindo had reported that the government had given Panama large parcels of land to develop and extended other privileges to it that might "open the door to communism." Harry Lawrence was also critical of the government's "rush" into Third World maneuvering for aid. "Look what happened to Jamaica, Trinidad, and Guyana when the socialists took over! Belize is a small place—it wouldn't take much to make it sink fast. I'm in no hurry at all for independence. At present we have to rely on British troops to keep Guatemala from invading. Our survival is at stake!"

In order to continue surviving, I wondered, would Belize have to become an authoritative Marxist state, as the conservative opposition fears? Or would it, as critics from the left predict, turn into another scruffy banana republic dependent on handouts from the US?

"Neither!" I was told by Assad Shoman, Belize's Attorney General. "For God's sake—this is Belize!" The colony, he believes, is unique in having a small population, plenty of land, and a treasured history of democracy—valued resources that need not be dominated by any foreign model for development. "People who are screaming that we are being influenced by 'communists' are the sort of people who are by nature frightened of any change in the *status quo,* or who want to protect their privileged positions. Belize needs all the friends it can get—including Panama. But the link between Panama and communism—that's pure fiction. Our government has no plans to turn the country into a socialists workers' paradise!"

Shoman did want to see a policy of economic planning continued, in order that independence, when it comes, will not be a mere political formality. "It that sounds like socialism, too bad! There's no point in having freedom if the people can't benefit from it."

Assad Shoman, when he smiles, looks a little like a Bollywood film star. He is, in fact, of Lebanese abstraction, a 33-year-old London-educated attorney. And he is the man the opposition loves most to hate. His reputation as a radical stems from his youthful arrest at an anti-Vietnam war rally outside a theater that was showing the John Wayne epic, *Green Berets*. What inflames the opposition most are the occasionally flamboyant statements he has made to the foreign press about Belize's willingness to accept aid "from anywhere"—the sort of remarks that wouldn't raise a single eyebrow at the United Nations nowadays. He didn't look particularly flamboyant to me, dressed in slacks and an open-necked short-sleeved shirt. His office contained nothing more imposing than a cheerful wall-map of Belize colored in bold crayon strokes by some of his young constituents.

What would happen, I asked, if Guatemala would succeed in annexing Belize? "The place would resist like a territory occupied by an enemy power," Shoman said. "Belizeans would suffer repression, especially blacks. Guatemalans are notoriously prejudiced against them. I'm talking about the people in power there. I don't believe the average Guatemalan peasant gives a damn about Belize. The government's threats against us, though serious, are mainly attempts to divert attention from internal problems in Guatemala—severe problems...."

He showed me a report on Guatemala published by Amnesty International which stated that since 1966, more than 20,000 Guatemalans, mostly Maya Indians, have been the victims of extrajudicial executions and "disappearances," as they are called. Mass assassinations of people believed to be critical of the government have been carried out by police, soldiers, and right-wing civilian vigilante groups operating with the approval of the authorities. The report states that

Many victims are found with signs of torture and mutilation along roadsides or in ravines, floating in plastic bags in lakes and rivers, or buried in mass graves in the countryside. Other victims are shot in their homes or in the street.

"This sort of thing is unknown in Belize," Shoman said. "We would fight it to the bloody end!"

The dispute between Belize and Guatemala has been the subject of some whimsical reportage in the North American press, but to the people who live in the colony, the issue is no joke. Shoman reminded me that in the past few years, two former colonies—Spanish Sahara and Portuguese Timor—have nearly been swallowed up by larger neighboring countries with scarcely a murmur from the United States and other Western powers. In East Timor, supporters of independence have been slaughtered in appalling numbers by the invading Indonesian army. This year, Djibouti on the northeast coast of Africa has been claimed both by neighboring Somalia and Ethiopia. Only Djibouti's strategic location near the oil-rich Arabian peninsula is keeping French troops there to insure its autonomy.

Belize has no strategic location. Though its untapped natural recourses might make it one day a profitable area to develop, the colony is at present a drain on Britain's economy. Belizeans feel that the United Kingdom has a moral obligation to continue protecting their land, but are also aware that the question of independence cannot remain in limbo forever. Hopes for a Commonwealth peacekeeping force, tenuous ones at best, were dashed at this year's Commonwealth Conference. Soon afterwards, British troops were flying into Belize—for the third time in five years.

Last year, the *London Observer* ran an item headlined BELIZE DEAL IS NEAR. British foreign secretary, David Owen, reportedly worked out a plan by which Guatemala would sign a non-aggression treaty with Belize, in return for an agreement from Belize not to sign military pacts with left-wing countries inclined to guerillas on hostile visits to Guatemala. Britain would build a highway linking Guatemala and the Caribbean coast through Belize—something it had promised as part of the 1859 treaty but hadn't yet gotten around to doing. If Mr. Owens' efforts are successful, Belize will become fully independent this year.

Maybe. In the archives of the national library, I read headlines like BELIZE DEAL IS NEAR at least twenty times in papers going back thirty years. Belizean have been wary of "deals" before, and will no doubt reject this latest offer to give them independence unless it can guarantee them real security against Guatemala.

Assad Shoman wonders what will become of a "transplanted people" like those of Belize. Can the descendants of aboriginal Indians, African slaves, and various immigrant groups who have found themselves living within arbitrarily-drawn colonial boundaries now maintain those boundaries against larger and stronger neighbors?

So far, Belize has survived. The phones don't always work, the electricity fails, teachers struggle in one-room school-houses to turn out a literate population, the speakers platform on the city wharf is hammered out of scrap wood. The Swing Bridge rotates slowly, inconveniently, by hand. But it works; Belize gets by: an anomaly among the Third World's nations, a colony in an era in which there are practically no colonies left, a place without telecommunications in an age of satellites, a land where personal and political freedoms thrive in times marked by a worldwide collapse of human rights.

As my fisherman friend said, Belize is different. I hope that the place can stay that way, at least until it's safe for it to join the rest of the world.

EL SAPITO

Boarding a bus on my first day of Language school in Santiago, Chile, I spotted a sticker on the plastic partition behind the driver: a green cartoon frog in a circle with a diagonal line through it. *No Entrar Sapitos,* read the caption. For me, a beginner in Spanish, it was a language lesson: picture + words = "No entry to little frogs." But why prohibit frogs on buses? I made a note to ask a teacher when I got to my school.

Every experience I had in the bustling modern city of Santiago was a kind of interactive Spanish class. I was on one of the language-immersion programs that have recently become popular all over Latin America and Europe. Rather than looking only for recreational or sight-seeing experiences abroad, travelers are taking classes and boarding with local families—and enjoying the experience of discovering what it's like to actually live in other countries.

Amerispan, the program I signed on with in New York, encouraged me to use public transportation between my host's house and my school in Santiago. Learning the routes for my 20-minute ride twice a day helped me feel at home in the city; I enjoyed reading signs and trying to pick up the Spanish words flying around me. As for the frog on the bus, my teacher at the Linguatec Center (a language school whose headquarters are in Denver, Colorado) got me so involved in learning how to greet people in Spanish that I forgot to ask about the amphibian.

I've been a college teacher for about twenty-five years, and found I enjoyed being a student for a change. Though my instructor, a woman named Ximena, was about the age of my students at home, I could tell she'd been thoroughly trained in helping us to feel confident about speaking Spanish right away. During the coffee break, I met people from Canada, South Africa, Japan, Holland, Britain, and Brazil, as well as the States. My youngest classmate was thirteen, the oldest in her 70s. Many already knew some Spanish, and were at more advanced levels than I was. Some had enrolled for just a week, others for longer. In my group were embassy staff, business people, retired couples, university students and a variety of tourists. Classes were small—four students or fewer—and we met for four hours a day, five mornings a week.

I also signed up for afternoon excursions led by teachers to local points of interest. Santiago is a big place, with more than four million people, but the central district is easy to get around. I found the journeys as interesting as the destinations.

On Santiago's metro—a clean, efficient subway system whose stations are decorated with colorful murals—I hoped to find another frog sticker so I could ask the teacher about it, but I saw none. Instead I busied myself reading other people's newspaper headlines, picking out new words I could decipher from their context. I also overheard conversations, and could actually understand some of what people were saying—two men's comments about a local football team, stock tips exchanged by chic women with briefcases. I wouldn't have paid that much attention in a New York subway, but under the streets of Santiago, in Spanish, everything was fascinating.

We visited a busy fish market, a crafts village (where I discovered the local word for tchatchka was *cachivache*. (Yanglish?) and a museum full of pre-Columbian treasures. In the Parque O'Higgins, the dusty but delightful Museo Municipal de Insectas y Caracoles (admission 20¢) contained not only exotic bugs and snails but iridescent swallow-sized butterflies, crocodile skulls, and a reputedly genuine 700-year-old *momia* (mummy) that looked like a prop from a 40-year-old horror film. The Museo de Bellas Artes, rising majestically from the trees in the Parque Forestal near the Mapuche River, housed an eclectic collection of 19th century Latin American landscapes and genre paintings. Schoolboy art-lovers in British-style uniforms clustered before pictures of a naked slave girl (*la esclava*), a teenage washerwomen (*la lavenderia*), and a dashing cowboy (*el huaso*). More words for my notebook, though probably not ones for everyday use.

I learned as much from my host family as I did on excursions or in class. The family had been chosen for me by Amerispan, but I could have changed families easily through the Linguatec School if I'd wanted to. I stayed with a young married couple, Christián and Marie-Esther, a public relations manager and real estate agent. They lived with their two small children and Marie Esther's father, Vicente, an architect, in a pleasant modern apartment in downtown Santiago. I paid about $20 a day, which included two meals and a much more congenial atmosphere than I've ever found in any hotel. My bedroom was simple and comfortable, with five blankets on the bed and lots of hot water in the adjoining shower—much appreciated, since it was June, the middle of Chile's winter, with the temperatures between the high 30s and low 50s. I had the run of the place, studying in the living room, snacking in the kitchen.

My hosts seemed to enjoy helping me with my primitive Spanish. At the dinner table, I sometimes consulted a pocket computer-dictionary whose chirping voice caused much amusement. Within a few days I felt like a member of the family. One evening when Christián and Marie-Esther came in late from their offices, Vicente and I scrabbled together leftovers for everyone, and I acquired a cooking vocabulary, including some expletives to use when you scorch the rice. I picked up more mellifluous words when a family friend came over to teach me some Chilean music on my guitar. Everyone gathered to sing songs late into the night. I realized that not once since I'd arrived in the country had I been lonely.

I visited parts of the city with the family I wouldn't have seen on my own—from luxury high-rises whose balconies overflowed with greenery to home-made brick dwellings in the *poblaciónes*—working class neighborhoods—where Vicente had designed a community center. I got close-up views of the snow-capped peaks that surround the city. At a roadside restaurant on the drive home, we stopped for a lunch of empanadas, pillows of bread stuffed with meat, onions, and sauce baked in a clay oven over a wood fire. We ate at a table beneath the trees; in a meadow behind us white horses grazed in the long shadow of the Andes.

The Santiago area is full of surprises that aren't listed in most guidebooks. In the South Central area of the city is the Parque O'Higgins (named for the country's national liberator, Bernardo O'Higgins, an Irish immigrant who married a Peruvian woman in the 1820s.) There's a lovely "Tibetan Garden" and a lake where families in little plastic pedal-boats chase flocks of quacking ducks around the water. What I liked best were the kites, hundreds of little diamond-shaped paper *volantines* diving and soaring and bobbing above the park's parade ground like a cloud of exuberant birds. In a row of booths bright banners proclaimed the names of kite-flying clubs—*Los Halcons* (falcons), *Los Cometas* (comets), *Los Dardos* (darts), and *Los Ases del Aere* (Aces of the Air).

My Spanish had improved enough so that, with help from my family, I could talk to Don José Yevenez, the president/founder of Los Ases. Don José, a middle aged man with black hair, almond eyes, and a gold ring with his club's logo on it, told me he'd become a volantinero at an early age, like most working-class kids in Chile. Now he and his wife organized about thirty teenage club-members for Sunday afternoon outings. With kites they had made at home, they were practicing for the big October competitions—a kind of World Series of kite flying. During these events, pairs of kids would stand in spaces three meters square, skillfully making their kites thrust and parry in the air. With string coated with powdered glass and dried glue, each *volantinero* tried to slice through the opponent's string and keep his or her kite flying victoriously until the end of the day.

DRAMATIC DANCES ABOVE THE TREETOPS: I translated a newspaper headline Don José showed me, along with a photo of *Los Ases* kneeling in rows like members of a championship soccer team. In Aerial Battles, Kites Win Cherished Trophies for Clubs, read the sub-headline. The competitions sounded especially exciting in Spanish—

the word *volantinero* had a flare to it. These kids weren't just kite-fliers; they were a corps of bold young sky-warriors. For a few hours each weekend, their hard lives were filled with adventure.

In this park, General Augusto Pinochet, Chile's dictator from 1973-91, had once reviewed his troops, and his detention in England was often the lead story in the newspapers while I was in the country. Nowadays, democracy has returned in strength, and the revival of *peñas*, or folk music clubs—centers of revolutionary idealism during the years preceding Pinochet's coup d'état—is a sign of the country's reclaimed freedom of expression.

The club I visited with friends from my school was decorated by nostalgic posters and lit by candles on the tables, reminding me of smoky Greenwich Village hangouts in the 1960s. Charcoal braziers glowed out of the darkness to keep the place warm. A folk-singer performed passionately. Middle aged couples and local college students joined in, sipping hot mulled wine. Everyone seemed to know all the words of the songs. Now I was confident enough—the excellent Chilean wine helped—to sing, too.

One Sunday, I visited the vast municipal cemetery where a memorial has been erected to those who were executed and "disappeared" during Pinochet's dictatorship. On a slab of white stone about three stories tall, over six thousand names were inscribed. The most prominent was the name of Salvador Allende, the socialist prime minister who died during the coup. I translated a line of poetry by Raul Zurito that appeared across the top: *Todo mi amor esta aqui y se ha quedado: Pegado a las rocas, almar, a los monañas..* (All my love is here and stays imbedded in the rocks, the sea, the mountains.) As at the Vietnam War Memorial in Washington, DC, visitors stopped to find the names of relatives and friends, and to leave flowers at the monument's base.

Like cities of the living, the Santiago's vast necropolis was divided into poor, middle-class, and wealthy areas. Framed by the ever-present mountains, fields of white crosses, carefully maintained by middle and working class families, stretched as far as I could see. In a different neighborhood, where the avenues were lined with tall pines and palm trees, I found myself walking among the eerie mausoleums of the aristocracy. They were about the size of small houses but had been built to look like grand edifices ten times their size. Miniature stone cathedrals faced pillared Greek temples guarded by marble goddesses with five-foot wingspans. Sphinxes crouched on the steps of lavish Egyptianesque palaces. Flowering vines climbed the walls of Moorish temples whose minarets were silhouetted against the reddening sky. The last rays of sunlight gilded windows and cast long angel-shaped shadows on the grass.

I felt as if I were walking through an oil painting, a silent crepuscular landscape bereft of human figures. Even the ghosts, imprisoned behind the mausoleums' heavy doors, seemed to be missing. Perhaps they were staring forlornly through the doors' little barred windows, longing for some family member to let them out for a stroll. Or perhaps for a carriage ride under a parasol—clip clop down the avenue behind a white horse, ladies with downcast smiles behind fans, gentlemen tipping broad-brimmed hats, *Buenos Tardes, Senorita*, good evening....

It was nearly dark now. I was lost, and very glad to meet someone who wasn't a statue: an elderly attendant who directed me toward the exit—*La Salida*. When you're pursued by the stares of *los fantasmos* (ghosts), words like *a la derecha* (to the right) and *a la izquierda* (to the left) are very reassuring.

At the end of my four weeks' stay, I was able to talk about my adventures at dinner with my host family. And in my last class at school, I finally remembered to ask about the no-frogs decal I'd seen on the bus. My teacher that day, an expressive young woman named Lily, used gestures and facial expressions as well as Spanish to help explain that a *sapito*, in Chilean slang, was someone who read other people's newspapers and listened in on their conversations on a bus or a train. The person she described, I confessed, bore some resemblance to me. Laughing, she told me that by now I could buy my own Spanish language newspapers and make my own conversations. My days as a *sapito* were over.

QUEENS, DEMONS, AND SAINTS: INDIA'S FOLKLORE HERITAGE

In the nearly three decades since I first lived in India in 1986 on my first Fulbright grant, the country has been through great changes, but much of the modernization, as far as I can tell, has effected the more secure middle class and the richer elites. The poor—among whom I spent much of my time--have benefited as well, but at a much slower rate. During my last visit to Rajasthan in 2011, the urban slums and more isolated rural areas appeared to have altered little except for the increased presence of television and cinema. I was told that folktales are less frequently transmitted orally as a form of popular entertainment nowadays. On the other hand, everyone assured me, their dramatic plots and sentiments are thriving in the new electronic medias.

India is a vast land of mountains and deserts, plains and jungles, ancient villages and sprawling modern cities. Over a billion people live there, comprising all the races of man and speaking over a hundred different languages. Each region is like a country within a subcontinent, with its own distinctive landscape and cultural traditions. If any one thing unifies this nation, it is the radical transformation that its citizens are undergoing as the ideas and technology of the 20th [and 21st] century begin to encroach upon their lives.

In India, however, the people have as strong a desire to preserve the richness of the past as to embrace the promise of the future.

Nowhere can you find a land where folk traditions are more alive than they are in this country today. People's dress, their architecture, their food, the complex fabric of their social life—all reflect an awareness of a culture that has been handed down through centuries. The religions of India are the richest repository of traditional art, music, and lore of every kind. Indeed, it is difficult to find any spot in the nation from which one cannot see some bit of religious or folkloric symbolism.

A charioteer from an heroic legend glares at you from a film poster. A goddess smiles from a package of fireworks. A truck painted all over with sacred lotus blossoms careens through a marketplace. Along the side of a building someone has left red handprints to ward off evil spirits. On the dashboards of buses, you can see plastic figurines of Hindu deities, Sikh gurus, Christian or Moslem or Jain saints, or any combination of these sacred personages, often with a smoking stick of incense beneath them, sweetening the scent of diesel fumes. Hardly a day goes by when there is not a festival in some village or city, where events believed to have occurred thousands of years before are reenacted, with everyone from the beggar to the bank manager watching or participating.

The state of Rajasthan, where I collected tales for my book, *The Pomegranate Princess,* is one of the least developed areas of the nation, and one where ancient traditions are most in evidence. In the northwest of India, bordering Pakistan, the state is home to more than forty million people who belong to over two hundred ethnic groups, each with its own dialect and customs. It is a land as harsh as it is beautiful. Mountains and valleys which centuries ago were covered with forests are now burning deserts. Patches of green are likely to be the result of ingenious irrigation schemes the people have evolved to water their crops. In the thirty thousand villages where ninety percent of the people live, humans and plows still guide the plow across the fields. On rural roads, camels wagons are nearly as common a form of transport as bullock carts. Electrification has reached many of the villages, though the lines run mostly to government facilities like clinics, not private homes. Someone in almost every village has a transistor radio and can inform the neighbors of events around the nation, but little is known about the world beyond India. All the social groups in the nation are represented in Rajasthan, from the Untouchables [who prefer now to be called Dalits] and desert tribes to the famous Rajput families whose brave deeds are recounted in epics and legends. Until 1947, when the status of the maharajahs was abolished, there were twenty-two princely states in the province; their monarchs claimed descent from the sun, the moon, the sacred fire of the god Agni. Along the mountain tops, massive ancient fortifications still guard the land. The people of Rajasthan point with pride to these monuments, identifying in the stories they tell with the kings and queens, princes and princesses whose heroism in the face of hardship provides inspiration for their own daily struggles.

Rural life still follows ancient rhythms, with each caste contributing its skills to the network of economic and social relationships that allows villages to maintain considerable self-sufficiency. Villages are busy places, and poor ones, but existence at a subsistence level does not mean a life devoid of meaning and enjoyment. There is always time after work to visit the temples, to decorate houses with designs of white lime, to join the neighbors for festivals and weddings. Folk music, art, and drama go on. And the great rural literature of India continues to be created and recreated, not usually by writers, for few villagers are fully literate, but by story-tellers. The tales they relate are still among the most popular forms of entertainment in rural India.

Stories are told in a variety of settings and contexts. Tales that feature gods and goddesses or that have specific religious meanings are told on ritual occasions in temples and in the courtyards of people's homes. Women may join together at a home to honor a deity or remember a revered village ancestor. A design in lime or flower petals is made on the ground, or figures are fashioned from clay or cow dung. The women sit around this temporary shrine, each holding a handful of grain. When the story is completed and its message absorbed, the women throw down the grain as an offering.

These sessions may include songs and recited verses as well. Though women usually initiate them, men and children come and go and can become part of the audience if they wish. Castes sometimes mix socially, and the same tales, with variations, can be told by members of all castes, high and low.

In some areas of Rajasthan, large painted scrolls are taken from village to village and unrolled slowly before local audiences, revealing in small pictures—like a very long comic book page—the exploits of heroic ancestors. A balladeer recounts the tales in detail, pointing out areas of the scroll corresponding to his verses, sometimes singing to the tune of a stringed instrument, sometimes dancing. These mixed media events can include small troupes of singers, dancers, and even acrobats. They are social and recreational occasions, but they have important religious significance as well. Villagers invite a balladeer to tell about the lives of epic heroes in the belief that these ancestors will help them overcome family problems, protect them from illnesses, aid barren women to produce children, or in some way alleviate the hardship of rural life. Thus the tale itself is believed to have power to affect lives; the telling of it becomes a ritual act. Sometimes the balladeer becomes possessed by the spirit of a mythic hero. In any case, he is considered a *bhopa,* or priest, and performs an important priestly function for the audience.

Religious stories are told at specific festivals such as Diwali, Teej, Holi, and Dashara, at particular times of the year. Some tales are "mythic charters"—they explain the origins and meanings of the festivals being celebrated. At fairs in Rajasthan, tales and religious epics are recited at the temples, usually by men. And at the temple rest houses, the fairs' pilgrims from all over the state exchange stories as much for the sake of entertainment as spiritual renewal.

Indeed, it is often as difficult to differentiate between sacred and secular tales as it is, in other contexts, to separate religious concerns from social, political, and economic ones. What sounds like a pure adventure story may involve a folk hero who has been deified in some local area and may be considered an avatar of a Hindu god. However, stories with deities as characters may attribute non-godlike qualities to them or even include jokes that seem very profane. There are of course a great many oral entertainments not associated with any deities.

These include tales about wily animals, foolish peasants, wicked kings, ogres and demons and witches, and—nowadays—about exchanges between clever Indians and naïve foreign tourists. Such stories might be told anywhere: in a home at night around a fire, by men resting in the fields or gathering at village tea-stalls, by women keeping their children amused as they do household chores.

However entertaining a tale may be, it is always possible to find in it some moral that is more than secular. Hinduism is so all-encompassing, and its literature—both written and oral—so rich in folk material, that all tales reinforce in some way the belief system that forms the basis of the people's religious life.

In 1986 and 1987, I lived in Jaipur, Rajasthan's capital, where I was affiliated with the English Department of the University of Rajasthan as a Fulbright Indo-American Senior Research fellow. I was fortunate to have as my translator and guide Mrs. M. K. Mukerjee, a retired school administrator who had spent many years working in rural areas as a UNICEF education officer.

Four or five days a week, we traveled to two villages, Bassi and Watika, both located about forty miles outside the city. We were often given tours of farms and shops, invited into homes for tea, shown family photo albums and treasured mementos. I spent about a month getting to know the villagers before asking them to begin telling me tales.

Bassi, to the east of Jaipur, is an agricultural center of about five thousand people, larger than most Rajasthan villages, with some paved streets as well as dirt roads. A few people have *pukka* houses of stone and stucco; most live in houses of mud brick with thatched roofs.

What Can You Do

Parvati and Chhoti, two sisters who told me several tales, lived in a small Dalit area near the village administrative center. Here, a dozen thatched houses were arranged around a swept dirt courtyard. Most had cylindrical chimneys provided by a government program promoting an improved smokeless cook stove.

A relative of the sisters, a young tailor, was pressing clothes with a charcoal iron on a stone slab outside his house when we arrived. His specialty was turning worn-out adult clothes into serviceable children's outfits. Three other men shared his house; their beds were leaning against the wall, their bedrolls folded tightly. The house was cool, immaculate, and so small that the beds, when set down, must have taken up all the floor space. Wooden shelves contained simple china, a mirror, a kerosene lantern, and a small shrine with plastic-covered pictures of Hindu gods. Just outside the door, a round clay water jug rested on a stone shelf built into the wall.

Parvati and Chhoti, though women in their sixties, had part-time jobs repairing the local roads. They had spend most of their lives as hired laborers on farms. Almost everyone in Bassi who was not in the fields or tending animals seemed to be making or repairing something. In the West, one rarely sees everyday items being manufactured because the process is done out of sight, indoors, in areas set aside for factories. Walking along the dusty streets of an Indian village, however, one can often watch things being made in courtyards or in front of the shops that sell them. The men of Bassi were turning scrap metal into farm implements on smithy's anvils, spinning pots on wheels, tanning cowhides to be cut and hammered into shoes. Women were making jute into string for weaving carpets, grinding wheat into flour, making clothes and quilts, brooms and bricks.

The two story-tellers liked being invited to the courtyard of the small stone administrative center. Parvati, unused to sitting on a Western-style chair, squatted on her haunches under a tree, the folds of her voluminous red Rajasthani skirt gathered beneath her. As she spoke in a high, sing-song voice, winkles fanned down her cheeks. She waved her hands and grinned and scowled with such expression that it seemed as if she herself might have lived the stories she was telling. Her sister Chhoti was similarly animated as she spoke. Adults peered through the gate at her; children perched on the wall and ventured inside to sit on the ground around us.

Another story-teller in Bassi was a man named Babu Lal, a thirty-five year old office massager who, it turned out, was a *charan,* a member of a caste of bards once attached to important families. For centuries, *charans* sang heroic ballads to inspire Rajput warriors going into battle, and recounted deeds of bravery to be saved for future generations. Nowadays, *charans* can be found in many professions, and though they no longer serve military functions, are often valued repositories of memorized folklore. Babu Lal, a Hindu like all my informants, also knew a lot about folk beliefs. He explained that the *bhootnays*—witches—who appeared in some of his tales were often people who had died unnatural deaths by falling into a well, being burned to death, or dying in childbirth. Witches lived in isolated places: abandoned gardens and lonely forests. Tamarind trees were popular roosts for witches, who could steal children and even adults who walked beneath the branches. Witches also gave people diseases by looking at them with the evil eye. Fortunately, there were specialists who knew how to chase away these creatures and cure the spells put on victims.

Other, less progressive villages, Babu Lal added, pointing to the horizon, were infested with witches. But there were none in *this* village, Bassi. The children sitting nearby laughed nervously at this last statement, which they seemed to think was as fanciful as any of Babu Lal's other stories.

Watika, to the west of Jaipur, is a smaller village whose mud walls and thatched roofs are dominated by the high ramparts of the hereditary ruler's fort. Though still occupied, the fort is nearly in ruins today. At one end of the vast outer courtyard, I explored a domed palace that was in a state of collapse, its rooms inhabited only by stray goats and buzzing wasps. Water buffaloes found refuge from the sun in stables that had once houses purebred horses. Slits in the wall showed where, centuries before, archers stood defending the palace against rival armies. The crumbling walls could barely keep back the dry winds now. But the *durbar* hall, where the *thakur,* the landlord, once held audiences with his peasants, was in fairly good repair. Its painted floral designs were still visible at the tops of marble columns that grew into the ceiling like rows of flowering trees. Here a servant invited Mrs. Mukerjee and me to sit on a rope bed to wait for the landlord to come greet us.

After our walk through the hot, busy street, we found this terrace cool and peaceful. Green parrots swooped above the treetops. An ancient family retainer, wearing a white *dhoti* and spectacles tied around his ears with string, made a slow, shuffling journey across the courtyard, carrying a wooden pitchfork loaded with straw. The usual village sounds—children shouting, dogs barking, hammers pounding—faded on the other side of the walls. I felt isolated from the world in time as well as space. This could have been any century.

A middle-aged man in plain white cotton trousers and jacket approached, watching us out of dark, deep-set eyes. In a quiet voice, he introduced himself as Devi Singh, the *thakur sahib.* He had once been the hereditary ruler of the entire town and its fields, a distant relative of Jaipur's royal family, which is still one of the wealthiest in Rajasthan. When Devi Singh was sixteen, in 1947, the year that princely states were abolished, his family was forced to give up his fifty horses, fifty servants, a pet elephant, and all its land but the hundred acres the family was still farming today. "I am an ordinary farmer," Devi Singh said, expressing no discernable longing for the past.

He was conscious of his family's history, however, as he showed us around the grounds. His collection of old swords and firearms was well kept up; they had recently been used ritually in the festival of Dashara, when the Rajputs, descendants of Rajasthan's warrior kings, commemorate the victory of Rama, the hero of the sacred *Ramayana,* over his enemy, the ogre Ravana. "We are descended from Rama," Devi Singh said. His family's gun collection was temporarily incomplete: two of his grown sons were out hunting with flintlock rifles at the moment.

The elderly village schoolmaster, who was also a *bhat*—a historian retained by the family to keep its records, was summoned, and two massive, hand-bound, leather-covered books were brought out for us to inspect. One had been printed in 1917. The other, almost a foot thick, dated back more than three hundred years, I was told. On its flaking pages entries were written in an archaic Rajasthani script no one but the *bhat* could read. When he died, the family's history would be lost unless scholars were to rescue the books.

The historian read to us about one of Devi Singh's ancestors: "He was killed in battle with Moslems by the wound of a lance. Two of his wives threw themselves onto the funeral pyre to die with him. Their markers are located...." The ink faded out. The man waved his hand toward the far wall. "...located outside," he improvised the entry's conclusion.

My translator and I visited the fort many times, and eventually were invited into the *zanana*, formerly the women's quarters and now the residence of Devi Singh, his wife Murudha Kumari—whose name means "Desert Princess"—two of their sons, and their sons' wives and children. The *zanana* was of stone and brick, three stories of rooms and balconies looking out on an internal courtyard. As we walked across it, two young women fled before us and ducked into a smoky kitchen. These were the daughters-in-law, who were keeping *purdah*, the state of seclusion for women that has been abandoned in most of Hindu India but which in Rajasthan still decrees that women cover their faces with the veils of their saris when any adult male approaches.

Murudha Kumari (who did not keep *purdah*), a quiet, attractive woman of forty-nine in a plain cotton sari, moved with the graceful bearing of a Rajput princess. She had been married at thirteen and had the first of her six children two years later. Except for a trip to

Bombay after her wedding, she had never left the Watika-Jaipur area, and in recent years rarely went out of the fort. She helped take care of her grandchildren and directed the few servants the family still had left.

"They are very progressive couple," Mrs. Mukerjee whispered to me in English, noting that the *thakur sahib* and the *thakrani* sat side by side on the carpet in their bedroom to entertain us. (In former times, the wife would have remained out of sight.) The room, the best one in the fort, was at the top of the courtyard, its windows screened in ornate plaster designs, its walls painted a dark glossy green with frescoes of flowers and gods decorating the corners. Unlike the administration center's courtyard in Bassi, this room was a traditional setting for the telling of tales.

Tea and crisp snacks made from maize grown in the family's fields were brought. Grandchildren ventured in and were seated in a semi-circle. Stories were mixed with chatter about household matters and gossip from Jaipur. After several months of our visits, the daughters-in-law shyly joined us. An elderly maidservant, Sujan Bai, was given the place of honor at times; her stories about witches and ghosts enthralled the children. Murudha Kumari's tales were, predictably, about the exploits of princes and princesses, and often ended with elaborate weddings, perhaps reflecting her ongoing efforts to arrange a good marriage for her youngest son.

At the end of my last visit to the fort in Watika, the family waved good-bye from the steps of the *zanana*. At the rear of the outer courtyard, a derelict 1946 Chevrolet Fleetmaster, almost all that was left of Murudha Kumari's dowry, gazed out of its stable from glassless eyes. Behind the *thakur sahib*, painted horsemen and an elephant bearing a turbaned prince led a parade of elaborately costumed musicians across the façade of the *zanana* wall.

Recent and past times melted together. I had often watched real costumed musicians trouping down village streets; bridegrooms on elephants and bejeweled horsemen were a common sight in Jaipur during the wedding season. I had also seen, in traditional folk paintings, cars and airplanes and other modern vehicles mixed with the elephants, horses, and camels that decorated the whitewashed sides of houses. The family's Chevrolet was already fading into the status of an antique, an object of nostalgia. Yet like the swords and muskets, a use might still be found for it, if only a ceremonial one. The twentieth century, it seemed to me, had made little impact here. Its material artifacts had merely been integrated, like those of previous eras, into the surface of the family's life. The family itself, with its traditions and beliefs and stories, were what remained constant over the centuries.

The tales I collected in Rajasthan are both characteristic of the specific area where people told them and are universal in many of their themes and ideas. Like stories from other parts of the world, they contain the extremes of human capabilities, and are not prettied-up to avoid shocking audiences. Murder, incest, cannibalism, and all sorts of social chaos are in them. Also present in abundance are courage, kindness, purity, restraint, justice—the forces of social order. Good and evil are in constant conflict. The plots are full of fascinating complexities, the heroes and heroines are tested to their limits, and in the end—though the way this happens is rarely predictable—virtue always prevails.

Folktales do more than entertain; they help to explain the world to us. If we believe in Western rationalism, we have faith that science can explain *how* things happen. Mosquitoes (not curses) give us malaria; electricity (not spirit voices) brings us radio music. But the scientific method is of little use to explain *why* certain people are so unfortunate as to come down with malaria, and why other people are lucky enough to be able to afford transistor radios. For these sorts of explanations, many people in the world look to folkloric beliefs and the stories that spring from them.

According to folklore, the ways we treat each other and interact with the mysterious forces of the universe help to determine why our lives are what they are. Reasons for disaster or good fortune often seem capricious, but we cannot accept a capricious world, for if we did, we would have no power over our destinies. If we can find explanations for life's mysteries, as folklore seeks to do, then we can feel justified in having faith in ourselves and in an ordered universe.

Another function of tales has always been to provide relief from the tensions of everyday life. Around the globe, not just in India, old tales remain alive in the countryside and some urban neighborhoods, and new stories—usually reworking the themes of old ones—spring up in schools, in workplaces, at sports events, and in the film studios of Bombay and Hollywood. In popular culture, movie stars replace goddesses, teachers replace demons, unreasonable bosses replace wicked kings. Using out imagination, we admire them, we outsmart them, we laugh at them. By telling new-old tales about them, we express our anxieties about the increased complexity of the modern world and better understand (we hope) our places in it. And if we believe that folk heroes and heroines still exist around us in spirit form—as millions do around the world—we can prevail upon them to intercede in our lives to help us deal with our troubles.

Indian tales share many motifs with stories from other regions of the earth. They often use the theme of a quest: a young man must undergo tests in order to prove that he is worthy to be a husband, a leader, or just a mature male. Young women, too, are tested in stories, accomplishing brave deeds and gaining stature in the process. Sometimes a misguided king banishes future heroes or heroines, who return at the end to right wrongs done to them. On their journeys, the young are sometimes helped by a wise surrogate father or mother in the form of a holy person or a bird. These figures who encourage them represent the spiritual qualities that always help those who seek them.

Gods and goddesses occasionally make appearances in Indian tales, too, but rarely play major roles, as they do in myths. As the folklorist A. K. Ramanujan states, "myths divinize the human, folktales humanize the divine." In one story, the god Vishnu employs dancing girls in his palace. In another, Durga, the most powerful of the goddesses, plays a brief scene of comic relief. In another, the goddess Kali appears as a cannibal monster who is outsmarted by the hero.

Often the characters encounter magic along the way. White magic miraculously brings riches or vanquishes enemies. More often, forms of black magic are employed against the protagonists. Foes take the form of djinns, witches, ogres, and giants with seemingly invincible powers. These villains, even though they employ supernatural means to achieve their ends, are no matches for the forces of virtue. This is a reassuring message to the peasantry who are often beset with inexplicable catastrophes in their lives, against which they have few defenses except traditional good behavior and stoicism.

The stories instruct audiences, defining goodness and displaying its triumphs. Heroes sometimes start out innocent and foolish, but they quickly become brave and clever, never losing sight of their goals. Good women are above all loyal to the men they love; their purity and devotion give them extraordinary power to rescue princes and ultimately be chosen as queens. Heroes and heroines alike display restraint in their endeavors, as their success often rests on their ability to remain calm in the face of destructive passions.

Evil, too, is carefully defined, so that audiences can recognize and avoid it (even while enjoying its glamour.) Those who scheme against the authority of a father or a king eventually meet with terrible punishment. Women who give in to wantonness also come to a bad end; female sexuality outside of marriage is viewed as a dangerous force. The various monsters and supernatural villains in tales all have in common a disregard for the ideals of restraint and spirituality. Excess of any kind is punished. One of the functions of folktales is to reinforce the belief that virtue itself produces power to triumph over the forces of chaos and destruction.

The tales I collected are, I believe, both eloquent reflections of the great cultural traditions of India and stories that can bring enchantment to audiences everywhere.

The following three stories from The Pomegranate Princess and Other Tales from India *illustrate some of the themes discussed above.*

The Princess and the Witches

There were once seven sisters who sat in the branches of a tamarind tree on the Rajasthan desert. They looked like any beautiful girls, in their long red skirts and sequined bodices, but they were witches. You could tell by their feet, which were on backwards: the heels in front and the toes behind.

One day a wedding procession passed by the tree. A prince was riding toward his palace with his new wife. The princess was dressed in a red and gold wedding sari and was as radiant as a desert sunset. The prince wore white breeches with a purple coat. His silk turban sparkled with precious jewels. All of the witches, gazing down from their branches, fell in love with him.

"Let's see where they stop for the night," one witch said. "Then we can decide how to steal him."

The prince and princess made camp near the tamarind tree. That night, the witches crept into the royal tent, lifted the couple's two beds, and flew away with them. The witches lived in a nearby jungle in a tower seven stories high. In its topmost room, they set the prince and the princess down, still asleep on their beds. They threw the princess out of the window, thinking that she would be killed and they could have the prince all to themselves.

Each morning, before they went away, they lay his sword near the foot of his bed, causing him to die. Each evening, when they returned, they put the sword at the top of the bed, bringing him back to life again. Then they danced in a frenzy around the room and sang beautiful wailing songs, inviting him to make merry with them. They draped garlands of flowers around his neck and brought him the finest food and drink—bowls of steaming basmati rice with rich sauce, along with goblets of sparkling wine. But he was so sad about the loss of his princess that he would not look at them. In the mornings, the witches had to throw all the uneaten food out the window.

Now, the princess had been saved from death by catching hold of the branches of a lime tree that grew beside the tower. She hid beneath it, surviving on the thrown-out food. Every day, while the witches were away, she climbed the pile of food to visit her husband. But because of the witches' spell, she could not move the sword and bring him back to life. Finally she said to herself, "I cannot just keep coming here. The witches may find me and cause more harm to my husband. I must do something to help him!"

Every morning she watched the seven sisters fly away in a palanquin. One day, she grabbed its corner just as the witches were starting their journey and, unseen by them, flew off across the desert, too. Beneath her, she watched camel caravans laden with marble blocks leaving lines of footprints in the sand. Tribesmen in orange turbans galloped their horses over the mountains. The hot wind blew in the princess's face. Swirling sand made her weep, and often her fingers ached from gripping the corner of the flying palanquin. But she held on until it reached the palace of the god Vishnu. There she jumped free and mingled with the crowds.

Vishnu sat on his throne wearing a golden crown, his forehead smeared with stripes of white sandalwood paste. In one hand he held a sacred conch shell and in the other a scepter. This he pointed to the people as they told him of their good deeds that would decide their fates after death. As they spoke, the seven sisters danced for him before the throne.

All at once, the princess approached him across the marble floor. "Lord Vishnu," she said. "These women are keeping my husband a prisoner in their tower. There they tempt him every night, and by day cast him into the sleep of death. Please, rescue him from their enchantment!"

When the god heard this, he told the seven sisters to lift the hems of their skirts to their ankles. Their twisted feet were revealed to everyone. People leapt back, covering their eyes.

Vishnu ordered the witches to remove their spell from the prince in the tower. The princess thanked him and returned to her husband. Now she was able to pick up the sword easily and set it beside his head. He awoke from death and embraced her.

And so the royal couple were set free. The wedding procession proceeded as before. The bride and groom rode on the backs of brightly painted elephants, followed by attendants on white horses whose saddles were studded with jewels. Women carrying candelabras on their shoulders walked behind, and the music of a brass band echoed all the way to the prince's palace.

Vishnu banished the seven sisters from his kingdom forever. They returned to sit in their tamarind tree, where in the glare of the sun, they have sometimes been mistaken for crows perched among the branches. They remain there still, waiting for another handsome prince to pass by on his way across the desert.

The Song of Naina Bai

In Rajasthan there lived a pretty young girl named Naina Bai who was the pet of her father and her five brothers. She had cheeks as round and shiny as the fruit of the *ber* tree. When she smiled, her teeth sparkled the way a stream does as it rushes into a patch of bright sunlight.

Her father liked to hear her sing in her high, quiet voice as she played around the hearth. Her brothers never scolded her when she ran indoors dripping wet from the monsoon rains. Her youngest sister-in-law was fond of her, too, and spent hours chatting with her and plaiting her long, silky hair. Naina Bai did her chores faithfully each day, but her father did not give her much work to do. It seemed a sacrilege to imprison her soul in household drudgery.

Everyone loved the girl, everyone but her four eldest sisters-in-law. They were jealous of her beauty and sweet nature, but of course they never dared complain about her to their husbands or father-in-law.

There came a time when the father and his sons had to go on a long journey to earn money for the family. As they were leaving, the father spoke to his daughters-in-law. "You must now take good care of Naina Bai, since she has no mother to protect her," he said.

The sisters-in-law nodded their agreement. But as soon as the caravan of camels had vanished over the horizon, the four oldest women turned on the girl.

"Go the well and fetch water for all of us," they ordered her.

"All right," said Naina Bai. "But I'll need a rope to lower the pitcher to the water, and a pad for carrying it on my head."

"Don't bother us about such things!" the eldest woman said. "You get no special favors now."

Naina Bai trudged off to the well. The other girls in the village gladly lent her their rope and a pad for her head. By carrying the pitcher back and forth in the hot sun, she was able to fill the water pots of her four sisters-in-law. She did this for weeks on end, sometimes crying from weariness, but she never complained.

"You're getting lazy," the eldest sister-in-law told her one day. "Go out into the forest and bring back fuel for our cook-fires."

So Naina Bai set out for the forest beyond the village looking for branches and twigs. Her friends helped her as much as they could, but as night began to fall, she still did not have enough wood in her basket for her sisters-in-laws' fires.

"Night is coming," her friends told her. "You must return to the village with us."

"No, I've given my promise," she said. "I must stay here until I've gathered enough wood."

The girls left her sadly, knowing that she might never finish her chore, because at night wild animals prowled through the forest. Naina Bai went on picking up sticks and putting them in her basket.

She tried to sing one of her high, quiet songs, but her voice had lost all its gaiety.

Suddenly a giant appeared before her, huge and hairy and horrible. "Why are you staying so long in the forest?" it demanded, flashing its sharp tusks at her. "Go home, or I'll eat you!"

"I can't go home until my work is finished," Naina Bai said, sighing.

The giant snarled and leapt about some more, but as the girl seemed too sad to be frightened, it went back into the forest.

Then a group of witches dropped out of a tamarind tree, screaming and chanting. They were filthy and old and ragged. "Go home before it gets dark!" they screeched, dancing around her on their twisted feet. "If you don't leave now, we'll eat you!"

"If you eat me, at least my troubles will be over," Naina Bai said. "Do as you like."

The witches danced faster and faster around her, but still she refused to flee. Finally they, too, faded into the forest.

Naina Bai began picking up more branches. Suddenly a wolf ran out from the bushes, its yellow eyes gleaming in the moonlight. In one leap, it ripped out her throat with its fangs. When it had satisfied its hunger, it howled and dragged her away. Her basket of firewood, nearly full, lay behind on the floor of the forest.

The wolf left her body near the well where Naina Bai had once drawn water for her sisters-in-law. On the spot where she lay, a *ber* tree sprang up. It rose up quickly out of the earth, and in a few days it began to bear fruit.

One evening, her father and her brothers returned from their journey across the desert, laden down with goods and gifts for the women of their family. They watered their camels at the well and bathed themselves.

"Look, a *ber* tree," the youngest son said. "*Ber* are Naina Bai's favorite fruit. Let's pick some to take home to her."

The father and his sons approached the tree, but as soon as they reached up into its branches, they heard a faint, high voice that seemed to be coming out of the tree, itself. Sometimes it sounded like weeping, and sometimes it sounded like singing, and sometimes it sounded like the wind blowing through the leaves. The men gathered around. The only words they could make out were, "Pick the fruit carefully...it is surrounded by thorns...."

The men were so amazed that they dug up the tree, brushing the dirt from its roots gently so as not to harm them. The father brought it with him to their home.

The women prepared a big feast. There was much celebration while the women tried on their new clothes and showed off their other gifts.

Soon, though, the father began to miss his youngest child. "Where is Naina Bai?" he asked her sisters-in-law. "We have gifts for her, too, and are eager to see her."

"Oh, that girl has been so lazy while you've been gone," the woman said. "She just wanders off every day to play. We don't know where she is."

Now the youngest son noticed that his wife was sitting in the corner, hiding her eyes behind her hand. When he went to her, he saw that she had been crying.

"Where is Naina Bai?" he asked her.

At first she was too frightened to speak, but finally she told her husband, "The other women sent her into the forest to gather firewood many evenings ago, and she did not come back. I went looking for her the next day, but I never found her."

The father and the brothers rushed off to the forest to search for her. Soon they came upon her basket. Nearby was a patch of blood-soaked earth. Then they knew what had happened. They remembered the voice they had heard in the *ber* tree, and knew that it had been Naina Bai's.

"The thorns that surrounded the fruit," the father said, "must be destroyed."

He ordered the brothers to blacken the faces of their wives—all but the youngest one, who had been good to Naina Bai—and take them deep into the forest. There they were buried alive and left to die.

The *ber* tree was replanted in the yard of their home, and since the spirit of Naina Bai was in it, the tree flourished. In time, the four brothers married other wives. Every night, the father sat by the hearth and listened to the faint, high voice of his daughter singing to him as the wind blew through the branches.

He gathered his sons and their new wives around the tree.

"The youngest sister-in-law will be the senior wife in this household," he said to them, "for she alone among the women obeyed my orders and was a friend to Naina Bai."

The new wives, knowing what had happened to their husbands' former wives, nodded in agreement.

"Do you see this tree?" the father asked them. "It is your sister. From this day on, you will water the tree faithfully, and prune its branches carefully, and accept with gratitude the fruit that it gives you. You will love it as if it were a goddess living among you."

And this is how the people of Rajasthan came to worship the *ber* tree.

The Flying Prince

A prince and a carpenter went walking in the forest. The carpenter wanted to find a tree with just the right wood to make a present for the prince as a token of his friendship. After examining many trees, he found one that he wanted. They cut it down and brought it home with them.

From the tree the carpenter built his friend an airplane and an engine to make it fly, At first the prince could only travel a few meters in it, but soon he was flying back and forth above the rooftops of the village.

One day he flew the plane across an ocean until he came to a white marble palace on the shore. On the palace roof, a beautiful princess was drying her hair after a bath. When she saw the plane, she ran indoors, covering herself.

The prince landed on the roof, "Don't be afraid," he called out to her. "I won't stay long."

"You have to stay," said the princess from behind the curtain of her chamber. "You've seen me undressed. Now you have to marry me!"

"Well, perhaps I'll stay a while," the prince said.

He and the princess spent the afternoon playing chess on the roof. Many times after that, the prince flew back in his plane to visit the princess in her palace, where they often played chess and made merry. After many months of this, the princess discovered that she was with child.

"I can't stay here any longer," the princess said. "I'll bring shame to my family and become an outcast. You must take me away with you!"

"If only I could!" the prince said. "But my plane's too small. There's just one seat in it."

"If you don't take me away, I'll kill myself," the princess said, tearing her hair.

"I suppose you could sit on my lap," the prince said.

"They flew away together across the ocean. But with two people in it, the plane was too heavy to fly very far. It was about to crash into the water when the prince saw a thatched roof of a house floating on the waves, and managed to land the plane there.

No sooner were they safe on the roof than the princess began to have labor pains. The prince told her, "Stay here. I'll go get a midwife."

"Hurry!" the princess said.

The prince took off and flew to the nearest shore, where he landed the plane on the edge of a forest. He hid it in some underbrush so that no one would steal it while he was away looking for a midwife. But when he was in the village, some men sat down near the plane smoking cigarettes. One of them threw a match into the underbrush. The plane caught on fire and burned to a pile of ashes. When the prince returned and saw what had happened to his airplane, he knew he would never be able to return to his beautiful princess again. He was so unhappy that he decided to cast off all his worldly goods and spend the rest of his life as a wandering holy man.

Meanwhile, on the floating thatched roof on the ocean, the princess gave birth to a baby boy. That night, there came a terrible storm, which broke the roof into two pieces. The princess was carried off on one piece, and the baby floated away on the other.

Now it happened that a rich merchant was sailing by in his ship and saw the baby lying on the thatched roof. "What good luck!" said the merchant, who had no children of his own. "I'll take this baby back to my wife." So he rescued the baby and sailed home with it.

Meanwhile, the princess floated until she came to a beach where some prostitutes were bathing. They swam out to the roof and pulled her up onto the land.

"How can I ever repay you for rescuing me?" the princess asked.

"You can come work in our house with us," the woman said.

"But I'm a princess."

"Of course you are," the prostitutes said, but they didn't believe her. "Your yacht was sinking when we reached you. Your royal jewels must have fallen overboard."

The princess realized that she had no way to earn a living. "All right, I'll come with you, but on one condition," she said. "I'll accept only customers of very high status. You must announce that my price is one thousand rupees."

The women agreed, and took her to their house in the town.

As the years went by, the boy whom the merchant and his wife had adopted grew into a strong and clever young man. He was given a good education, and took up the merchant's trade. One day, he traveled on business to a town where he happened to see a house of prostitution with a sign outside that caught his eye. It announced that there was a woman inside who was charging a thousand rupees.

"This must be a marvelous woman, to be charging so much!" he said to himself. "I'll just have a look at her."

He entered the house and walked up the stairs to meet the woman. When he saw her, he was amazed by her beauty. But as soon as she look at him, she burst into tears.

"What's the matter?" he answered.

"Nothing," she said. "Please do what you came for and then leave me alone."

But he insisted on knowing what was troubling her. Finally, she told him how she had come to work in the house of the prostitutes many years ago.

He took her hand. "If you pray to the sun god, perhaps we'll find out why you remembered this sad story today."

So the woman filled a brass bowl with pure water and prayed to Surya, the sun god. Suddenly her breasts filled with milk. They became so full that milk squirted from them into the young man's mouth. So now she realized that she was his mother, and he knew that he was her son.

He went to the prostitutes and said, "I want to buy this woman and take her with me."

"All right," the women said, and agreed to sell her for all the money in his purse. "She's earned nothing here, because her fee is so high."

The young man and his mother returned to the merchant's house. When the merchant and his wife heard her story, they took pity on her and gave her a room to live in.

The young man went on another business trip. In a village near the sea, he happened to meet a wandering holy man. The man told him all the unhappy events that had led to his leaving all his worldly possessions behind.

"A woman who turned out to be my mother told me a similar story about a prince and an airplane," the young man said.

"Then you're my son!" said the holy man.

"And you're my father!" said the young man, and they embraced happily.

The young man took his father back to the house of the merchant and his wife.

"First you bring us a prostitute, now you bring us a man dressed in rags with a long beard and matted hair! What are we to do?" the merchant asked.

But when he heard the holy man's story, and saw how happy the young man was to be reunited with his parents, the merchant welcomed the holy man into his home as well. So the young man lived happily there with his two families, dividing his time equally between them.

ANANDA'S DOVE

"Dear Foster Parent, I am well and happy," an eleven-year-old girl named Ananda wrote me from the slums of Mumbai, India. *I am enjoying at school. I like to play volleyball and sewing. I hope your family is having good health.*

I'd been sponsoring Ananda for several years through an agency that connects people in
Western countries to kids in developing ones, writing letters and sending annual checks to pay her school expenses. Now I was in India, myself, teaching at a university in Jaipur, and was about to meet Ananda for the first time. Arriving in Mumbai, I began to wonder how on earth I'd ever connect with this child, a Dalit or member of the "Untouchable" caste, who was growing up in extreme poverty. The agency had asked me to send her photos of my children and also of my home, a modest one by the standards of Ithaca, New York, but a palace compared to India's slum dwellings. Wouldn't Ananda be uneasy, too, perhaps even resentful when I showed up in person—a rich foreigner she might feel she had to be thankful to all afternoon?

Mrs. Iqbal, her social worker, and I started up a steep, winding footpath through one of the city's vast, suburban shantytowns. In the 100-degree heat, the air seemed to hum faintly around us. From narrow lanes that wove between the shacks, crowds rushed out to stare at us. Everyone was lean and sinewy except some of the small children whose swollen bellies were signs of kwashiorkor, a disease brought on by malnutrition. A soupy sewage ditch gave off a stench that made me gag. Greenish bulges bubbled up along its surface like the snouts of excremental bullfrogs.

At the top of the hill I probably looked as bedraggled as I felt, and Mrs. Iqbal was staggering in the heat. A woman took her by the hand and led us to a tea-stall, a patch of open dirt where, incongruously, two red beach umbrellas had been set up. There we sat on metal stools to drink little glasses of sweet milk tea that no one would let us pay for. All around me were more and more hills covered with shanties, their roofs forming patch-work quilts of tarpaper and rusted metal sheeting. Across a wide valley, I saw tiny figures standing on roofs, arranging the stones that held them down, or spreading out wet laundry that must have just been washed in the murky streams visible among the huts.

On the slope below, adults and children dragging huge canvas sacks swarmed over a mountain of garbage. They were sifting through tons of plastic and rags, glass and metal, searching for anything they could sell to recycling plants. The mountain smoldered; tall plumes of smoke fed into a grimy haze that made my eyes sting. On one side of the dump I saw a settlement of huts, prime real estate where families got the first pickings when trucks deposited their loads of valuable pestilence.

More and more people crowded around the patches of shade where Mrs. Iqbal and I sat, quietly watching our every movement. I supposed it wasn't often they got to see a plump lady nicely dressed in a sky-blue *salwaar kameez* and a pale-skinned foreigner wearing a wide-brimmed, canvas hat. Now I was seeing them close-up, too: a man with a polio-withered leg, a woman whose face was gruesomely pitted by smallpox, a baby with ribs showing through the taut skin of a concave chest. Polio and smallpox were on the verge of being eradicated worldwide, but too late for these people standing a few feet from me. I had an impulse to turn away from them, but they didn't look ashamed of anything, so why shouldn't I return their gaze, at least communicating that I knew they existed? I did look back, and gradually they seemed less alien, more like people I saw every day in Jaipur.

Still, the hush that surrounded me was beginning to feel tense, as if my intrusion had created an unnatural silence. Then a little boy of perhaps ten sat cross-legged on the ground at Mrs. Iqbal's feet and pulled a small bamboo flute from under his shirt. Staring up at her, he raised it sideways to his lips. As his fingers moved over the openings, lovely high tones rose and fell through the air. The notes danced, they looped and scampered around us. How did a kid so young know how to make all these miraculous sounds? When he put down his flute, people were smiling. Mrs. Iqbal began to clap, and everyone joined in the applause.

The musician ran ahead of us as we started down the slope. From the valley below I heard a powerful murmur—the voices of almost a million crowded, busy people. Now I *felt* the sound, like a warm wind rising against my face in waves. And I was aware that though appalling distress was here, it wasn't the entire story of the slum; a powerful energy was also being given off by the people who struggled hard to survive here, living ordinary daily lives, purposefully and bravely.

A few parched scrub trees began to appear beside the path, which widened enough for the occasional bullock-cart and pony-trap to pass. I smelled charcoal smoke and the tang of spices sizzling in pans. A woman sat in a doorway shelling beans; further on, a boy milked a bleating goat tethered to a stake. Wires ran every which way from what looked like confused octopi nailed to poles outside house roofs; some homes in this area were evidently electrified. Many of the houses had cement bases with upper sections of woven matting; few of them were much higher than my head.

On one hand-painted door-sign, I recognized an address—C1245—that I'd written on so many envelopes I'd mailed to India. It was the house of Ananda, whose blue aerogrammes with the foreign stamps had arrived at my own house in America. Having walked across her neighborhood, I realized that her brief letters hadn't given me the faintest idea of what she was really like. And what had my cheerful communications told her about me? Almost nothing, I thought—except how little we had in common.

A stocky girl stood in the doorway, grimacing in my direction. As I approached, she straightened her back as if defending her ground. Her skin was so dark that her yellow dress appeared luminous as a paper lantern in the shadows. A shaft of sunlight caught a sprig of purple jasmine in her tied-back hair. She looked rougher than the girl in the photo the agency had mailed me. Her eyes were still huge and dark, but she didn't gaze fetchingly; she checked me out as I were an approaching storm.

I pressed my palms together. *"Namasté,* Ananda! I'm happy to meet you, finally,"* I said. Mrs. Iqbal translated.

"Namasté," Ananda replied in a faint, scratchy voice, and stared down at her slippered feet.

When Mrs. Iqbal rested her hand on her shoulder, Ananda appeared startled but obviously delighted "I've been here before. She knows me," the social worker said to me. Then a puffy-faced woman in a stained cotton sari stepped into view: Ananda's mother. Mrs. Iqbal spoke to her in Hindi and introduced her to me. The ghost of a bruise discolored the skin below one of her eyes. "I asked her how she got that shiner," Mrs. Iqbal told me. "She said her husband got drunk and beat her. Ananda, too."

Now I noticed a purplish mark along the girl's jaw. I'd seen kids with uglier scars, but that didn't make Ananda's any easier to look at. Her frown twitched; she ducked inside. Stooping, I entered the first of the house's two rooms, leaving my shoes just inside the door. Ananda's mother was barefoot, the tops of her feet pinkish brown, the bottoms black with dirt. This room was a kitchen area, with a smoking stove in the corner. The back room was more spacious, though still smaller than my bedroom in Jaipur. Three *charpoys*—Indian rope-strung beds—leaned against one wall. On a shelf were some calendar prints of Hindu deities, and a small plastic radio. Ananda immediately switched it on for us, making the air bounce with staticky film music. Clothes hung on nails. Ananda took down a gray blouse and blue skirt on a hanger and held them out for me to admire: her school uniform.

"They're very nice," I told her. "Are they new?"

"She says they are," Mrs. Iqbal translated her reply. She took the clothes from Ananda and fingered the material. "Good. I wondered if her mother might use the agency's money to buy hooch. But she seems to be managing the household well enough—*insha'Allah* [May it be God's will]." Ananda pointed to little leather sandals in the corner. Their shiny straps were buckled in twin arcs, as if an invisible schoolgirl were standing in them. I admired them, too, nodding my head from side to side, Indian fashion. Her face flushed. She pointed to two chairs set up near a wall.

"You could try your English!" Mrs. Iqbal said to her, in English. "You're learning in school."

Ananda took a deep breath, then whispered "S-sit."

Mrs. Iqbal cocked her head, one hand cupped behind her ear.

"*Sit!*" Ananda let out a harsh, loud command. Suddenly she was transformed from the sweet urchin to a street-wise toughie, and I could picture her holding her own in kids' neighborhood brawls, even defending herself against a drunken father. I sat. She spoke in Hindi to Mrs. Iqbal.

"She wants to know about Christmas in America. She saw a program about it on the agency center's TV," Mrs. Iqbal said.

I skipped the complicated religious aspect of the holiday and told her about family dinners, gift-giving, and Santa Claus. He was a fat man who wore a red suit and rode over the rooftops in a....what? This girl had never seen snow or a sleigh. "...on a palanquin," I said, knowing they were familiar to Indian children through folk-tales; gods often rode in them across the heavens. When I mentioned the reindeer that pulled the palanquin, she gave me a puzzled look.

"Like, um, thin bullocks," I said, "with horns that have...many fingers." I made antlers out of both hands on top of my head, fingers extended. Ananda giggled, pressing her knuckles to her lips. Then, hearing her mother shout from the kitchen, she said, *"Chai."* Taking a big breath, she tried it in English. "Tea! Tea...is cooking. Is coming soon."

"Good!" Mrs. Iqbal smiled at her.

Ananda walked to the shelf to take down something wrapped in immaculate white cloth. Returning to my chair, she carefully uncovered it a flap at a time, revealing a polished wooden box full of the photos I'd been sending her for years. She stood beside me, watching my face as I turned over each picture. The first one was one of my wife and me standing in our yard with our red-shingled house in the background. It was strange to sit in this scorching little hut in India, smelling the scent of palm-matting walls, hearing roosters crowing in the lane outside, and seeing my green American lawn with patches of left-over snow visible beneath a pine tree.

I looked at a picture of my kids, aged eleven and fifteen. My daughter grinned as she reached up behind her big brother's back to make rabbit-ears with her fingers; my son was trying to assume a hard expression but a smile was showing in his eyes.

"Dan." I pointed to my son, "and...." I pointed to my daughter, "Lana."

Ananda whispered the names.

Also in the box were postcards I'd sent. One showed my college, another a waterfall in

Ithaca, another a farmer's market there which wasn't all that different from many Indian ones. Ananda leaned over, rapt, as she studied the pictures with me.

After we'd had our tea, Mrs. Iqbal asked Ananda to show us her school. In the lane, my hat attracted stares from the local children. I

was glad the words "Cricket India" were stitched on the crown. Then I remembered that very few if any of Ananda's neighbors could read English, or any other language. By paying for Ananda's schooling, I was setting her apart from the people she'd grown up with. If she finished high school, she'd be so much more skilled than anyone in this neighborhood that she'd find it difficult, perhaps impossible, to keep living here. Was I helping to make her an alien in her own community? I asked Mrs. Iqbal.

"I know what you mean, but the nation can't develop if the poorest people can't move up," she said. "They ought to be able to get education, to have indoor toilets and scooters and radios if they want them!"

"Nowadays they must see other people owning them every day. It has to make them furious."

"Yes, but you don't notice the anger. Until one day, it erupts in violent street demonstrations, food riots...." Mrs. Iqbal glanced around. "So we try to make things better one family at a time."

Ananda was making little scuffs in the dusty road as she walked along with us in her bright green cloth slippers—probably brought new for my visit. I pictured her sitting at a roadside shoe stall, proudly trying on pair after pair as other kids watched enviously.

I began to hear a roar of voices up ahead, then saw its source: Ananda's five-story brick school rising above acres of metal rooftops. The racket kept increasing as if we were approaching a vast factory with all its machines whirring at a frantic speed. Inside the school gate, we had to shout at each other to be heard. Ananda glanced at me and gazed up proudly.

Most of the hallways had been converted to classroom areas. Crowds of small children sat on the floors, leaned over little exercise books, and colored in the outlines of purple mimeographed pictures. The teachers, all young women, shouted through the din; somehow the pupils heard their questions and screamed back high-pitched responses in unison. Walking carefully so as not to step on some child's fingers, I entered a classroom where kids sat crammed two to a desk. Laughing nervously, they stole looks at me, and at Ananda who appeared both pleased and anxious to be seen with two formidable-looking strangers.

Bright red cut-outs of flowers were taped to walls. On the chalk board were squiggly rows of sentences in Hindi, which the students read aloud in unison as the teacher tapped each word with her pointer stick. I realized my face was clenched as if against a hard spray: the perpetual din. It came from this room, the halls outside, four more floors of rooms above me, and a brick courtyard—which also was packed with children sitting in neat rows, writing and screaming. Each teacher I passed seemed to have control of her class, though, and the children looked happy to be squashed in together. And why wouldn't they be? So many kids their age couldn't go to school at all. Some were out scavenging garbage, or picking up bits of coal from along dangerous railroad tracks. Others were squatting on factory floors earning fifty cents a day as they wore out their eyes tying tiny knots in carpets that would sell for thousands of dollars abroad. These schoolboys and girls, in their scrubbed uniforms and neatly oiled hair, were the elite of the neighborhood. One day, they might go to work in offices, wearing clean clothes to sit at desks and use typewriters or even computers. I could see why Ananda was smiling.

I spoke with one of the room's two teachers, Miss Murthy, a slim woman in a pink sari and tortoise-shell spectacles. She told Mrs. Iqbal and me that two classes of about forty students like Ananda occupied each room and hallway. I asked her how many pupils were in the school.

She smiled wearily. "I am estimating…fifty thousand."

"Fifty *thousand?*" I stared at her.

"Oh—no, no!" She laughed. "There are *two* shifts, you see! We are having only twenty-five thousand in each shift."

Oh. *Only* twenty-five thousand little kids in the school building at one time. Ananda had already been to the morning shift, from seven-thirty until one. Most teachers, mercifully, worked just one shift a day. Miss Murthy squatted down to compliment a boy on how well he was coloring in the stripes (orange and green) of a tiger—an animal he'd be very unlikely to ever see, though tigers attracted masses of foreign tourists to Indian game parks. Miss Murthy asked Ananda if one day she might like to be a teacher. The girl nodded emphatically; she seemed to have already made up her mind.

Back at Ananda's house, her mother stepped outside, agitated about something. From her mouth spilled a jumble of Hindi words with a high-pitched, ragged edge to them. Mrs. Iqbal spoke to her, sounding angry. Ananda looked stricken with embarrassment. Mrs. Iqbal shook her finger—a gesture not taken lightly in India—and suddenly Ananda's mother collapsed to her knees in sobs. For a moment, Mrs. Iqbal watched her, frowning. Then she helped her up and, using the edge of her head scarf, wiped the tears from the woman's cheeks.

When Ananda's mother had gone indoors, I asked Mrs. Iqbal what had happened. "The mother wanted to know if the family would still get agency money if she married Ananda off now. Ananda has just been asked for by a 'good man.' He is a forty-year old bullock-cart driver, a drinking companion of the husband. He is pressuring Ananda's mother about this—" Here Mrs. Iqbal raised her fist to demonstrate the nature of the pressure. "But I told her absolutely not!"

"Good." I hated the thought of eleven-year-old Ananda, with her huge eyes and shy smiles, being forced to marry a middle-aged man and never seeing her school again.

"I said, 'Don't you dare take that child out of her classes!'" Mrs. Iqbal continued. "'This man with me has come all the way from America to see that Ananda finishes her schooling! If I hear that she's married, then you and all your family will be taken off our rolls forever!'"

"It looked like you got your message across," I said.

What Can You Do

Mrs. Iqbal sighed. "I wanted to be hard on her, but perhaps I went too far. She has a difficult life." She glanced toward the house. "*Insha'Allah,* you'll be able to keep helping Ananda get an education!"

Would Allah be better at protecting a young Hindu girl in Mumbai than a lapsed Christian from upstate New York? I hoped so.

Mrs. Iqbal took Ananda's mother into the kitchen to talk with her privately. I was left alone with the girl in the other room. Silence. We stared at each other, me sitting awkwardly on a hard chair and she standing, shifting her weight from one foot to another. The cramped space was baking hot; my shirt was soaked with sweat and my mind was incapable of producing anything to say. I stood and beckoned Ananda to come outside with me. I had no idea what I'd do there, but at least we'd have more room to breathe.

The lane was just a short expanse of dirt where I could see the scratch-marks made by home-made twig-brooms. The air, as always, hummed with collective voices: a baby crying down the street, men laughing over a card game, a woman singing Hindi devotional songs somewhere. I glanced down at Ananda, who had finally stopped standing straight as a toy soldier and was slouching as she scratched an ankle with her fingernails.

"You got…pet in Amrika?" she asked in her small, hoarse voice.

"I don't," I said, and immediately wished I'd spoken more agreeably. "My daughter has a cat, though." I think she understood; she seemed to blink the information in with her eyes. "Do *you* have pets?" I asked her.

She nodded.

"Can I see them?"

"Yes! Show you…." She walked—strode, really—up the lane, gesturing for me to join her. We stopped at a shed where a dovecote was set on the low roof. Inside the rusted tin cage, I heard the cooing of birds. Ananda unlatched a wire, reached deep inside, and pulled out a silver-gray dove.

She passed it to me to hold. I took the bird carefully, my hand cupped beneath it. One of its eyes was round and sleepy-looking, partially scabbed over; I saw a raw patch where some tail feathers were missing. The body gradually relaxed in my palm. The dove reverberated with a purring sound. I could feel the throb of its heart inside the warmth.

"I like it." I smiled.

She explained slowly, with pauses for eye-rollings at her impatience with her English, that she had six birds; they flew around the neighborhood but they always came back to her at night. She'd once owned eight, but one had been killed by a hawk, another by a stone from a boy's sling-shot. I handed the dove back to her. She pressed it gently against her cheek. I had a feeling this was a girl who didn't get much cuddling, herself.

"What's this bird's name?" I asked her.

She shrugged. Then she stared up into my face. "Name... Lana," she said. "All right?"

"All right—yes!" I said that I'd write to my daughter and tell her about the dove. "She'll be very happy about this. Thank you!"

Ananda's expression changed; her lips relaxed into a smile. She held the bird expertly, smoothing down its feathers with her thumbs. I was glad to see that she didn't look camera-sweet any longer, but like a pretty, sweaty-faced kid who was growing up fast in a tough place and loved her scruffy doves. I held the cage door open for her. Carefully she placed the bird in its dovecote, and we walked together back to her house.

THE WITCH TEMPLE

The folktales that Indian villagers told me teemed with witches and eerie spirits. In one story I collected, seven hags cast a spell on a prince that made him catatonic while they danced in a frenzy around his bed. Another tale featured a man driven to madness when a demonic serpent crawled down his throat into his belly; only a wise priest's white magic could force it to leave. The hero of another story had to strangle a duck into which an ogre's life force had been transferred.

Some of the elderly women who told me these tales looked a little like witches themselves, I thought, with long, lumpy chins and eyes that bulged during the scary parts. They enjoyed cackling for the awestruck children who often clustered around us to listen. But I was assured by the local people that in *this* village there were no witches, because everyone was a devout Hindu ... but in *that* village—my gaze was directed across the fields to the horizon—many witches flourished.

The translator I'd hired with my Fulbright research funds told me that witches—as well as demons, *cherels, bhuts, djinns,* and other supernatural beings—were believed to be the souls of people who had been murdered or who had died in some other violent or "unnatural" way, such as falling down a well. They were condemned to drift restlessly around the earth before being reincarnated again. Some wanderers took human shape, often as mysterious crones, but many were invisible, and all were dangerous. People trained in witchcraft could summon them to put spells on enemies, causing illnesses, stillbirths, crop failures. Victims had to consult ritual healers to have curses removed and demons chased away.

I thought of these animistic ideas as holdovers from more primitive times, persistent scraps of tribal beliefs that had once been blended with the far fringes of Hinduism. In the Hindu temples I enjoyed visiting in Jaipur, the capital of the northern state of Rajasthan where I lived, I found no signs of such disturbing forces. The temples were serene, often lavishly decorated places dedicated to benevolent deities. I found them havens from the crowded markets, the crush of urban traffic, and especially from the severe, unsettling loneliness that often beset me living so far from home. Their floors were cool marble, their walls decorated with paintings of colorful deities: Lakshmi, the glamorous goddess of wealth; Ganesh, the chubby elephant-headed deity whom children loved to propitiate with candy; and noble Hanuman, the monkey-faced god who helped the hero Rama rescue his beloved Sita in one of Hinduism's holy books, the *Ramayana*. Such divinities made cameo appearances in villagers' folktales, too, rushing to the aid of brave warrior princes and faithful princesses. It always amazed me that busy peasants—men who plowed all day behind bullocks, women who cooked endless meals over wood stoves—carried in their heads so much rich and elaborate literature. To me, witches, like the heroes and heroines, were characters in endlessly fascinating fiction.

When a visiting American anthropologist asked if I'd like to accompany him to a town called Mehandipur, the site of a "witch temple" where he'd started doing fieldwork, I was eager to go, hoping to learn more about some of the spirits I'd heard about in the villagers' tales. The temple, he told me, was the only one in India where pilgrims could bring insane family members to be cured. This aspect of the place sparked my interest, too, though I didn't say so. When the anthropologist came down with a sudden illness that confined him to his room at the university guesthouse, I decided to hire his driver and make the 60-mile journey by myself.

On the road, the driver was reluctant to talk about our destination. Perhaps to stop me from asking so many questions, he handed me a book the anthropologist had left in the car; it was about nuns who had run amok in a 17th-century French convent, believing themselves possessed by demons. Now I recalled that, while teaching in Kenya years before, I'd read reports of uncontrollable laughing fits that broke out among students in several mission-run girls' boarding schools; "mass hysteria" or "emotional contagion" had been blamed.

But France and Kenya seemed far removed from the peaceful scenes I was passing today. Out the window I watched turbaned men driving camel wagons, women in bright saris filling clay pitchers at a hand-pump, boys playing tennis-ball cricket in an alley. The driver's car was a Maruti, an Indian-made model named for one of the avatars of Hanuman; since the temple I'd be visiting was dedicated to Balaji, another of the same god's avatars, I asked the driver if he thought this coincidence was auspicious. He made no reply. As we drove farther into the desert, his cheerful expression faded.

I began to feel a little apprehensive myself as we approached the rocky Aravalli Hills that jutted up from the desolate landscape. We passed gullies so raw they seemed to have been gouged out of the earth by enormous pickaxes. Wind-tormented thorn trees were the only vegetation. Just outside the town of Mehandipur, the road, nearly empty a few minutes before, became congested with traffic—cars and rumbling old buses, horse-drawn *tongas,* and bullock carts packed with pilgrims. People wandered the town's one main street in a dusty haze the vehicles stirred up. Men's clothes were shabby brown and gray; ghostlike women covered their heads with dark shawls.

The temple itself, rising between two hills, looked like none I'd seen before. Massive as an armory with tall columns, built of grimy stone and brick, it took up all one side of the main street. Many of its arched windows were blocked up, its balconies crumbling. Crows swirled above the roof like ashes rising from a smoldering fire. As I stepped out of the car, scrawny children clustered around me. They thrust their hands into my face, clutched at my pants. *"Hallo sah! Rupee sah!"* they shrieked. Frightened, confused, I pushed away the little fingers. Rags flapping, the kids flocked off to accost some Indian pilgrims climbing down from a bus. One old woman was knocked to the ground. The children dove at her, heads bobbing as if they were trying to peck her to death.

The driver slipped away to a roadside tea stall. I approached the temple. Normally I didn't think twice about leaving my shoes outside temples—the custom in India—but today I slipped them between two blocks of cement at the base of some stone steps. Barefoot, I felt vulnerable and precarious as I climbed the uneven stairs toward the entrance.

The foyer was gloomily lit, with no paintings of elegant goddesses on the walls, just smoke-smudged plaster. The air reverberated with murmuring voices and muffled thuds. I stood still, squinting curiously as the crowd shoved around me. Ahead of me was a woman sprawled on her side, her hips thrusting violently, her eyes jumping back in their sockets as if she were having agonizing orgasms. When a man knelt to hold her still, she tried to bite his arm, teeth flashing.

I was knocked sideways, my shoulder slammed against a wall. A crush of men crowded past carrying what looked like a door. It *was* a door. A man was lashed to it with rope. His bullet head clunked against the heavy wood. Thrashing against his constraints, he'd torn away most of his clothes; his uncircumcised penis flapped like a frenzied fish. Wincing at his screams, I turned away. My impulses to both stay and flee were so confused that I found myself stamping my feet in place.

Someone tugged my arm. "I will guide you!" A boy in a long, patched tunic shouted at me over the racket. His hair was matted with dust; one of his eyes was milky white. "I am Praful. Knowing all temple things. Other *forengee* always hire me." He spoke in a low, gravelly voice, as if he were a stunted adult masquerading as a kid. "Hundred rupees only!"

His fee seemed high, but the sound of his English reassured me. "Yeah, all right," I agreed.

Eyes watering from clouds of thick smoke, I shuffled behind him, holding his shoulder. I made out a woman sitting cross-legged on the floor, her head and shoulders shaking hard, her face nearly hidden behind a tangle of black hair. According to Praful, she was "possessed by a *preta,*" or evil spirit, as a result of a curse put on her by malicious neighbors. Men and women squatted close around her, stroking her and speaking urgently to the *preta*— "Get out! Leave her!"

The woman's lips curled back; the *preta* screeched through her mouth: *"You people get away! Go fuck your sisters! Eat shit!"* Praful grinned as he translated, his good eye glowing.

A boy about Praful's size but much darker came stumbling toward me. I tensed as if for the impact of his body, but he swerved away. Turning, I saw him caught by a tall man who tried to console him as he whimpered loudly. A memory came rushing back: once, a student at the school where I'd taught in Kenya raced up a hall and threw himself into my arms, gasping and weeping, before dashing erratically away. For days, the boy remained confused, trembling, unable to eat or sleep. Very concerned, I took him to the modern hospital in Nairobi where a psychiatrist tried in vain to diagnose his case. "Send him back to his village," I was told—by both a British and an African doctor. That meant, one of my Kenyan colleagues said, that he needed to be seen by a *nganga*, a traditional healer. Since the boy was nominally a Christian, one of the more religious teachers objected to sending him to be treated by a "primitive witch doctor." He was overruled by the other teachers; a passage from the Bible [Matthew 8, 28-33] was found that reported Jesus healing a man by casting out the demons that had possessed him.

What Can You Do

After two weeks at home, the boy returned to school his normal, lively self, as if nothing had happened. His brothers, jealous that he'd been sent to school, had hired a sorcerer to cast a spell on him. But how had the spell been transmitted? What had the traditional healer done to remove it? I was told that these were matters a foreigner had no business asking about.

I thought I'd never forget that first brush with witchcraft, but so many people in Africa told me about similar experiences that they stopped seeming memorable. The Indians I knew in Kenya were slightly scornful about traditional African beliefs. Here in Rajasthan, my Indian university colleagues, who as children had enjoyed ghost stories told by household servants, were more tolerant of uneducated people's ideas. They were glad, they said, that I was recording and writing down tales in the villages to preserve the nation's oral heritage.

Yes, good ... but how did the uneducated Indian pilgrims in the witch temple like having me in their midst? So far, they hadn't taken much notice of me. They had a lot more pressing concerns.

Now I stood with a crowd before a cave-like altar illuminated by eerie red bulbs. Worshippers shouted chants and clanged a bronze bell that hung from the low, soot-stained ceiling. Behind a low fence, priests in grimy robes snatched puffed-rice balls from the pilgrims and thrust the offerings into glowing braziers. Plumes of sickly sweet smoke gushed up from the coals. Supplicants leaned forward *en masse*, mouths open as they tried to eat the smoke rendered holy by the priests. Farther along, people clutched at the sticky offerings which the priests had touched against the altar before handing back. Some people squashed the ash-smeared balls between the lips of relatives too weak or confused to feed themselves. The god on the altar was Balaji himself: a stele painted a gleaming ocher with a monkey's mouth below two black eye-dots. Hanuman in this form appeared drained of all nobility, reduced to a stony lump of raw capricious power.

Praful led me to a bigger stone image with an ocher-splotched face that peered out from necklaces of flower garlands that people had draped around its neck. He said this figure was a helper of Balaji, a "judge" called Mahakel Bhairev, "the god of punishment," whose "court" this area was. His black eyes appeared fixed on a circular cavity in the stone floor—a place for "hanging," Praful said. "There—*see!*" He pointed to two brawny men carrying a woman whose loose hair swept along the flagstones. Her legs were bound in clinking chains. The men lifted her and hung her upside down over the dark hole. Her head dropped out of sight. They bobbed her down and up, down and up. Over and over her forehead struck the hole's stone rim, already stained dark with old dried blood. Her agonized voice echoed through the shadowy room.

"What's she screaming?" I shouted at Praful.

"Her *preta* is speaking—not her!" he said. "It says it refuses to leave her."

I heard the men pleading with the spirit to stop tormenting the woman, and clenched my teeth, praying that they'd stop cracking her head before they knocked her even more senseless. Finally they raised her high off the floor. One of the men cradled her gently in his arms and carried her past me. Her eyes were rolled back in their sockets. She looked battered but peaceful.

"She has come from Bengal," Praful said, overhearing the men talking. "Confined on a bullock cart."

"That's over a thousand miles." I gaped at the woman. "All that way—in chains?"

"It must be." Mahakel Bhairev had helped her, he explained; her *preta* had driven her mad, but had been punished so harshly that it fled. Now the woman could go home with her husband, sisters, and brothers.

We climbed some stone steps and entered a big room where a loud chanting session was in progress, led by a priest who stood in a sea of nodding turbans and hooded women's heads. Sitting or squatting, people packed the room so tightly I didn't see how I'd push my way through. I felt tremors against my leg: several people were vibrating with palsy. But I stopped noticing them as I stared hard at an adolescent boy who pressed himself into a corner. He was sobbing continually; high-pitched notes spurted from his mouth as if from some inner abscess of misery. For long moments I couldn't stop listening, trying to hear familiar words in his voice. Then I needed to flee the room. Pushing, dragging my feet as if through quicksand, I forced my way to the temple's back door.

Daylight! I stood on a terrace outdoors. Pacing around, I tried to clear my head. The floor was strewn with crushed flower petals, dust, random brown lumps. I jumped back as a woman collapsed with a long wail. Two priests turned her face-down, then pinned her ankles and shoulders to the floor with their hands. Another priest slowly set a thick, flat stone down on the middle of her back. Then he hefted another slab onto her buttocks. The priests chanted quietly. Her moaning subsided. Her lips opened and I heard steady, rasped breathing.

"She is starting to vomit a *preta* now," said Praful, who had followed me out.

"How—how long will it take?"

He shrugged. "There can be many different kinds of spirits in her. She must stay under stones all day, I think."

Blinking in the light, I saw two other women and one man lying face down on the terrace with huge, flat rocks resting on their backs. All the people having spirits crushed out of them were attended by family members—men, women, and children—who sat nearby on benches, taking turns wiping the patients' faces and murmuring into their ears.

A scab-eared dog sniffed at the face of a collapsed woman; her relatives gently pushed it away. Dogs were sacred to Mahakel Bhairev, Praful said; throughout the temple they were considered auspicious, and were free to roam. In a stone pool, children washed a puppy in filthy water; people caught the overflow in clay cups and gulped it down. I padded away, feeling headachy.

Around this area of the temple were smoky little stalls where people were eating or pushing finger-loads of food into ill relatives' mouths. Cups of steaming tea were passed around, some of it spilling on the clothes of patients who were gesticulating or trembling too hard to drink. More dogs pushed in and out of the crowd, food dripping from their mouths.

Praful watched me scrape my bare heel against the stone. "That is shit on your feet, sir," he said, smiling.

I looked down. Shit was indeed what had been making my feet feel so sticky. Dog turds littered the terrace. I felt grimy, my shirt sticking to my back, my face damp with sweat. Clouds had drifted over the sun; the afternoon was heavy with shadows. On a hillside rising from the terrace I saw upright slabs of stone.

"Are those tombstones?" I asked Praful.

"No, they are markers for *preta* who were left behind. If a family buys a markers, the *preta* must stay here under it, not bother the people after they go home."

Now I could see that the entire hillside was covered with little stone slabs, some leaning, some collapsed—like houses in a derelict toy necropolis. Though the terrace was crowded, no one was walking among the little structures, and I could understand why. Crows were perched on the spirit houses as if they were *preta* searching for their departed victims.

I wondered if some sort of "emotional contagion" had been going on inside. Probably not: the patients seemed engulfed by individual torments. Also, healthy people were mixed among the ill ones, family members calmly consoling afflicted relatives during this lengthy process of pilgrimage and exorcism. Indeed, if anyone were cured here, I thought, the families must get most of the credit.

Praful pulled me into an open doorway. Here was a big, well-lit reception hall full of much better dressed people. Men in white bush suits and women in silk saris were being attended to by several priests who smiled and nodded a lot. They wore clean robes with burnished leather sandals. Some mildly disturbed people were here, too, a few trembling or making soft squawking sounds, but they seemed otherwise under control.

A man in a white robe strode up to me smiling, his thick, tortoise-shell glasses forming two squares like reinforced windows in his pudgy face. "I am head priest of Balaji temple," he said, greeting me with his palms pressed together in front of his face. As I made the same gesture, I saw a flash on his wrist—a heavy gold watch, its face sparkling with jewels. "Welcome to you!" he said, leaning forward. "What is your country, please?"

"America." I stepped back. He reeked of cologne.

"*Am-rica.* Yes, of course!" He nodded. "Have you questions for your field work?"

He'd mistaken me for another *forengee,* the university anthropologist. I tried to think of something to ask, anyway. "Um ... how do you exorcise spirits?"

"Myself, I do no exorcising." He pushed out his lower lip, smiling beneficently. "All good works here are done by Balaji!"

"I see. How do the people who come here get possessed by spirits?"

"Most were doing bad things in previous lives. Now they must suffer." The priest's eyebrows flipped up as he watched me for a response. "But in the court of Balaji, very many are pardoned."

"So they only have to come once?" I asked.

"Some, once is enough. But if the *preta* are very strong, then people must stay several days, several weeks, making small contributions. We are having *dharamsala* for them—rest houses."

"Convenient," I said.

The priest smiled. "Families save for years to make long journeys here with afflicted ones. This temple is their only hope for curing, so naturally they wish to make good offerings."

"Offerings like your wristwatch?"

His heavy-lidded smile faded, and he wordlessly slipped away to join some men in suits who'd just entered the hall. Around me, other priests were seated on floor-mats consulting thick astrology books with clients, or humming prayers in a slow-rolling surf of sound. I headed outdoors again.

The temple scenes I'd witnessed brought back some vivid memories. The teen-ager I'd watched weeping in a corner reminded me of another kid of about the same age—me—who'd had long jags of uncontrollable sobbing, too. Locking myself in my room, I'd sat on the floor nodding my head slowly for long spells as I wept and gasped. I recalled my mother screaming through the door, "What's gotten *in*to you?" The jags let up eventually, but dark depressions started settling over me, sometimes making it hard for me to leave my room. Lying awake in bed, I pictured the mood as the heavy, leathery wings of an enormous blackbird trying to suffocate me. At 19, I once gave in to a fit of rage and flung a carving knife at my father. I missed, but I laughed to see his face go pale with sudden dread. What the hell *had* gotten into me?

If I'd been the son of destitute Indian peasants, I'd have been dragged off to this temple to have whatever-it-was exorcised. Instead, my parents drove me to an elegant hospital in Connecticut and left me there to be cured. The place had a meeting room not unlike this temple's reception hall. There the patients—except we were called "guests"—heard cheerful lectures each week. I went for staff-guided walks in the tranquil woods that surrounded the hospital grounds. Three times a week I met with a psychiatrist, who over a period of months stripped away most of my demons. Later, I wanted to believe that I'd left them all behind when I went to Africa to teach for three years. But of course they couldn't be left behind; old and new ones visited me there, and elsewhere from time to time over the next 20 years. Even here in India, I was sometimes beset with bouts of loneliness and culture shock and, yes, weeping, that had kept me confined for days to my room at the university.

Praful and I didn't have to descend back through the temple to reach the street; he showed me to stairs leading down a steep alley. My head throbbed with a heavy, dizzying ache, and I had to stop now and then to sit on the steps. From there I looked down onto the street, where people swarmed slowly among animals and vehicles. Beyond the shop roofs, the Aravalli Hills rose into the stone-colored sky, their rounded peaks straining against dark clouds that pressed down on them. I felt oppressed, myself. The dusty air I'd breathed burned in my lungs; I wondered if I'd inhaled some of the temple's expelled spirits.

I pictured some of those *pretas* swooping and diving in the air like a flock of red-eyed crows; they settled in cackling clusters all over the temple roof. Closer up, many had the curved fangs and horns of demons I'd seen painted on the backs of trucks. All were creatures of the dark side of the religion I'd thought so gentle and welcoming, the raw underside of the folktales whose heroic princes and glamorous princesses I'd admired so much. In earlier times, the faith I'd been born into, Christianity, had inspired great literature but also preyed on the weak and the deranged, too. Its priests, like the man with the gold watch upstairs, had enriched themselves by periodically scouring witches from the land. If I wanted to open myself to the peace I'd felt radiating through Jaipur's temples, I also had to choke on the gritty sanctified smoke that India's most wretched people offered here to the fearsome god Balaji. I'd been enchanted by folklore's magical beings; now I had some idea of what it felt like to be cursed by them as well—not as characters in stories, but as forces as real and capricious as illness, insanity, and other inexplicable tragedies of life.

I continued to the main street, then sat down hard on a low stone wall. Praful pointed to my bare feet. Their soles were black. "Are you wishing to clean?"

I wished I could scrub myself all over with soap suds and a wire brush, but had to be content to splash my feet under an outdoor spigot near the cement blocks where I'd left my shoes.

"Two hundred rupees!" Praful said in his gravelly voice, thrusting out his hand.

I scowled at him. "You said a hundred!"

"I go find your shoes. Two hundred rupees!"

I leaned over to peer between the blocks. My shoes were missing. *"Aw, fuck you!"* I screamed.

The boy—or dwarf, or whatever he was—laughed. I paid up. He sloped off. I dug my bare toes into the ground, my eyes half shut in exhaustion. Finally he stepped before me again and flung the shoes down at my feet. I half-expected him to vanish like a puff of dust, but he turned and quickly climbed back up the stairs.

When I got back to the university guesthouse, I had to go to bed, my head was pounding so hard. I wept and vomited all night. The crushing ache kept me in bed for three more days until finally, I believe, it flew back across the desert to the Balaji temple in Mehandipur.

THE VILLAGE ARTIST

"My wrist-watch." Karyan Singh pointed to a painted silver orb that shot light rays toward a galaxy of stars. His signboard had been nailed, not quite straight, to the wall outside a tiny shop whose owner, sitting cross-legged on a frayed blanket inside, was fast asleep with his turban drooping to one side. A bullock cart passed, clunking and groaning along the dirt street. The artist wiped a layer of dust from his painting. Now the watch glowed, a hovering celestial body.

The actual watches for sale on the shopkeeper's bench were tinny-looking specimens, and I feared that the magnificent illustration might have the opposite effect on business than intended—making the merchant's wares look pathetic by comparison. Evidently Karyan Singh's calling wasn't just to sell material objects, but to transcend them.

I'd come to his village in the Indian state of Rajasthan in 1986 while on a Fulbright grant doing research in folklore. A retired social worker, Mrs. Mukerjee, was my guide and translator. In this area, I'd been fascinated by the traditional images I'd seen painted in bold colors on the outside walls of thatch-roofed huts: graceful maidens and regally caparisoned elephants, flowers in vases and warriors with flintlock rifles, even—concessions to the modern era—diesel locomotives and airplanes with multiple daisy-like propellers. But Karyan Singh by-passed them quickly as he moved along the street in his peculiar swagger-like gait. A stooped-shouldered man of about fifty, in baggy trousers and a shirt that hung down so far it resembled a smock, he sported the kind of beret that artists wear in movies. His looked home-made, like a cheap cotton ice bag, but he wore it at a jaunty angle I found it endearing—out here on the edge of the desert, he brought off a bohemian look, including a pencil-thin mustache that smiled when he did.

The entire town was his gallery. We stopped before a CHEMIST & BEUTY SHOP where his sign depicted a sleepy-eyed lady with silky black hair cascading over her shoulders. She smiled mischievously, as if about to flick her hair softly against my cheek. Beside her was a curvy bottle shaped just like her. SHAMPUU was written across its bosom.

"My mer-maid," the artist said, and then I noticed that below the hem of her sari a silver fish-tail glittered above frothy surf.

"A beauty!" I said, and Mrs. Mukerjee translated this into Hindi, making Karyan Singh grin. "Have you ever been to the ocean?" I asked.

He reported he'd visited the beaches of Goa on the country's west coast, and near Madras, on the east coast. I wondered what had taken him there. Most Rajasthan villagers never traveled so far.

We walked on. "My bicycle!" he announced, sweeping his hand toward a repair shop. Over its door hung a painting of a riderless bike careening down a snow-capped mountain peak. I snapped a photo of it. Farther along, a dark orange, mustachioed circus strongman in purple Y-front underpants flexed his muscles outside a clothing store. I stopped to admire a golden loaf of bread that glowed outside a shop where a miller ground local farmers' grain in a roaring, boxy machine. What the paintings lacked in realism and perspective—quite a lot—they made up for in boldness and enthusiasm. Karyan Singh had evidently become part of an age-old economy in which a town artist was as indispensable as the town miller, the merchant, the mechanic.

He had his own shop with a signboard outside: a portrait of a broad-shouldered, black-haired young artist brandishing a dagger-like brush before a canvas aflame with color. His face was Karyan Singh's, yet it seemed…familiar. Of course it was: all the male painted figures in town had the same facial features. Karyan Singh was, literally, Everyman.

His shop, open to the street, consisted of a bare counter and a display area behind it where wedding portraits rested on home-made easels. "People like to stop and watch him work." Mrs. Mukerjee translated what he said, but looked dubious. "They think what he does is magical."

"So do I," I said. In his vivid wedding portraits, the brides wore radiant saris and more heavy silver jewelry—on noses, wrists, earlobes, necks, and ankles—than any living woman could move around in. The grooms, in silk turbans, long collarless jackets, and curly-toed slippers, were local farmers and artisans dressed as princes-for-a-day. On such an important occasion as a portrait-sitting no one wanted to look frivolous, so each face wore what looked to me like a lugubrious expression, though I knew that the subjects must have seen themselves depicted with dignity and pride. The portraits had been commissioned by couples' families but hadn't been paid for yet, and might not be for months. Sometimes Karyan Singh accepted partial payments in clothes for his daughters or flour for his wife. He said that she had enough flour to bake a stack of rotis (flatbread) that would rise to the moon.

He unrolled some wall posters, extravagantly colored fireworks ads for which he'd made the original paintings. One print featured Lakshmi, the goddess of wealth, wielding sparklers in two of her four hands. Several featured the chubby, elephant-headed god, Ganesh, my favorite deity, surrounded by starry bursts of light. I handled the posters gingerly so as not to tear the cheap, brittle paper.

Karyan Singh's wife wanted him to design more of these posters, he said, and to paint advertising slides shown in the area's cinema houses. He handed me a tin-framed glass square not much bigger than a postage stamp. The glass was filled mostly with Hindi script, with a miniscule painting of a razor blade in the center. "I know this is the latest technology," he said, "but there's too much lettering!"

"It must be hard to work around," I said.

"I need space to draw!" Karyan Singh spread his arms wide as if trying to take flight. His beret slid off. He caught it deftly in the air and replaced it, but not before I saw that, unlike the artist on his signboard, he was completely bald.

"My studio—come!" he said, and led me to a door at the back of the shop. With a flourish, he produced an antique key for the lock as if he were about to open Ali Baba's cave. Inside, he pulled the string of a dangling light bulb and, despite the dim wattage, the walls glittered with treasure: canvases of brawny gods and folkloric action-heroes, luscious goddesses and film divas. They, too, looked a little like the artist, especially a suave purple Krishna cuddling his silken-haired goddess consort, Radha—the original shampuu girl. In one painting, a young Karyan Singh pointed a huge pistol at a tiger, bloody in tooth and claw, that had just attacked an elephant. These paintings, he said, he did only for himself nowadays. I knelt to get a better view of them as he turned them toward the light. Mrs. Mukerjee wrinkled her nose, sniffing the air. Her steel-rimmed spectacles glinted; despite the heat, not a strand of her silver hair escaped its tight bun, and her sari had stayed neat and trim.

Karyan Singh opened an album whose photos showed him in his "glorious years," as a painter of cinema billboards. In one shot, he rode a scaffold ascending the arm of an enormous cobra-wrapped goddess. In another, he gripped the scaffold's ropes like a sailor hoisting a mainsail. He'd learned the artist's trade on these cinema billboards, working in backstreet sheds to sketch outlines in squares marked out on thin canvas stretched on huge wooden frames. After his apprenticeship, he'd graduated to a full-fledged artist, coloring in the bodies and faces of film actors using thick poster paint that could withstand sun and rain. Then he'd hoisted the billboards into place. All over India he'd created larger-than-life film stars who rose two, three, even four storeys above the ground. Giantesses in golden saris twirled parasols or knelt in ecstasy before savage idols or wept tears the size of hand grenades. Musclemen posed in wizards' capes, mod-squad bellbottoms, and blood-drenched camouflage fatigues. They shot arrows and leapt from tall parapets and fired bazookas at charging lions. The phantasmagorical billboards were as much a part of India's urban landscape as temples and minarets. They announced the week's attractions outside lavish cinema palaces where arrivals of new superstar vehicles were celebrated by mobs of patrons as avidly as they'd been in the States in the 1930s. Smaller hand-printed film posters were plastered on walls everywhere. Indians loved their movies, the more lavishly advertised the better. If the actors on the screen inside didn't quite live up to the ads' spectacular images, nobody minded. Admiring the outdoor artwork was part of the fun of going to a show.

At election time, cinema artists were hired to paint billboards depicting political candidates, who often looked as impossibly glamorous as film actors. The hand-painted Bollywood style influenced millions of product ads, as well. Posters featured housewives in golden saris happily scrubbing with DIZ soap flakes, baby-Krishna-plump children reaching out for HORLICKS malted milk, raffishly sideburned teenagers waving like matinee idols from BAJAJ motor scooters. In the West, this work would have been thought "kitch" or at best "commercialized folk art." Some educated Indians, including Mrs. Mukerjee, found it embarrassing garish. She thought I was slightly mad to take so many photos of billboards and posters, but my camera lens was drawn magnetically toward them. I loved their vibrancy, their unabashed sentimentality and surreal derring-do.

Karyan Singh himself had once been a star in the world of billboard-painters, traveling all over India. His work blazed above avenues and rooftops of its biggest cities. But one day he came to the job drunk, fell from a scaffold, and fractured his leg in several places. It healed crookedly; no one would risk hiring him again. Mrs. Mukerjee face softened she translated. The twin dagger-blades of Karyan Singh's mustache drooped at the tips, and red veins throbbed in his eyes; he'd had a few drinks this afternoon, too. I noticed the cobwebs in the studio's corners, the peeling plaster, and the dizzying odor of old paint. This room hadn't been opened in a long time.

"When I can find time to paint here," he said, smiling, "I am rising up the scaffolds again!"

Hearing someone call, Karyan Singh opened the studio door. A middle-aged woman in a faded gray sari stood barefoot in the shop, hands on her hips. She spoke in a sharp voice to the artist, then paused, touched her fingertips to her forehead as she bobbed her head at Mrs. Mukerjee and me. We greeted her. "Please, come next door for tea," she asked. Following her, we left the shop to cross an alley where goats chewed on rotted clumps of plants that gave off a powerful stench.

The air in the artists' small sitting room, though, was fragrant with incense smoke rising from a brass bowl in a corner of the carpet. I sat on a covered mattress beside Mrs. Mukerjee, adjusting a bolster between my back and the wall. "The woman is the artist's wife," she told me. "When he came back to this village after painting billboards, he was not in a good condition, but she showed him how to start this business. Now she takes orders and does all the accounts. He cannot do it, himself."

"Why not?" I asked.

She spread her hands at her side, palms up. "You have seen him."

A beaded curtain in the door rippled. The woman carried in a tray of teacups, followed by her husband. When he sat, one of his legs protruded at an angle; with his skinny chest and sharp nose, he resembled a collapsed crane with a broken wing. His wife lingered in the doorway, murmuring to Mrs. Mukerjee with her face nearly covered by the end of her sari head-cloth.

"She is telling me she doesn't want him to work in that small studio. The smell in it is bad for his respiratory organs. He uses cheap paint, and he has breathed too much of it." The wife's voice grew tearful. "She found him a job, but he is refusing to do it," Mrs.

Mukerjee continued, her own voice conveying frustration. "Do you remember the houses we saw with the ladies and elephants and whatnots on the walls?"

I smiled. "Of course!"

"He doesn't like to make those pictures. To him they are like the simple drawings of children."

"That's too bad," I said, but I could understand that, after seeing Goa, Madras, and the bright lights of Bollywood, he couldn't work up much enthusiasm for painting figures on thatch-roofed huts.

Karyan Singh twisted around to speak to his wife. She gazed back from the shadow of her hood-shaped sari end, her eyes wet-rimmed, her lips turning up in a smile. Though her face was deeply lined, I could see that once she'd modeled for Krishna's consort and other goddesses.

"Now he says he will make pictures on those houses. Because he doesn't like to see her crying," Mrs. Mukerjee said. "She has to push him along. There are four daughters who will soon need dowries."

"Four!" Karyan Singh said in English. He gave me a what-can-you-do?-look, the bags beneath his eyes drooping. I smiled back in sympathy.

When I finished my tea, we all stood up. Karyan Singh had to hold the wall to get his balance. Watching him leave the room, I could see that what had looked like a swagger in his walk was a carefully disguised limp. He rushed to his studio and returned with some prints. He handed me one of Ganesh with firecrackers. When I offered to pay for it, Mrs. Mukerjee frowned, as if worrying that I might be cheated.

Then she translated what Karyan Singh told her: "The printer has given him extra posters at no charge, he says, so it would be wrong to ask you to pay for them." When he handed her one of Lakshmi, her face broke into a smile. I carefully tucked my rolled-up poster under my arm. With my palms pressed together, I raised my hands to my forehead, a gesture of acknowledging a great favor. Karyan Singh made the same gesture to me.

What Can You Do

When I visited India again in 2008, I was glad to see how much prosperity had come to the country, or at least parts of it, over the past twenty-three years. But something was missing from the landscape. I saw too quickly what it was: the hand-painted ads and signboards were gone. I could find no more commercial artists working in any of the villages. Gone, too, were the urban artists whose enormous billboards added such dramatic color to the skylines of India's cities. How I missed those sultry-eyed cinema divas with dangerously heaving bosoms, the fifty-foot tall supermen with tombstone teeth and shirt-bursting muscles! They'd all strode off the subcontinent for good. I learned that the downfall of the gods and goddesses had come at the end of the millennium with a terrific boom—the one that happened when India developed its own information technology as dynamic as any in the world. Suddenly computer-generated imagery provided a cheap and easy way to proclaim the arrival of blockbuster films and to advertise products.

Today's billboards and posters feature elegantly coifed ladies and tailored men who have stepped from the pages of glossy fashion magazines rather then from the imaginations of individual artists. The advertisements are slick, sophisticated, and repetitive, showing the same images in city after city. Unlike the hand-painted work, their style isn't unique to India; the same pictures, with a few costume changes, can sell movies and products in Singapore, Buenos Aires, or New York.

The figures in the old film posters resembled characters from Indian folk tales and legends; they embodied easily-grasped qualities familiar to everyone: courage, sensuality, virtue, malevolence, foolishness. The heroes and heroines may have been outsized, but they retained a common touch that allowed viewers to imagine themselves transported into their fantastic adventures. What qualities do figures in today's outdoor advertisements stand for? Sophistication and consumerism, and a certain blank-faced anomie:

the bored narcissism of the fashion model which discourages the viewer from identifying with any human qualities, rather focuses attention on the product itself. Instead of gazing up at billboards the way I used to do, I instinctually try to look away as I pass—the way I've always responded to advertising in America.

Many of the new female fashion idols have almost-Western faces; only the eyes, almond-shaped and Orientalized to resemble assimilated Western fantasies of the exotic East, look vaguely Asian. No young Indian farmer in town to mill his grain could fantasize about winning the heart of one these stylish ladies; the girl in the modern shampoo (not shampuu) poster will never flick her silky hair in his direction.

The new billboard man grasps the wheel of a BMW. He's debonair and sleek, in a Western sports coat or silk smoking jacket, and he's got power on his mind, the kind that comes from manipulating stock portfolios, not from lifting barbells in Y-front underpants. No village girl could imagine this gent approaching her father to begin negations about her dowry.

In the days when town artists and billboard painters ruled the world of public art, the figures they painted looked unmistakably like Indians, with dark orange skin tones slathered on by the bucketful. But today, the country's better-educated, internationally-oriented people don't want to see themselves like that. I can understand why, and know that it's time for me to see India as part of the changing, modern world, too. But I'm still uneasy noticing that the film stars and models who smile distantly down from billboards have complexions airbrushed to an any-racial homogeneity. Symbols of India's rising prosperity, they reflect the aspirations of the nation's new moneyed class, not the fantasies of the common people who, from what I can see, have sometimes been left far behind.

I was never able to find out what happened to Karyan Singh. I hope he had time to raise his daughters' dowries before the boom arrived. Perhaps he was able to get by painting traditional elephants and ladies and warriors which still appear on people's thatch-roofed houses in some parts of India. Though he thought them child-like, these examples of older folk styles have proved more resilient than the commercial work he preferred.

Occasionally, upwardly mobile home-owners hire artists to make copies of simple village illustrations beside the doorways of their elegant new houses—a sort of nostalgia for days that they wouldn't want to come back again. Either would I, but I can't help feeling sad that the painting Karyan Singh liked to do has had its day. I'm glad, though, that I was able to meet him, to admire his home-made signboards, and to live in India during a time when a race of giants frolicked high above the nation's dusty bus stations and tin-roofed slums, acting out dramas that everyone could enjoy.

CHILDREN OF THE MAZE

Walking up the driveway to Jaipur's prison complex, I recalled shadows of similar places falling over me, and nearly turned back. Then behind a window I saw an Indian woman who must have been the social worker I'd contacted about my visit. A blurred figure, she seemed to be pressed against the heavy glass as she stared out at me. I stepped up to the main gate. A buzzer rasped, the gate's steel teeth slid sideways; when I'd stepped inside, it clanked shut behind me, making the floor shudder beneath my feet.

Mrs. Romila Sharma and I exchanged stiff *namasté* greetings, each pressing palms together. Her supervisor had ordered her to take me around, she said in a weary voice. In focus now, she looked alarmingly thin, and too young—30 at most—for the gray streaks in her hair. Her pale blue sari was gathered around her so tightly that her movements made only faint whispers.

"I'm very new to this posting but I will try to show you...." She narrowed her eyes at me. "Professor, what is it that you are looking for here?"

In my letter to her supervisor, a friend of one of my colleagues at the University of Rajasthan, I'd said I hoped to explore research possibilities for my Fulbright grant, and offered to teach English to make myself useful here. I'd written about my experience teaching in prisons, and the five years I'd spent counseling delinquents in reform schools a decade ago. Suddenly I missed those kids, and for a moment felt a rush of old worries that I might have caused some of them more harm than good by intervening in their lives. The taut, wary look on Mrs. Sharma's face reminded me of an expression I'd often seen in my mirror during my own years as a social worker.

"I'll be interested in anything you can show me," I said, wishing I could have been clearer.

"Yes, all right." Adjusting her sari at the shoulder, she walked ahead of me down a long, twisting corridor. Somewhere farther inside the prison more gates crashed shut; I felt metallic echoes gust against my face as they rushed through the tunnels. Some guards marched past me in khaki uniforms with *képi*-like billed caps; they reminded me of soldiers at the desert fortress in *Beau Geste,* the old film about a French Foreign Legion outpost.

We were in the men's detention area, most of which, as a woman, she couldn't take me to. A few prisoners, wearing gray drawstring pants and sleeveless gray shirts, kept their eyes to the ground as they passed us. Inside an empty barracks, double-decker beds were neatly made; the scoured floors gave off a dizzying tang of ammonia. The convicts were at work now. We walked outdoors and crossed a sandy courtyard to the factory. Like the other buildings, its high crenellated roof-line was topped by coils of razor-wire like elaborate man-traps. Through a window, I could make out men at benches assembling what looked like office desks. Along the wall, massive robotic machines clattered as if in a frenzy to bash their way out. The entrance was locked, and the racket swallowed the sound of Mrs. Sharma's small fist rapping on the door.

"They tell me I am to show you this building—then no one will let me in!" Scowling, she wiped beads of sweat from her face, smudging the dark mascara around her eyes.

"Never mind, I can see fine from here," I said. The sun's glare was blinding; I shielded my eyes to squint inside. "The conditions look pretty good." This was true; I wasn't just trying to cheer her up. An article I'd read about the notorious Tihar Jail in Delhi reported that over 12,000 men awaiting trial—"undertrials"—were kept in unspeakable squalor.

"I should take you to my work area, but I've never gone to it from here. There are so many corridors and courtyards!" Mrs.

Sharma swayed in place. Then she led me back into another long, dim hallway. Our footsteps echoed out of sync. The deeper we went into the maze, the hotter and closer the air felt. A reek of disinfectant gradually gave way to a strong odor of smoke and spiced food that made my eyes sting. Mrs. Sharma paused at an open door. "The mess hall's kitchen," she said.

Two prisoners, their bare chests glistening, stirred a cauldron of brownish stew. Other men wielded huge spatulas to scoop rotis—discs of bread—out of a wood-fire oven, an iron furnace that blasted red-tinted heat into the room. Through an inner doorway I saw about a hundred men in gray file into the mess hall. They gave off a low, collective murmur like the approach of rolling boulders in a subterranean cavern.

A kitchen worker in an apron approached me. His eyes bulged, his hollow cheeks looked sanded down to the bone. A burly guard in khaki tried to push him away. The prisoner didn't budge.

"Who are you?" He squinted at me, his jaw thrust out.

"I'm a teacher," I said.

A gap-toothed smile cracked his face. "Years ago, a meditation teacher came! He made my mind so much at peace!" Suddenly he grabbed my wrist in both hands. I started, frightened. But his grip was light, and I recalled the way my American prison students had shaken my hand good-bye after each class, just wanting to touch someone from the outside world.

The guard gave the man a sharp prod with his truncheon. He let go of my wrist, but held me with his gaze a moment longer. "You want curry," he said.

The guard tensed. Mrs. Sharma was at my side. "You don't have to eat!"

Hesitating, I wondered what I was being invited to put into my mouth. Then I said, "I'll try it."

The man went to the stove and returned with a metal bowl. I used a folded roti as a spoon and took a bite. The food was unexpectedly tasty, better than I'd eaten in most American institutions. When I told the man this, he beamed proudly and strode away.

The guard, glowering at me, took the bowl. I'd made him look bad by accepting it from the prisoner. Pay-back time. "You liked this curry?" he asked me. "That convict, the cook—he was chef for big restaurant. Do you know why is he is here?"

I had to lock my jaw to keep from smiling. "Okay, tell me."

"Poisoning," he said, and walked out of the kitchen.

The social worker stood beside me again. "What he told you," she whispered. "I don't think it can be true."

"I know. It's an old joke—what visitors get told in places like this. I didn't know it was international." I saw her brows tense; she wasn't amused. "It's all right, Romila!" I said, then wondered if I should have used her first name.

I walked with her out to the corridor again. Her sandal heels clicked rapidly along. "If that man wasn't a chef," I asked, "what was he?"

"He is Munji Bhil—the leader of a famous gang of dacoits." Gradually she slowed her pace.

Dacoits, she said, were bandits who lived in desert ravines and ambushed camel caravans, leaving behind many dead. They also stopped trains by rolling tree trunks onto the tracks. When the locomotive crashed into them, derailing the train, the dacoits would leap aboard, guns drawn, to rob passengers—just like the Wild West in America. Munji Bhil had also been a smuggler. He trained his camels to out-race the mounted soldiers across the Rajasthan desert as he carried gems to Pakistan. He brought back raw opium as well as wagon-loads of cameras, video players, and other Western luxury items; because of India's trade restrictions on foreign goods, only smugglers could import them.

She paused by a door that led outside, glancing around as if lost. "Perhaps we can go this way...."

We walked out into another high-walled area. I looked down a long row of gray steel doors with thickly-screened windows. When I asked Mrs. Sharma what was behind them, her face went ashen.

"I am not supposed to take you here!" she whispered.

In this area were solitary confinement cells, mostly for "VIPs"—high-caste offenders and foreigners. Often upper class Brahmin men were kept in isolation for their own safety, she explained; one man here would surely be murdered if he were put among the other prisoners, who knew he'd once led a mob that had beaten to death some low-born "Untouchables" who'd "polluted" his well by daring to draw water from it.

"*Hola! Hola!*" I heard someone calling to me in a muffled voice from one of the cells. Behind the window in its door, I saw a bristly pale face. "*Señor*—come! Please—talk to me!"

"*Don't!*" She stepped between me and the man's door. I walked away beside her. The prisoner was a Spaniard, she explained, who'd been convicted of smuggling explosives to Pakistan where they were used against Indians in the disputed state of Kashmir. I recalled reading about women and children blown to pieces by road bombs there, and felt a surge of loathing for him. But why him—when the dacoit I'd met hadn't upset me? This place was disorienting me. The sandy ground muffled our footsteps.

"How long is he here for?" I asked Mrs. Sharma.

"I don't know." She glanced ahead into yet another courtyard. "He—he may be executed."

We walked on, entering an open area that appeared to be a century older than the rest of the prison; its stone walls were streaked brown as if rusted by time. In the center of the yard stood a platform made of heavy planks. A wide staircase led up to it. At one end a steel pole rose high into the air. A crossbeam jutted out from its top like the narrow beak of a monstrous black crane. The gallows.

I felt a chill rush down the back of my neck. "Is that where the Spaniard—where he might be going?" I asked, my voice hushed.

"Yes. I feel very bad to see that thing! It's against all I believe...."

"Me, too," I said. But I couldn't stop staring up at the gibbet. From beneath, it looked huge, predatory. The plank steps sagged. How many men had climbed them, flanked by guards and a hangman, to confront a dangling noose? The courtyard was terribly still. The great bird waited. Never before had I felt so close to the instantaneous process of passing from life to death. I was appalled, yet felt an urge to walk up those steps, myself—to stand on the planks right beside the trap door, to stare up into the beak of death. I took a step toward the platform. Then I saw the social worker watching me—her eyes widening, her lips pressed together as if to restrain a cry—and quickly turned around.

She moved on quickly. I stammered encouraging things about the place to try to dispel her uneasiness, and my own.

"We're doing our best," she said, "at least for the convicts."

"Who else is here?" I asked.

She looked down. "We also have undertrials. They have a different status."

"I thought they were all kept at Tahar, in Delhi."

She shook her head. "Undertrials are a high percentage of this jail's population."

At the end of the yard the walls narrowed into an area of deep shadow. Slowing, we walked close to an old brick building with one long, barred, glassless window. The stench hit me first—piss and shit and rancid sweat. Through the already roasting air rushed a wave of body heat—from the men behind those bars.

"The undertrials," Romila whispered.

They'd spotted us. Suddenly they began shouting, wailing, calling out to us in Hindi. I halted, my heart racing. The long, kennel-like cell was so dark that at first I couldn't make out complete faces, only grimy foreheads. And a long a row of knuckles—men's fists gripping each metal shaft. For an instant, I saw deeper into the low-ceilinged room; it squirmed with near-naked bodies squashed together, surging toward the light. Anguished shrieks ricocheted off the walls, piercing me in the crossfire. The social worker was frozen in place, one hand pressed against her cheek.

"*Romila—come on!*" I shouted to her over the racket, and gripped her arm. We ran together, my legs rubbery. I yanked open a door and we rushed through, slamming it behind us. Gradually, the screams outside faded.

On a bench in the corridor, she leaned forward, wiping her face with a handkerchief. I sat back, trying to catch my breath. I recalled what I'd read about Delhi's prison where "undertrials" lived in horrific conditions, thirty men to a room designed for ten. They slept in shifts on filthy floors. Gangs roved the cell blocks, demanding food and drugs, raping boys. Latrines overflowed, insects swarmed over the walls. Prisoners' throats were slit in the night. Those men waited to appear in court for many months, sometimes for two or three years, or even longer. Conditions must have been as bad, here.

"Are you all right?" I asked finally.

She raised her head. She'd rubbed the skin around her eyes nearly raw. "Still dizzy, a little—"

"Me, too."

"I—I know where I am now! My work area is not far." She blinked hard. "But you may have seen enough…?"

I stared down the deep corridor. "Let's go on."

She opened a door at the far end of the hall, and we were outdoors again. From the other side of a high wall came twittery sounds, as if from a hidden aviary. I cocked my head to listen.

"Those are the children," Romila said.

"What are kids doing in a place like this?"

"They belong to the female inmates. A small prison within a prison is here—for ladies. They can keep their children until they're about six years old."

She called to a guard in a khaki sari who unlocked a steel door for us. I waited inside as Romila started across a big open courtyard. Several woman rushed forward to grab her hands. She squeezed their fumbling fingers, smoothed the saris back from their cheeks, spoke in soft Hindi to them. Her face glowed. The voices of the women splashed around her. Spotting me, though, they backed off quickly. Romila turned and beckoned for me to join her. Fifty-one prisoners, she said, lived in this area, some with their children. Now I saw little girls in brightly colored dresses, boys wearing neat shirts and shorts—all shrieking and laughing as they raced around in the hot sunshine. Many were playing with plastic toys on the loose ground; the yard was a giant sandbox for them. With cups of water, they'd created a small complex of mud fortress-like buildings whose rooftops were crenellated like those of the prison walls that loomed above them.

At the far end of the area was a loom about twenty feet long that resembled an enormous harp lying gracefully on its side. Women in hooded white saris were working the strings, pushing and pulling at wooden rods. More women in white glided along a dormitory verandah and hovered about in ghostly groups. As soon as I started walking toward them, they rushed away, pulling down the ends of their saris over their faces as they ran.

"They must hide their faces from men who aren't their relatives." She said. "Many Rajasthani ladies still practice *purdah*. Even in prison, the custom remains."

"Those white saris—are they the prison uniforms?"

"Oh, no," she said. "Hindu widows wear white."

"You mean...each one of these women are widows?"

"Yes." Her voice dropped. "They killed their husbands."

"*All* of them?" I stared at her. Hearing my voice rise, the children suddenly went silent. An echo of their cries rang against the far wall.

"Often their husbands abuse them," Romila said. "The beatings go on year after year, from the time they are married at twelve or thirteen. And they can't escape anywhere. So one night, after the man has been drinking and passes out, a woman might pick up a heavy stone—" She raised her hands in the air. "—and smash it down on his head." She sighed. "Then if the men in her husband's family don't kill her, she is dragged off to the local constabulary."

Several women peeked warily at me around the side of a building. I glanced down, pushing the toe of one shoe into the sand. On a road outside Jaipur, I told Romila, I'd watched from a car as man pounded a shrieking woman with a heavy tree branch as she lay collapsed in the dust. I'd wanted to jump out and help her, but the driver grabbed my arm to keep me from risking my life and his: it wasn't safe, he said, to intervene in a dispute between a man and his woman. I hadn't told anyone about this incident until now. "I still wonder if I should have listened to him," I said.

"I'm afraid the driver was right," Romila said. "And there was nothing you could have done."

I was silent for a moment. Then I asked, "How long are the women's sentences?"

"Fifteen years, minimum, for murder," she said. "But some of them stay longer. Often their families refuse to take them back in their villages, so they've no place to go."

"And the children haven't either?"

"Not usually," she said. "You must have been seeing how many street urchins there are in Jaipur. We don't want to add to their numbers."

She waved at the kids. Racing forward noisily, they crowded in close and gripped the folds of her sari in their tiny fingers and nuzzled their foreheads against her like baby goats wanting their necks stroked. She smiled; her whole body loosened, as if a steel rod had slipped out of her spine.

With the kids tagging behind, she took me along a verandah to the "vocational learning area" where huge manual typewriters squatted on desks like prehistoric armadillos. Two more looms were strung with white thread. The ladies made their own saris, as well as bed-sheets that were sold to a hospital so they could use the money to buy small things for themselves and their children, Romila said. She taught literacy, typing, and weaving, and arranged for teachers to give classes to the children. "In their villages, they could never get the schooling we give them." She pointed to a television set. The ladies and their children could view educational programs, and also see the Monday night Bollywood movie along with millions of other Indians.

My old social worker life was coming back to me here. One day at a reformatory, I told Romila, I'd supervised a kid named Minesha, a 17-year old former prostitute from Harlem, while she was visited by her 3-year old daughter. Minesha's aunt came into the reception room with the wide-eyed little girl, whom she'd dressed as if for church: pink pinafore with white stockings and shiny patent leather shoes. I'd loved watching Minesha play with her daughter; she hugged the child and braided her hair, murmuring to her in a soft, musical voice I'd never heard her use before. It was hard for me to pry mother and daughter apart at the end of the visit; they clung to each other with tears streaming down their cheeks. After the heavy front door had clunked shut behind the little girl, her wails from the parking lot made my eyes damp, too. Now, recalling the bird-like cries of the kids at the Jaipur prison, I wondered how it was that India, supposedly a less developed country than mine, had found a way to keep children with their incarcerated mothers for years.

"Being separated from her child—was that part of the girl's punishment?" Romila asked me.

"Oh, no," I said. But then I frowned. "Maybe it was, though, in a way. For years, I thought I understood how things worked in that place. But then I realized I didn't."

We were sitting at some school desks while children nearby stacked wooden blocks. Romila squinted hard at the far wall. "Today, I had confusion like this, too," she said. "About this prison."

"When we saw the undertrials?"

"Yes!" She pressed her knuckles against her lips.

Pok! A little boy in a red sweater threw a block against my desk. He grinned at me when I picked it up. A few other kids, more curious than shy, ventured closer to me. I took a big picture book from a desk and sat down cross-legged on the sand with it on my lap.

"Won't you spoil your clothes?" Romila asked.

"It doesn't matter." I turned a page. Gathering her sari loosely, Romila squatted beside me.

The boy's huge eyes were level with mine as he watched my face. I pointed to a drawing of a cat, then mimed the Hindi name of the animal, which fortunately I knew, and smiled expectantly at him. In a sing-song voice, he said the word for "cat..." then for "dog," "cow," and "donkey," as I pointed to different animals. I applauded each time he spoke. Kids clapped, too. Now Romila was joining in the applause. Finally she spoke, smiling and patting the air with her palms. The noisy recitation ended in a shower of laughter. She and I got to our feet. The kids leaned against Romila and stared at me.

"Every child in India has seen those animals," Romila said, "except Rahul." She rested her hand on the boy's shoulder. "He was born in here, so he knows animals only from picture books." This didn't seem to bother him; he kept gazing at the book and chattering away in Hindi. I turned pages, and we looked at more exotica: squirrels and fish, trees and flowers. Other kids crowded around, and I smelled the sweet scent of laundry soap their clothes gave off.

Suddenly, growing agitated, they all turned toward a woman dashing across the sand. Her sari swept out behind her like a long, white cape. An "unbalanced" prisoner, Romila explained; she had to work out her mental stress by running. "We should leave now." Romila glanced around. From the opposite end of the courtyard I saw dark eyes glowing at me through gauzy white veils. An agitated whispering swelled like the sound of leaves at the approach of a storm. "The ladies are frightened," Romila said. "There are some here who haven't been this close to a man in many years."

In an empty office near the gate area, Romila talked to her supervisor on the phone. Then she told me that she was sorry, but it had been decided that the prison couldn't offer me any research or teaching opportunities. A man couldn't be admitted regularly to the women's section; the male convicts had no need to learn English, and no "outsider" could be permitted near the undertrials. The decision made sense to me; I could see now that I'd been admitted only as a courtesy to the university. For a moment I was disappointed. Then the feeling passed.

"I'm afraid your time has been wasted—"

"No, the opposite," I said. "I'm very grateful to you."

Romila smiled faintly. Then she leaned toward me. "I did not tell my supervisor that we saw those men, the undertrials," she said.

I nodded. "I won't say anything."

"Thank you. I knew that they were in the prison, of course. But I never really saw them before today." Sighing, she sat down beside the desk. "You know, Edward, I have been blind to many things. Sometimes I wonder if I ought to be working in a place like this."

I pulled over a chair and sat beside her. "I used to wonder that, too, in America."

"Surely, where you worked, there were no people like the men we just saw."

"There must have been. I think there are people like that everywhere," I said. "Maybe we all have to stay blind some of the time, Romila. If I hadn't, I couldn't have been any use to anyone."

"And here, I couldn't help the ladies if I were always thinking about what happens on the other side of their walls." She tapped her fingers quickly on the desk. "Normally, I just rush as fast as I can from the front gate to their section. And then, when I walk through the door in their wall, I feel so—I don't know—"

"Safe?"

"That's right!" She blinked hard. "It is remarkable, because…they tell me that *they* feel safe when *I* come."

"I used to hear that, too." I met her gaze. "I think when the women and the kids see you, they know they're not forgotten. They're still part of the world. That's what you do for them."

She nodded slowly. The room was quiet; even the echoes of crashing inner doors had stopped. "And that's what they do for *me*, too," she said in a hushed voice.

I smiled. "I remember that feeling."

We walked down the dim corridor together toward the front gate. It slid sideways for me. We stepped out onto the driveway's light. She pressed her palms together and said, "*Namasté.*"

"*Namasté.*" I made the same gesture, and stood there for a moment enjoying the stillness with her.

SCANDALS

During our first years together, Amy and I, recovering from terminally stalled marriages, transformed our new bed (so we said) to a train rocking through the darkness almost every night. But in India, when she came to join me after a separation of four long months, we didn't put much mileage into the bed in the house I'd rented. From the railway depot down the street we heard locomotives give off enthusiastic sighs of steam, but our room stayed torpid in the 110 degree heat that blow-torched our lungs. Sand from the Rajasthan desert stung our eyes and crunched in our rice. I'd grown used to life in India, but Amy wept when, as she tried to get a drink, the tap gave out only a cough. When water did flow, it smelled like the sewage ditch outside where feral pigs woke us at daybreak with their raucous wallowing. We fantasized about cool air and fresh water more than we did about each other.

Amy pressed her lips tight to keep from complaining, but I saw that if she were to survive the final month of my research grant, I'd better get her out of this broiling suburb of Jaipur for a while. A university colleague, Ashok, suggested we visit a town called Mt. Abu, a popular mountain resort. There, he said, the days were breezy and the evenings sparkled with cool mist. We headed there on an all-night train, so tired we hardly heard the snores of the two other couples cocooned on the bunks of our compartment. In the morning, a battered taxi drove us up the mountain. The temperature seemed to drop five degrees a minute.

Ashok's sister, Mira, who'd recently started teaching at the town's primary school, had booked us into a centuries-old converted palace with rusty cannons guarding the gate and a courtyard exuberant with flowers. On a mural in our room, gazelles gamboled over lush, green fields. The four-poster bed looked so inviting we wanted to try it out right away, but I glanced at my watch and remembered we were due for dinner at Mira's house. Quickly we changed out of our traveling clothes. Amy put on the silver-gray blouse I'd bought her in a Jaipur market.

"You look pretty in that," I said.

She shrugged. "The style's not right for me. But at least it goes with my hair, now." Because of the unreliable water situation at our house, she hadn't been able to use her blonde rinse.

I hoped our dinner would be brief.

Bordering the paths of the school grounds, white-washed rocks glowed like big electric bulbs in the twilight. I spotted a woman in a pale blue sari—Mira, presumably—in the doorway of one of the staff houses. She was waving excitedly as if to flag us down before we might rush away.

"*Namasté! Namasté!*" On the doorstep, we all pressed our palms together at chest level, dipping our heads. She beamed, "Welcome—Professor Hower, Mrs. Hower."

"Edward," I said.

"Just Amy is fine." Her smile was tight. She wasn't used to constantly making a secret that she wasn't a "Mrs." In our American university town, no one cared that we'd lived together eleven years without a wedding, but in India such a relationship would have been considered beyond the pale of respectability.

"Oh please, please—come in!" Mira's voice sounded ragged. As she showed us into the front room, we glanced at her bare feet and we removed our shoes, according to custom. "Just sit anywhere you will be comfortable."

The only place to sit was a square, firm mattress that took up most of the floor space; its cotton cover was printed with a flowery design. Mira hovered around us with dishes of nuts. Tendrils of hair escaped her bun, dangled over her ears and neck. An attractive, heavyset woman in her early forties, she moved precariously, her toes curling on the linoleum like a tightrope-walker's. Sweet incense smoke floated from a corner niche where small sandalwood deities perched: several elephant-headed Ganeshes like children's action-figures; Hanuman, the heroic monkey god; and amorous Krishna cuddling his devoted paramour Radha. Amy, a devout atheist, ignored them, but their company relaxed me. Mira swayed in place, smiling down at us.

Um...." I chewed a cashew. "Amy and I bought a spread like this," I said, pointing to the cloth we were sitting on.

Amy glanced at me, nodded at Mira. "Yours is very pretty."

"Oh, thank you! So few high-quality things are available in this exile outpost!" Mira wrinkled her nose. "How is my brother, in his big university posting? So near he is to Mt. Abu, yet he hasn't visited here in all these months. I suppose he has sent you to check up on me!"

I shook my head. "He just suggested—"

"Of course—never mind! It's very kind that you've come." She sat cross-legged, leaning toward us. "And what is it that are you both doing in Jaipur?"

"Amy's working on a novel." I shifted my position on the mattress. "I'm collecting folktales out in the villages."

"Tales." Mira narrowed her gaze. "Brave kings and virtuous queens, isn't it? And the wicked adulteress buried up to her neck in the dirt."

Amy's nervous laugh quickly turned to a throat-clearing when she saw the look in Mira's eyes. "But the stories can't all be like that," she said.

"True. Sometimes I told folk fables about amusing jungle animals to my daughters." Mira sighed. Silence. I heard the ticking of an invisible clock. Mira stared off into the kitchen, then faced Amy again. "And how are you adjusting to life in Jaipur? It must be so scorching, scorching, this time of year!"

Amy let out her breath. "It sure is!"

"I am so sorry. And you are just arrived here...."

What Can You Do

I heard a door click, a sudden swish of cloth. Mira scrambled to her feet. "*Guruji!*" her voice rang out as she dashed into the kitchen. "*Oh, Guruji! You have come!*"

Any shot me a raised-eyebrow look, which I shrugged back. A plump-faced young man had come in the kitchen doorway without knocking and now padded into the sitting room with Mira at his heels. He appeared to be wearing a long white dress. No, it was a kind of sarong worn with a knee-length silk shirt. Wavy hair caressed his shoulders. As he gazed around at us all, his lower lip swelled as if he'd just bitten into a piece of candy so sweet he could barely contain his elation.

Mira introduced him to us only as "Guruji." ("Ji" was a suffix appended to the names of respected people; "guru" meant simply "teacher.") What followed was something I'd hadn't once seen in this country where men and women never touched each other in front anyone but immediate family: the guru wrapped his arms around Mira with a bear hug. His eyes closed in a serene expression. She collapsed against his chest, her cheek nuzzling his shirt.

"Guruji has been so very sensitive to me during these past months!" she said to Amy, stepping back unsteadily.

"Oh—no, no, no!" he cooed, pursing his mouth.

"Without him, I might have taken my life!" Mira gazed up at him, her face glowing. "Guruji, will you stay for dinner—please?"

"Oh—no, no, no!"

We sat again, and Mira brought a cup of tea for him, which he drank with soft, slurping sounds, sitting in a lotus position on the mattress. He said almost nothing, just smiled dreamily as the rest of us chatted about Mira's school. She was desperate for a transfer, she said; the girls were angels, but the teachers here were hopelessly provincial. She fetched more nuts, which Guruji refused with a wave of his fingers and then proceeded to gobble down by the handful.

He turned to Amy, his eyebrows tilted. "Amy, I feel you are so uncomfortable!"

"Oh, no—I'm okay." She managed to smile but I knew that sitting cross-legged, the custom here, always made her back ache.

"I must prepare rice," Mira said. "Now you and Edward can take an amble around the school, stretch the legs."

"I will help you in the kitchen, Mira!" Guruji beamed at her.

We walked past a playground for faculty children: a slide, a sandbox, a metal frame with three swings hanging from the bar. A pleasant breeze blew through the darkness but I could sense Amy's tension in her quick gait. "I don't get Mira at all," she said. "Or maybe that's just India being inscrutable to me again."

"Ashok didn't tell me what her story is. She seems very glad we've come."

"She has her holy man to keep her company. What's *that* all about?"

"I don't know...." The best I could do was explain to Amy that gurus in India, unlike the characters whose fuzzy faces appeared occasionally in Western screen comedies, were taken seriously in their own country. They founded charities and study centers that people visited to renew their spiritual beliefs. Unofficially, though, stories about randy "godmen" were part of folklore here, traditional and modern, like tales of lascivious friars in old England and corrupt televangelists in America.

"Right...." Amy said, meaning: I'll wait and see.

We strolled along in silence, passed a palm tree leaning like a switched-off gooseneck lamp, then headed back toward the playground area. My heart sank as I spotted a chubby white form sitting on a swing. Guruji. With a clatter of chains, he jumped up and joined us.

"How I love the cool fragrance of these evenings!" He swept both arms high in the air. His loose sleeves flapped like wings. "I feel light as a moth! Do you, Amy? I am having the sensation that we could just flutter away, utterly free! Just *skip* along!"

She pressed her arms to her sides. "I don't think so—"

One moment she was beside me—the next she was gone in an flurry of white cloth. Out onto the moonlit field she scrambled beside the flapping guru. He held her by the hand and danced across the grass, head back, hair flouncing behind him. *"Skip! Skip!"* he sang out.

"Hey!" I shouted, rushing toward him.

Amy skidded to a halt, yanking her hand away from him.

"You see?" Guruji's eyes bulged mischievously. "I was sensing the eagerness of your footsteps!"

"*No!*—" Amy leaned against me. Feeling her struggle to catch her breath, I held her loosely around the waist. Guruji rocked his head, trying to coax a cheerful expression out of her with his marshmallow smile. Then he strolled off. In a few seconds he reappeared farther away, slipping back into Mira's kitchen door.

"Amy, are you okay?" I asked.

She jammed her fists against her hips. "That's the silliest man I've ever seen in my life!"

"I should have tackled him." Sweat was breaking out on my forehead.

"Why didn't I pull my hand away sooner? His grip was like…foam rubber. But I couldn't let go!" She shook her head. "Why on earth did Mira invite him here to meet us, anyway?"

"Well, she couldn't ask a man to dinner without someone else being with her."

"Great. So we're chaperones."

"Listen, she's lonely. Couldn't you see that?"

"Of course I could!" She glared at me. "But what d'you think *I've* been? I can't connect with anyone here and I miss my kids! While you're off gathering your folktales, I've got nothing to do all day but stare at the walls of your house!"

"I thought you were working on your book."

"I haven't been able to write a word! Sweat keeps dripping onto my keyboard. The local kids giggle outside the window! They reach in with a stick and poke the curtain aside to watch me!"

"I'm sorry, darling. You never said a word—"

"I don't want to be a drag on you here, but…" She took a big breath. "I'm all right, now. Really."

We went back inside. I was relieved for Amy's sake that Mira's dinner was delicious, a lightly spiced chicken dish with almonds. Though not used to eating with her fingers, Indian-style, Amy cleaned her plate and complimented Mira. Guruji, who'd decided to stay after all, busily soaked up gravy with finger-balls of rice.

For several lazy days, Amy and I wandered the streets of the town. We gazed at flowering vines in miniature gardens, paused outside a bakery to smell the sweet cakes, heard Bollywood film music squeaking out of curb-side stalls. Other tourists, all Indians, passed us in family groups. We strolled by shops and guest houses: TEA AND SAMOSA HERE, BEST SWEETS IMPORIUM, VISITORS WELL COME. Paddle-boats glided on a sparkly lake. We rented one and joined the flotilla. From cottages along the shore, soft voices floated out across the water. Mt. Abu reminded me of old resort towns in New York's Catskill Mountains: casual, cheerful, shabbily cozy. In our room, we lay about talking and talking, with no thoughts of heat, sand, or pigs. I was sadly aware that the soft, saggy bed was better suited to dozy affection than passion. Or were we just getting too old for this kind of travelling life?

I'd promised to call Mira that week, but every time I saw one of the ubiquitous red *Ten Rupees Only* telephones on a shop counter, I walked past it. On our last day, though, I did invite her to our hotel—for tea, since its dinners weren't as good as the one she'd cooked for us, and we had catch a midnight train later. At the entrance to the hotel grounds, Mira stepped out of a taxi looking radiant in a pink and gold sari. Then Amy and I suppressed sighs: behind her followed Guruji, doughy white and gazing tranquilly around him.

The sun's slanted rays ignited a row of cedars whose long shadows sprawled across the palace lawn and climbed partway up the ancient stone walls. From nearby I heard high-pitched chirps as if from an aviary—the cries of children whose families rented cottages on the grounds, each one guarded by rows of potted red geraniums like toy soldiers. Two barefoot little girls rushed past us.

"Look at them—how beautiful!" Mira cried, clapping her hands. "Can we sit here?"

"Of course!" I pulled over some cane deck chairs. Guruji flopped down in one beside Mira, who gazed after the girls. A starched, elderly waiter brought us plates of sugar biscuits, cups and teapots and tiny pitchers of heated milk. Teenagers ambled by in same-sex clusters; silver-haired grannies in somber saris shuffled along, tapping their canes. Not far away, base lines for tennis courts were faintly visible in the grass. The area was a big playing field now where fathers kicked soccer balls with their kids and pretty young mothers hit shuttlecocks into the air with plastic racquets. Middle-class Indians didn't get much exercise in crowded cities and tended to be pudgy, but here, with this rare chance to romp with their children on a large recreation area, they moved with an appealing awkwardness as if re-learning to use their limbs in ways forgotten since their own childhoods. I lay back, half-closing my eyes. Then I heard a rustling sound.

Mira was handing Amy a package. "Perhaps this will be helpful to you," she said.

"What? Oh...." Amy slowly peeled away the silver paper and pulled out a sandalwood figure—the elephant god, Ganesh. He sat on her palm with his trunk resting on his pot belly.

"Guruji and I chose him." Mira smiled. "You see, Ganesh is the remover of obstacles."

"Oh, Mira...." For the first time since Amy had arrived in India, I saw her examining the image of a god without wariness.

I'd hoped that she might come to like the country's amiable deities as much as I did, but I could see that she was getting tired of seeing them everywhere. Still, she awkwardly stroked the rounded image on her lap. "He's rather sweet, isn't he? Thank you so much!"

"Perhaps your children will like him," Mira said. "*Do* you have children?"

"I have three boys...." Amy paused. "By a previous marriage."

Mira sat up, blinking. "You had a previous...marriage?"

In India, Amy and I been warned, divorce was still rare, even scandalous, especially for women; we were careful not to share a lot of our personal information with people here.

"Yes, I did." Amy met her gaze.

"And...second marriages like yours and Edward's are common in America?"

"Pretty common," I said.

Amy gave me a long look. I finally nodded. "But in fact...." she said, "we're not married."

"This is true?" Mira's eyes widened. *"Ahh!"* She sat back, rested her cheek against the padded slope of the deck-chair, smiling. "I promise—I won't speak a word of this to a soul."

"Nothing needs to be spoken," I said, "about anyone."

We ordered more tea, as well as plates of scones, then samosas, then jam sandwiches. At one point, a cloud-white 1950s Packard floated along the drive, an arm waving from the window. When it stopped, Guruji walked over to talk to the driver. He was the old maharajah, Mira whispered to Amy and me; he still lived in part of the palace. "One of our donors," she said proudly.

"Donors?" I asked.

She didn't seem to hear me. The car rolled on. Guruji padded back to his chair and reached for another sandwich. Soon it was dark, time to "make a move," as Mira said. But at the driveway's end where we could have hailed a taxi for Mira, the evening was so pleasant that Amy and I continued strolling with her and Guruji into town. The shop-fronts and restaurants were strung with fairy lights. Mira stopped in front of a the elaborately carved open door of a temple.

"Since...since coming to Mt. Abu, I've hardly spent time in any temples," she said. "I haven't dared. The priests are too...busy to speak to me."

"You can go in, Mira. Our Ganesh will bless us!" He pointed to the bulge in Amy's straw bag.

This temple wasn't sacred to Ganesh; it was dedicated to the monkey god, Hanuman. Actual monkeys, finding sanctuary here, perched on the sills of the latticed windows. Fragrant clouds of smoke billowed inside the walls; a brass bell clanged.

In the foyer, a boy holding a long staff approached a very respectable-looking couple. "Guide, Sir? Madame?"

The woman gathered her silk sari to her, and the man, impressive in a tan safari suit, shook his head severely and strode inside with his wife. When the boy approached me, I heard the hiss of a nearby monkey and, seeing the guide brandish his stick, handed him a coin.

The first thing he did was bonk the monkey on the head as it charged toward us. Several of the beasts scrambled off, chattering and baring their teeth. Mira walked slowly, dreamily, caressing the wall's bass-relief gods with her fingertips.

Suddenly a woman's wail rose in the courtyard. We rushed into the open space to find the woman in the silk sari shrieking at a monkey that was sitting on a ledge high on the wall and dangling her purse from its paw. Her husband patted her shoulder, trying in vain to calm her. The monkey picked through the purse. A crowd of tourists gathered on the ground staring up, a crowd of monkeys gathered around the ledge grinning down. The first monkey turned the purse inside out to gnaw on its lining. A compact, a lipstick, some pills and coins rained onto the flagstones below. They were followed by the purse, which the monkey, evidently not finding very tasty, flung down. The animals scampered off across the roof.

Crossing the courtyard toward the gate, Amy and Mira waved merrily to the furry delinquents. Outside in the narrow street, the two women walked among the other pedestrians, deftly dodging the occasional bicycle or wandering cow. I strolled along beside Guruji, enjoying the hubbub around me.

Back at our room, when Amy and I had finished packing, we looked longingly at the bed with its soft quilts. But we were not done with Mira and Guruji. They'd insisted that they must make us comfortable at her home while we waited for the drive to the railway depot. Somehow Guruji had conjured up an elderly Ambassador De Luxe Saloon Car with linen curtains over the back window and a fan that perched on the dashboard lolling its whirry little head slowly back and forth. At the hotel gate he sat beaming beside the driver in the front seat as we drove to Mira's house.

When we were settled on the sitting room mattress again, he turned to me and asked, "Edward, do you know California?" When I replied that I did, he stroked his hair back with both palms and said, "Three visits I have taken to Santa Barbara, California." He had been invited to stay with an important Indian businessman and his wife who lived there. Sadly, the businessman had expired, and now the widow was begging Guruji to return to California. She promised to build him a house exactly like her own. "Four-burner electric stove and Formica-top counters in the kitchen!" Guruji said breathlessly. "A beautiful balcony outside each bedroom!"

"So generous she is," Mira said, and bit her lip.

He raised his palms slowly at his sides. "A gift of love. It was her husband's last wish."

"But you don't want to go?" I asked.

"I like to visit...." He glanced at Mira, whose face had frozen. "But Mira needs me here. Many good people in Mt. Abu have a great need of me. At present, they are building me an ashram with residences for pilgrims."

"The ashram will be very beautiful!" Mira smiled again.

"My dear friend in Santa Barbara has told me that many American foundations donate to support centers for religious studies in India." Guruji leaned toward me. "I believe your research is funded by a foundation."

"Right. But I'm afraid it doesn't support religious projects."

"Oh, no, no, no! Only educational ones, I am aware. I, myself, love education very much." He smiled, his eyes crinkling. "But just in case you should meet someone...." He handed me a printed card with his color photo on it.

"Right...."

"Already Guruji is educating many people in Mt. Abu," Mira said. "He has helped me so much with my knowledge of the sutras."

He stood now, shaking down his sarong with a wriggle of his hips. "Mira, my dear—I have just remembered, I must use your telephone. Ashram contractors are waiting to hear from me."

"Of course, Guruji!" Scrambling to her feet, she pointed his way down the hall.

I stepped out on the doorstep and Amy went into the kitchen with Mira. Their voices drifted through the open window, Amy's quiet, Mira's becoming increasingly high-pitched. Then Guruji's soothing tones reverberated. The front door opened, and Amy joined me.

"What an operator, that guy!" she said as we walked out into the darkened field.

"Sure." I turned over his glossy card in my pocket. "But still, he could have just stayed in California nibbling grapes from widow's fingers."

"What do you think he wants from Mira?" Amy asked.

"She can't have much money."

"I'll say she can't!" Amy lowered her voice. "She just told me she's in debt to a bunch of lawyers. Her husband left her this year for another woman. Then he accused *her* of adultery and divorced her!"

"That's awful!"

"She was headmistress of a fancy school in Delhi, so it was a big deal. TV spotlights outside the courthouse and everything. Then the husband got custody of the two daughters. Mira hasn't even got visitation rights!"

"No wonder—"

"She couldn't stop sobbing!" Amy squeezed my arm. "I kept mopping her face with my handkerchief."

I rested my hand on Amy's. We stood close, breathing slowly. We'd had no legal troubles at all with our former spouses. Each of us had gotten joint custody of our kids, now nearly grown.

"We should go back in," I whispered finally.

When we sat down again, I noticed children's crayon drawings framed on a shelf—a squirrel, some tigers, a temple with silver spangles pasted around the gate. Several dolls sprawled beside them, dresses mussed. One was bald, her legs in the air, staring up like a child just run over by a truck.

Mira shuffled past me to stand beside the shelf with Guruji. Her eyes shone wet. "I should have straightened things better! I should have—"Her body began to sink.

Guruji gripped her by both shoulders. He slowly raised her again. "So brave Mira has been."

"The judge said I was unfit!" Mascara dribbled down her cheek. "He was bribed!"

"He was." Guruji pressed his chin to her forehead.

"Do you truly think the court will hear my appeal?"

"Yes, yes, certainly! The ashram's solicitors have filed the papers for you." He turned to the shelf. "But for now, we must straighten the dollies—look, my dear!" He leaned them against the wall. "When your girls visit you, they will see them waiting as they walk in the door. Yes?"

"Yes...." Mira sniffled, blinking hard. "Tell me about the ashram, Guruji."

"When it is completed, you will shift there from this school. Families will stay in the cottages—like at the palace, today. All the children you will care for." He spoke with a sing-song cadence, as if repeating verses he'd often recited for her before. "So many children! How they will love you!"

He reached towards a basket of napkins. Amy picked it up, and I leaned sideways to hand him one. He softly wiped Mira's cheeks.

"Such a lovely school you will have there! It will have a playground...with swings....." His voice sank to a whisper. "Your daughters will come. You will swing with the children...."

"And you will, too, Guruji?" Mira whispered back.

"I will." He rocked her slowly. "We will all swing together."

With Amy and I in back behind the driver, the Ambassador De Luxe Saloon Car bumped down the mountain road to the railroad depot. Soon the train rumbled toward us, vibrating the ground at our feet. Steam sprayed from between the wheels of the locomotive as it halted. In our carriage, I rented two blanket-rolls from the bedding-man and slid open our compartment door, expecting other passengers to be lying on their bunks. But the compartment was empty.

On the rack we packed the bulging straw bag beside our suitcase. I thought other passengers would knock on our door at each station where we stopped along the line, but no one joined us, and when I took out my railway map, I could see that there were no towns now for more than fifty miles. I locked the compartment. Amy and I turned to one another, grinning. Our clothes flew onto the luggage rack.

Rolling on a bunk, we joined the swaying rhythm of the car. When the whistle wailed up ahead, I wailed back. The moon outside the big window raced along with us, flickering wildly. Amy had never looked so lovely.

We got too carried away to notice that the train was slowing. It rolled to a stop beside a maintenance shed. Somewhere outside, a spotlight turned. Glare flooded our compartment. On a raised embankment beside the track, turbaned workers walked beside the carriages. Some of them—*oh no!*—were grinning in the direction of our window. We flopped onto our bellies. The window had a curtain but neither of us could reach its cord. We lay bare-assed, motionless.

Finally the locomotive gave off a blast and the train jerked forward. I felt Amy's breath warm against my neck. She was laughing.

Ca——chunk!...ca—chunk!...ca-chunk-chunk-chunk.... went the wheels. Gradually the train rolled away from the shed until the only lights in our compartment were flickers from the careening moon. As the engine got up to steam again, so did we.

EXPLORERS OF THE SPIRIT WORLD

In 1992, while on my second Fulbright grant to India, I lived in a suburb of Madras where my tiny apartment block was on a street named, strangely enough, for an American—a Colonel Olcott. Over a century earlier, my neighbors told me, he had lived nearby with a Russian woman on an enormous, high-walled estate, now the headquarters of the International Theosophical Society. It turned out that I'd passed it on the Number 28 bus every day on my way to and from the university where I taught. Now, my curiosity aroused, I got off the bus at the estate's gate. What I found inside the walls fascinated me, and continued to do so on periodic visits I made over the following decade. This article, as well as my novel based on some of its material—Shadows and Elephants—is the result of getting to know the man my street was named for, and the mysterious woman who inspired him to make his home in India.

On a warm autumn afternoon in 1874, Henry Steel Olcott, an attorney and popular New York journalist, found himself in Vermont looking for ghosts. On assignment for his newspaper, he planned to investigate one of the séances, or "spook shops," that were enjoying a surge of popularity across America.

His credentials as a sleuth were impeccable. After rising to the rank of colonel during the Civil War, he had attracted national attention as the head of a commission that investigated the conspiracy to assassinate President Lincoln. Now 42, with his fashionable mutton-chop whiskers and pince-nez spectacles, he was an imposing media figure, and his readers expected a brilliant exposé. They were to be very surprised.

For Colonel Olcott was about to have one of the most dramatic mid-life crises in history. Changing from skeptic to true believer, he would become a leading exponent of occult wisdom in countries around the world, and the first American to popularize Eastern religions in the West.

What brought about the dramatic turn-about in his life? Her name was Helena Petrovna Blavatsky, a down-on-her-luck Russian aristocrat and mystic who had also made her way to Crittenden, Vermont that afternoon. Middle-aged and fat, fond of dressing in frumpish Gypsy-like costumes, she was no siren. Nonetheless, her round face, wiry hair, and huge eyes gave her a hypnotic attractiveness. She could converse brilliantly on any subject, and when Colonel Olcott met her, he was fascinated.

Inside an old farmhouse, they joined a hushed audience facing a wooden platform. The room darkened. Onto the stage stepped the "materialized spirit" of Honto, a beautiful Indian maiden. She did a dance with scarves, then vanished into the shadows. An Egyptian juggler appeared, offering an Oriental rope trick. A wizened old lady brought messages from the next world in a tiny piping voice.

Madame Blavatsky herself began to call forth spirits from the ether. Among them was her family's former footman, who wore a tall fez and sang folk songs, and her late uncle, a Russian judge wearing lugubrious black robes. He gave her a military medal which she told the amazed audience had been buried with her father many years before. For Colonel Olcott, the medal was proof of her genuineness as a medium.

To understand how he could take such theatrical apparitions seriously, I had to look at the history of the religious movements that swept across the country during the last century. Spiritualism, the conviction that the dead could communicate with the living, had many sober-minded adherents then. The belief occurred partly as a reaction against Charles Darwin's Theory of Evolution, which seemed to deny all traces of a divine origin to human history. Defying "materialism," clergymen and mediums alike brought reassuring messages from Heaven to their audiences. Many people like Colonel Olcott believed that investigations of into paranormal activity would eventually reveal ways in which spiritualist "phenomena" could be explained by natural laws.

Today, in another era of confusing scientific innovations, the growing New Age movement has revived considerable interest in communication with the spirit world. Channelers, shamans, gurus, and spirit guides attract loyal followers. The actress Shirley MacLaine, who has been satirized in the Doonsbury cartoons, has become a best-selling author with her books about her past lives.

But none of these figures can match Madame Blavatsky's flamboyance or the proselytizing zeal for which Colonel Olcott became famous a century ago.

At seventeen, on the run from an unhappy marriage in Russia, Helena Petrovna Blavatsky began a life of constant travel. She supported herself as a lady's companion, journalist, pianist, and even a circus bareback rider. She also held séances among society matrons in Europe, Colonel Olcott reported in his columns, and studied magic with a Coptic sorcerer in Cairo. Ever in search of occult knowledge, she claimed to have visited India and Tibet.

The colonel, whose joyless marriage was ending and whose law career was bogged down in routine, remained smitten with the exotic Madame Blavatsky after they left Vermont. Defying social conventions, he set up house with her in an apartment on 47th Street and 8th Avenue in New York. To her, he must have seemed a godsend—she had recently been reduced to working in an immigrant sweat-shop making artificial flowers. Now she had someone who would not only pay the bills but would introduce her to the many influential people he knew. She and Colonel Olcott were probably never involved sexually—her letters report that she had an aversion to physical passion, and he was known to keep mistresses—but their partnership was to last for over a decade. They spoke of each other as "chums."

The "Lamasery," as journalists began to call their apartment, was a joyously eccentric place. A mechanical bird and a golden Buddha perched on the mantelpiece, framed by tall potted palms. Stuffed owls, snakes, and lizards peeped out from the overflowing bookcases. The star of this menagerie was a stuffed baboon, wearing spectacles and a dickey, and clamping under its arm a lecture on Darwin's "Origin of the Species". The ape signaled Madame Blavatsky's contempt for scientists who she said ignored the spiritual wisdom of the Orient.

The place became a salon for truth-seekers who were attracted by the colonel's enthusiasm and the Madame's witty, irreverent conversation. Guests also hoped to witness one of her famous "phenomena." Like other contemporary mediums, she could make mysterious rapping sounds echo from under séance tables and cause pictures to appear on slates no visible human hand had touched. Unseen "astral bells" tinkled around the room as she sat mesmerizing her audience with tales of her adventures.

At one gathering, Colonel Olcott suggested that an organization be established to study "phenomena" and occult literature. Someone suggested calling it "The Theosophical Society," after a group of Third-century Alexandrian scholars. The name was adopted, and, in November of 1875, the colonel was elected the society's first president. Among the early members were Thomas Edison, the inventor, and General Abner Doubleday, who was later credited with originating the game of baseball.

The new society needed ideas to distinguish it from those of other Spiritualist groups. Madame Blavatsky, announcing that she was through with "spooks," began writing a compendium of ancient occult knowledge. She was a voracious scholar, who seemed to remember every book she had read since childhood. The colonel edited her manuscript as she wrote, skillfully packaging her arcane theories for public consumption.

When her book, *Isis Unveiled,* was published in 1877, it came to nearly 2000 pages. Reviews were mixed. The author pasted all of them in her 30-volume scrapbook, which I read at the Theosophical Society's headquarters in Madras, India. "The most remarkable production of this century," said the *New York Herald.* "A large dish of hash," scolded the *Springfield Republican.* Madame Blavatsky shot back letters commenting on the reviews, doubling her media exposure. If she were alive during our era, I'm sure she'd be a popular guest on television talk shows. Her book is still in print, having sold over half a million copies since its publication.

In *Isis Unveiled,* Madame Blavatsky laid out the fundamentals of Theosophy. Borrowing from American spiritualism, contemporary science, European mysticism, and the religions of the East, she explained our existence as an evolutionary process by which we progress through successive reincarnations toward a perfect understanding of the Absolute. We are governed by the laws of karma, which reward the good deeds we have done in past lives. Theosophy, as she explained it, encouraged an appreciation of all the world's faiths, and embraced the brotherhood of all men.

The author claimed that most of her book had been dictated to her by Masters, extraordinary men who for centuries had been guarding secret knowledge in Egypt, India, and Tibet. She said that they communicated telepathically with her on astral currents. They also wrote letters, some of which dropped from the ether onto the colonel's lap as he sat working across from her at their desk. Non-Theosophical historians, needless to say, have doubted the telepathic origin of these letters. But at the time, Colonel Olcott reported their contents with great excitement.

Rival journalists attacked this new development, and the Theosophical Society's paid-up membership began to dwindle. Then a new convert, a Bavarian aristocrat named Baron De Palm, promised to bequeath the organization his entire fortune, consisting, he said, of a silver mine in Colorado and castles in Switzerland. He asked only that Colonel Olcott make sure that he was cremated after he died.

Cremation was unknown in America at the time, so when the baron passed away and Colonel Olcott announced that the body was to be burned, journalists had a field day with the story. After the ceremony, The *New York Daily Inquirer's* headline announced, BROILED BARON: DE PALM DECENTLY DONE. Unfortunately, the deed to the Bavarian's silver mines proved to be worthless. His Swiss properties were nothing but castles in air. The estate could not even cover the cost of the funeral.

Colonel Olcott devised a new plan to increase membership: he would merge the society with the Arya Samaj, a large Hindu revivalist organization in India with which he had been corresponding. The two groups, the colonel believed, had similar aims: the awakening of interest in ancient religious wisdom. Madame Blavatsky, who was tiring of New York, proposed moving the society's headquarters—along with its two founders—to India.

At first the colonel balked at giving up his comfortable life, but the prospects of adventure won him over. He acquired a letter of commission from the Secretary of State to help him make commercial contacts abroad. Madame Blavatsky took out American citizenship—the first Russian native ever to do so—in order to enjoy the protection of United States consulates in India.

The contents of the Lamasery were auctioned off. Soon the apartment, once so splendidly exotic, was bare. The few remaining Theosophists sat on packing crates to drink tea together one last time. Thomas Edison made a recording of everyone's voice—including that of the society's cat—on his new invention, the phonograph. On December 17, 1878, Colonel Olcott, Madame Blavatsky, and two British friends sailed off across the Atlantic bound for the Orient.

A pleasant compound of tile-roofed houses in the hills above Bombay became the Theosophical Society's headquarters. Swami Dayananda Saraswati, the leader of the Arya Samaj, welcomed the two Americans. Curious pundits and priests of every Asian faith arrived in droves to meet them.

Colonel Olcott soon became a popular lecturer all over India. Never before had a Westerner so ardently espoused Eastern religions and so vehemently rejected the influence of British colonialism. Maharajahs sent processions of elephants to meet him and Madame Blavatsky, showering them with gifts. Everywhere he stopped, the colonel founded branches of the Theosophical Society. Its fame spread throughout the subcontinent.

One Indian paper reported that Colonel Olcott had "A Hindu heart and a Saxon energy." Another reporter described Madame Blavatsky as "a woman of extraordinary powers...whose life is full of romance and hair-breadth escapes on land and sea and from shipwreck, poison, sword, fire, wild beasts and pestilence." She must have given him quite an interview!

Despite their anti-colonial sentiments, the Theosophists found a friend in A.P. Sinnett, the editor of the most influential British newspaper, the *Pioneer*. Mr. and Mrs. Sinnett had long been keen believers in Spiritualism. They now made Madame Blavatsky a celebrity guest at séances given by the leaders of Anglo-Indian society. Tongues sometimes clicked in disapproval of her Bohemian contempt for conventional decorum, which she called "flapdoodle." But everyone loved the mysterious miracles she produced.

Astral bells tinkled. Handkerchiefs embroidered with people's names appeared from the ether. Mr. Sinnett began to receive letters from the Masters. On one occasion, the wife of A.O. Hume, a high-ranking civil servant, expressed a wish to reclaim a brooch she had lost years before. Madame Blavatsky said it had been "materialized" outside in a flower bed. The amazed guests dug up the treasure.

At another gathering, a visiting European professor challenged the Madame by declaring that no one, not even she, could produce a miracle the way the yogis of the Shastras (holy books) had done in ancient times.

"Oh, they say no one can do it now? Well I'll show them!" Madame Blavatsky replied. "If the modern Hindus were less sycophantic to their Western masters, they would not have to get an old hippopotamus of a woman to prove the truth of the Shastras." She made a sweeping gesture in the air, and a shower of roses fell onto the heads of the startled guests. Smiling, Madame Blavatsky handed a flower to the professor.

Events like these caused much public debate. Believing that sensational press coverage distracted the public from the serious mission of the society, Colonel Olcott went on extended lecture tours without Madame Blavatsky along to cause controversy.

His greatest personal triumph occurred in 1880, when he was welcomed in Ceylon (now Sri Lanka), a land he was to visit thirty-one times in the next twenty-seven years. In a public ceremony, he took vows as a Buddhist. As a Theosophist, he considered the faith part of the One Great World Religion, and vigorously defended it against attacks from British missionaries who were trying to Christianize the island.

Defying the colonial authorities, he set about founding Buddhist schools—well over a hundred, by the end of the century. He spoke to enthusiastic audiences in temples and town halls, at coconut plantations and village crossroads, always urging his listeners to take pride in their cultural heritage. Travel was exhilarating, he reported in his journal, but arduous:

journeys by clear days, and nights of pouring tropical rain...when sleep is broken by the ear-splitting sounds of the jungle insect world, the horrid yelp of the jackal pack, the distant noise of wild elephants pushing through the cane groves....

Summoning his Yankee ingenuity, he designed a two-wheeled bullock-drawn cart with springs and a rounded canvas top. It slept four, converted to a dining room or study, and contained lockers for storing camp furniture, cooking utensils, and even a library. Resembling a combination covered wagon and a modern R.V., it allowed him to travel to regions previously inaccessible to Westerners.

During one stay in Ceylon, Colonel Olcott wrote a Buddhist catechism that is still in use, and designed a Buddhist flag, which can be seen flying over temples around the world today. The colony's Buddhist priests appointed him to represent them in London. There he petitioned for various changes in policy, including the legalization of religious schools and the celebration of the Buddha's birthday as a national holiday. The bureaucrats in the colonial office must have been startled to see the robust American colonel, wearing his long white beard and Ceylonese sarong, striding down the corridors. But the government acceded to all his demands.

During another visit to the island, his ministry took a curious turn. He was asked to cure a man suffering from paralysis. Long a believer in magnetic healing, the colonel made passes with his hands above the man's body, transferring—he believed—his own revitalizing magnetic energy into the afflicted areas. The patient recovered immediately, and soon the colonel's services were much in demand. During the next several months, he treated hundreds of Ceylonese afflicted with epilepsy, dysentery, even deafness and blindness. To satisfy the clamoring villagers, he gave away thousands of bottles of "magnetized" water.

Suddenly, he was ordered to stop the curing because his vital energy was being so depleted that he could no longer carry on his important organizing work. It occurred to me that his fellow Theosophists may also have worried that the society's leading emissary was turning his mission into an American-style medicine show.

When I visited the headquarters of the present-day Theosophical Society in Colombo, the nation's capital city, I asked the officers if they believed in the colonel's reputed healing powers. The organization's president, a former Sri Lankan ambassador to Burma, was surprised that I had asked. Surely I was aware that, in Asia, there have always been extraordinary men with highly developed mental powers that allowed them to cure the sick. I apologized for my ignorance.

Today a statue of Colonel Olcott stands in front of the railway station on Olcott Mawatha (Street) in Colombo. Twice his picture has appeared on the country's stamps. Sri Lankans consider him the father of the Buddhist Revival Movement, and an important figure in the island's struggle for independence.

Flushed by success, the colonel returned to Bombay from Ceylon in 1880. He found trouble brewing. The society's housekeeper, a woman named Emma Coulomb, was feuding publicly with the two British friends who had accompanied the Founders from New York. The colonel and Madame Blavatsky decided to back Mrs. Coulomb—a decision they were later to regret. Then Swami Dayananda, irked by Colonel Olcott's refusal to submit to the authority of the Arya Samaj, broke off relations with the Theosophists. When A.P. Sinnett brought out a book of letters he said he had received from Madame Blavatsky's Masters, a clergyman confronted her with evidence that one letter was plagiarized from a sermon he had published in an American Spiritualist magazine. Anglo-Indian journalists rushed to satirize the Madame's astral communications system.

Theosophical headquarters were moved to Madras at the end of 1882, and for a time, public controversy died down. Colonel Olcott embarked on more lecture tours. While in London in 1884, he learned that the British Society for Psychical Research, an organization dedicated to the study of paranormal phenomena, wanted to investigate the Theosophical Society's activities. The group included the philosopher Henry Sidgwick, the politician Arthur

Balfour (who would become Britain's prime minister), and the physicist Lord Rayleigh. To Colonel Olcott, whose formal education had ended at sixteen, the attention of such distinguished men must have been flattering, and he cooperated fully with the investigators.

Their attention was caught by a sensational article in the *London Times*. Emma Coulomb, Madame Blavatsky's housekeeper, claimed to possess letters from her employer that instructed her to fake many of the mysterious events that had attracted so much controversy. The housekeeper published these letters—which the Theosophists insist to this day were forgeries—in the magazine of the Madras Christian College. For years, the society had been sparring with the missionaries. Now they appeared to be getting their revenge.

In one letter, it Madame Blavatsky reportedly instructed Emma Coulomb to display a bearded, life-sized doll in the moonlight so that it could be taken for a Master paying a nocturnal visit to prospective members. Another letter ordered the housekeeper to put faked notes from a Master in the Madras Headquarters' hallowed "shrine." This was a cabinet equipped with hidden sliding panels, allowing access to it from the adjoining room—Madame Blavatsky's bedroom, in fact—through a concealed hole in her closet wall.

The SPR's president, Richard Hodgson, left for Madras to have a look at the cabinet. But when he arrived at the Theosophical Society's headquarters, the British and American members there told him that the "shrine" had vanished. A few days afterwards, he discovered that they had chopped it up and burned the pieces.

The colonel rushed back to Madras with Madame Blavatsky. He insisted that the cabinet had been destroyed to save her unwarranted persecution, and that she had never ordered Emma Coulomb's husband to build its suspicious panels, as the housekeeper claimed. Instead, he asserted, the man had constructed the panels *after* the Madame had left for Europe, knowing that the SPR would be investigating the cabinet. According to the Theosophists, the Coulombs were out to ruin Madame Blavatsky's reputation, in retaliation for wrongs the couple said she had done them.

Hodgson visited the Coulombs' quarters in Madras. There, a mysterious letter fell into his lap, just as letters had fallen onto Colonel Olcott and other Theosophists. Mrs. Coulomb demonstrated how she had caused the letter to drop—by releasing it from a nearly invisible thread attached to a concealed hook in the ceiling. It occurred to Hodgson that a shower of roses might have once been released in a similar manner.

The SPR gathered evidence with the meticulousness of a police investigation unit. A handwriting expert testified that the letters produced by Emma Coulomb had been penned by Madame Blavatsky. Hodgson's committee published its report, which came to over three hundred and fifty pages.

Colonel Olcott, it stated, was "innocent of any willful deception," but guilty of "extraordinary credulity and inaccuracy of observation and inference." Madame Blavatsky was judged guilty of deceiving many people with bogus shrine messages and faked appearances of Masters. The report concluded:

"We regard Madame Blavatsky neither a mouthpiece of hidden seers, nor as a mere vulgar adventuress; we think that she has achieved title to permanent remembrance as one of the most accomplished, ingenious and interesting impostors in history."

Was Madame Blavatsky an imposter? The Theosophists still vehemently insist she was not. During my research, I found nothing fraudulent about the intellectual scope of her books, or the intensity of her belief in the esoteric ideas they contained. I can understand how people who believe in psychic intuition claim her as one of its greatest practitioners. But the SPR's evidence is convincing: it appears to me that she did sometimes use highly deceitful means to dazzle people.

Colonel Olcott understood the importance of her "phenomena" for winning converts, since he had initially been a true believer, himself. I believe that eventually he must have doubted their authenticity, though. He once argued vehemently with her about a Master's letter which she insisted ordered him not to visit Ceylon. After defying it, he reported in his journal, "I did not love or prize her less as a friend or as a teacher, but the idea of her infallibility...was gone forever." During the SPR investigation, however, he could not openly criticize her activities without damaging his own reputation for integrity and risking the good name of the movement to which he had dedicated his life.

The investigation nearly destroyed the Theosophical society. It certainly caused a rift between the Theosophical chums. Madame Blavatsky, who usually deflected criticism with her famous wit, insisted on suing a witness who she said had slandered her. Colonel Olcott, ordinarily a jovial and easy-going administrator, refused to back her lawsuit, fearing further public embarrassment for the society. She retreated to her quarters in a rage, accusing him of treachery, and announced that she was on her deathbed.

By this time she was truly ill with a serious liver ailment as well as nervous exhaustion. After consulting doctors, Colonel Olcott arranged for her passage on the first ship bound for Europe. On March 31, 1885, too weak to walk, she was hoisted in an invalid chair by cables onto a steamer waiting in the Madras harbor. She was never to return to India. And except for one brief, uneasy meeting in London, she would never see Colonel Olcott again.

To the astonishment of her critics, her career as a public figure was by no means finished. Miraculously recovering her health, she went on to write *The Secret Doctrine,* another enormous chronicle of occultism which caused as great a sensation as her first book. Taking up residence in England, she again attracted many of the leading intellectuals of her day. Annie Besant, a protégé of Shaw and one of the future founders of the Indian National Congress, converted to Theosophy. Another frequent guest at Madame Blavatsky's London salon was the Irish poet William Butler Yeats. A young Indian barrister named Mohandas K. Gandhi attended the society's meetings and was inspired by the discussions of Indian religions he heard there.

In her sixtieth year, Madame Blavatsky died in London during the influenza epidemic of 1891. Colonel Olcott, lecturing in Australia at the time, was not among the mourners at her funeral.

Ever since she had left Madras, he had been a driven man, travelling all over the world to establish Theosophical Society branches. He always praised Madame Blavatsky's work, but a time had come for him to move on without her.

During his frequent sojourns in Madras, he started free schools for children of the Untouchable caste. He also founded a library where scholars from many countries came to study ancient religious texts. Today, the society's headquarters, a beautiful palm-fringed estate, attracts thousands of visitors each year. The organization's profile is much lower than during the times when its leaders were making headlines, but it has steadily grown, with 33,000 members and branches in over fifty countries.

In 1907, Colonel Olcott took his last voyage back to Madras to give his annual presidential address. Too ill to deliver it himself, he was carried downstairs from his room to hear it read. A few days later, he died of heart failure at 75. Though he had often visited the United States during his lecture tours, he never returned there to settle. India was—and is—his final home.

ALONG SOUTH INDIA'S COROMANDEL COAST

Walking along the beach south of Madras, I saw what looked like a rainbow rising out of the palm trees. In fact it was one of South India's famous modern temples covered with radiant stone deities. Each one was painted in flame-red and sky-blue and sea-green and hues I couldn't possibly name. The colors were so fresh I could smell them—the sweet odor of new paint mixing with the smoky scent of incense and the salt spray from the Bay of Bengal. I seemed to hear them as well, but soon identified the sounds as the pounding of drums, the clanging of a brass bell, and the singsong chanting that traditionally accompanies Hindu prayer services.

The Ashta Lakshmi temple in the suburb of Besant Nager isn't one of the huge, important landmarks listed in the guidebooks, but I like its smallness and accessibility. Joining a stream of local people, I climbed narrow stairways all over the facade, pausing to meet the life-sized deities face to face. Vishnu, the Preserver god, was appropriately regal. His consort Lakshmi, goddess of love, beauty, and prosperity, looked very glamorous (raven-tressed Indian film actresses are often compared to her) as she smiled from the wall of a second story terrace. Worshipers touched her green saree and pressed jasmine petals into her hands. Their approach to the deity was relaxed, informal, personal.

South India is like that, I discovered, as I left the city and headed down the Coromandel Coast of Tamil Nadu state with a car and driver toward the former French enclave of Pondicherry. This round trip of a hundred miles is one of the most pleasant short excursions in India. Theoretically it can be done in a day, since the roads are good, but I took three days so I could stop and explore along the way.

The suburbs south of Madras are modern and upscale, but on the shore behind the marble-fronted apartment blocks, I strolled along rural village streets lined with houses made of woven cocoanut-fond mats. Chickens roosted on the sloping thatched roofs. Girls in sarees sat on the ground sorting trays of dried fish like silver jewelry. The handle of a pump creaked up and down as women gathered to fill shiny metal water pots. I stepped aside as a small boy led a loping, curly-horned buffalo down the lane.

Between the houses I caught glimpses of the surf where turbaned fishermen were poling a catamaran out into the water. Men sat on the beach mending nylon nets that lay on the sand like clouds of blue mist. Everyone was busy mending or washing or cooking or selling something, but no one was rushing. A constant buzz of conversation seemed to make every task a social occasion. Life in Indian fishing villages is hard, but there are compensations.

Continuing on fifteen miles south of Madras, I stopped at Dakshina Chitra, a remarkable living museum of architecture, crafts, and folk art. On an expanse of ten acres, beautiful old brick and wood merchants' houses, rescued from the wrecker's ball, have been moved and reassembled, complete with furniture, paintings, utensils, and toys—as if the inhabitants had just stepped out a few minutes before. The guide described the lifestyle of the owners in such vivid detail that I began to feel like a houseguest in another century.

The Madras Craft Foundation sponsors many demonstrations for visitors: weavers making silk sarees, potters working in clay, folk dancers performing dance-dramas, musicians playing traditional instruments. (It's wise to contact the Foundation's Madras office ahead of time to see what's scheduled.) I joined a sixth grade class as they crowded around a Foundation volunteer, Ms. V. K. Deveka, eager to see how she fed tufts of cotton into a portable spinning wheel. It was just like the one which Mahatma Gandhi turned as he spoke to his audiences, she told the kids. As they tried out the wheel,

I could see from their faces that history had come alive for them—which was the whole idea.

One continuous palm-fringed beach stretches from Madras to Pondicherry, and around Mahabalipuram, the approximate midway point, are a number of beautiful seaside resorts. The quiet little town itself, popular with young tie-dyed travellers, is full of no-star restaurants and tiny family-run "lodges." At one, the friendly Danussi Cottage, I rented a spotless room and a cot that I moved onto the roof so that I could sleep under the stars and watch the sun rise over the bay.

The next morning I swam at the beach beside Mahabalipuram's Shore Temple. This is a delicate, 7th century stone structure which is so worn away by the salt spray that it now resembles a filigreed sandcastle. Even older are the carvings on one enormous boulder that depict the hero Arjuna and a procession of animals from Indian folklore. A "tink-tink" sound accompanied my walk around the town's sandy lanes: the sound of chisels striking black stone. Sculpture is still the village's main trade; men in open sheds were busy carving images of deities to ship all over India. I bought an elephant-headed Ganesh that fit into the palm of my hand; I could have bought a flute-playing Krishna that would have taken up my living room.

Heading south again, I was enveloped by South India's lush greenness—plantations of shaggy-headed coconut palms and irrigated rice paddies gleaming in the sunshine. The streets of one town ran blue as a stream of teenaged girls in blue uniform sarees poured out the door of a convent school. A man lovingly washed a motorcycle half-submerged in a stream. Leaving my car, I walked into a field to get a close look at one of the equestrian terra cotta statues that potters make to guard their villages. Seated on his white-painted steed, this local folk-god wore a green sarong, gold crown, and a magnificent handlebar mustache.

Pondicherry, an enclave that remained under French rule for nearly a decade after the British left India in 1947, retains some of the flavor of its colonial years in the streets east of the central canal. I borrowed a bicycle from my hotel and pedaled past houses with graceful wrought iron balconies, carved wooden trim below the slopes of tile roofs, and walls in pastel shades of aquamarine, amber, and puce. I passed a miniature Arc de Triomphe nestled beneath the palm trees in a park where families sat on the grass eating pakoras (spicy fried snacks) and popsicles. Just off this square, the Pondicherry Museum was full of musty treasures: graceful Louis-Something furniture, ancient Indian coins, endearingly awful paintings, fossils, a palanquin, and a picture of a tiger made entirely of painted noodles.

Pedaling off, I inadvertently entered a main thoroughfare and found myself trapped in one of India's famous urban traffic crushes. A young policewoman in a white uniform and red beret casually raised her arm, and a thousand or so huge diesel trucks, packed buses, smoking cars, kamikaze motorcycles, plodding bullock carts and wobbly bicycles—including mine—all screeched to a halt. A graceful wave of her hand released another thousand insane vehicles that honked, snorted, growled, rumbled, roared past the traffic island. Then it was our turn to surge forward. But I wobbled off down a side street into the city's botanical gardens, where nothing fiercer than a fallen cocoanut confronted me on the road.

Back in the colonial district, I found several attractive churches, including one dating from 1770. My favorite was a Sacred Heart Church built in 1902 that looked like a castellated cake covered in gleaming vanilla frosting with cheerful raspberry stripes and lime-green trim. Inside, the brightly painted images of saints bore more than a passing resemblance to the deities I'd met at the Ashta Lakshmi temple.

Along the sea-front is a long, breezy promenade where Pondicherrians come to socialize in the evenings. I chatted with an elderly pensioner and some students from the new university. An eighteenth century French governor in wig, surcoat, and knee breeches gazed benignly down from his pedestal at Indian children racing cars in a sandbox.

At the south end of the promenade is the Park Guest House where the large, comfortable rooms have balconies overlooking a flower garden. I went to sleep to the fluttering of fruit bats swooping past my window. On the back of the door was a notice that cautioned me not to smoke, consume alcohol, or invite a guest to my room. The edict was enforced by a big photograph over the bed: a white-bearded Indian man and an elderly European woman whose steady glare said, "Don't even think about it!"

These folks were Sri Aurobindo, a revered spiritual leader, and his partner, a French artist who became known as The Mother. In the 1920s they founded a world-famous ashram, which now owns the Park Guest House and other Pondicherry property. After her guru died, The Mother started Auroville, a 12-square mile experiment in international living that I visited six miles north of the city.

European counter-culturists had moved here during 1960s and the place prospered as an agricultural commune. But when The Mother passed away at the age of 97 in 1973, hostilities broke out between the Auroville residents and the ashram's hierarchy. One Aurovillian—insisting that I not reveal his name—told me that during this period the French devotees forcibly expelled Indian families, including his own, and consigned "corrupt" books at his school to a bonfire.

This information made it a little hard for me to enjoy the beautiful park with tropical plants imported from many countries. But after a while the spiritual aura of the place began to waft over me—until I saw, rising up out of the foliage, the Matrimandir. This is Auroville's meditation center, a three-stories-tall cement globe resting in an artificial crater and pock-marked with hundreds of portholes—like a giant bathysphere dropped down from Mars to probe the depths of the solar system. The whole edifice was empty, I discovered, except for one dark, chilly, empty meditation room containing an empty glass globe on a pedestal. Now I'm glad to have seen this—possibly the most ludicrous building in the history of architecture—but at the time it inspired me to beat a fast retreat to the world outside the commune.

On my way back to Madras, my spirits were lifted again at the Golden Sands Beach Resort, a family theme park. The theme is a pop version of Indian culture and religion. Everywhere I walked I saw statues of lions and elephants and super-hero-like gods from Hindu folktales that every Indian child knows by heart. Crossing a drawbridge over a moat, kids crowded through a miniature Mogul fort. Parents strolled around a big flower garden planted in the triangular shape of India, each state outlined in hedgerows.

I passed walls where a series of painted bas-reliefs depicted the evolution of transportation (from bullock cart to Ambassador—an Indian-manufactured car) and the evolution of man (from an ape to a yuppie with sunglasses and tennis racket). Magicians and puppeteers put on free shows nearby. Customers at the snack bar were entertained by costumed folk dancers. Statue-Man, a mime in demon's garb, delighted giggling children when he suddenly brandished his cardboard sword at them. A Ferris wheel revolved against the pink twilight sky.

Finally I joined the families relaxing on the beach. Fully dressed, they sat on the sand and stared out at the Bay of Bengal. "So peaceful here!" one father murmured to me, smiling. Indian cities are among the most congested on earth; I could understand why the people viewed all this vast open space with a kind of reverence. Evening crowds were beginning to fill the park behind me, but I was content where I was, listening to the quiet voices and the waves splashing against the sand.

A VILLAGE ON THE BAY OF BENGAL

In 1990, when I first arrived in Besant Nager, a suburb of Madras (now called Chennai), I sensed a tranquility in the air that I'd missed in the rest of the enormous city. People had space to breathe, to relax and smile. They weren't jammed so close together that they had to clench their teeth to keep from screaming at each other. I remember walking onto the beach outside the Ashtalaksmi Temple, suddenly feeling the wide expanse of sea and blue sky open up around me. Exhausted by what seemed to me, a foreigner, the frantic pace of urban India, I lay down on the sand and watched an enormous, glossy buffalo wander by, led by a small boy holding the twine that connected him to the ring in the beast's nose. Families meandered along, gazing at frothy white breakers gliding up to the shore. A crab-man stepped stealthily, tiptoeing like a stork until he somehow sensed movement beneath the sand ahead and took a flying leap, digging his hand deep into the wet sand to yank out a wriggling creature. I watched barefoot children playing in the surf and suddenly had to take off my shoes and wade in, myself, the cool water soaking my trousers and refreshing me all over. I knew this was where I wanted to live.

I found a flat at the top of a small four-story apartment block overlooking what appeared to be a fishing village—small cement and thatch homes with sandy lanes leading to the beach where boats rested on the sand and heaps of fine nylon netting lay like clouds of blue-green mist. Facing the Bay of Bengal was a tiny temple that looked like a clay brick lying on its side; cement figures, faded and chipped, clung to the roof's corners. It was a Kali temple, I was told; the fishermen had build it and were maintaining it as best they could.

My neighbors in the building were upper-middle class professional people, but if there was any tension between them and the poorer villagers, I didn't sense it. In the pink light of dawn, I could look out from my tiny balcony and see the doctor who lived next door doing his meditation in lotus position on the sand while, not far away, a group of fishermen repaired their nets. During the monsoon, when the electric water pump in my building sizzled to a halt, ladies in silk saris waded down the lane with their plastic pails to take their turn with the village women pushing the lever of the hand-pump up and down. I don't say that inter-class harmony prevailed everywhere; I just sensed that there was enough space for people to live together easily, respecting each other's territory.

Returning eighteen years later, I found that—as in the rest of the world—most of the empty space had filled in. Besant Nager was chock-a-block with new offices and residences, and thriving. But I couldn't help feeling that all the upscale buildings seemed to be trying to push the fishermen closer and closer to the water's edge. And the fishermen appeared determined not to budge an inch. The physical landscape of the area seemed now to be deadlocked in a shoving match that neither side was winning.

Near the Ashtalakshmi Temple, I walked along a beach-side track past small brick, cement, and thatch-walled fishermen's residences. Up the narrow lanes, village life was going busily. Mothers sudsed squirming babies and hung out the wash. Children chased chickens; men sat on the ground repairing bicycles. I stopped to admire dried fish glittering like displays of silverware on straw mats. Film music squealed from open doorways. The air was scented with the aromas of cooking, making me hungry.

Then it occurred to me that this village stood in an area that used to be wide open. Where had the beach gone? The small sandy area that remained was strewn with the rubbish that people inevitably must make wherever they live; paper, plastic and rusted metal were everywhere. Heaps of old bricks and ragged, blackened cocoanut matting were, I was told, left over from dwellings destroyed during the tsunami.

A row of painted fishing boats now crowded the sand, their pointed snouts sniffing the spray that nearly reached them from the surf. There was little room to spread nets out to dry in the sun. It seemed now that the men were sitting closer together as they worked on the boats.

The houses looked closer together than I remembered them, too. Were there more of them than before? Yes, a lot more. And now the rounded, thatched hutments appeared to be leaning against one another for protection.

Protection from what? Not the sea, three years after the tsunami. I stepped as close to the water's edge as I could, looked up and saw the city looming over the little houses. The new residences gleamed in the sunlight, their graceful balconies and tile roofs basking among the palm trees. Unlike the fishing village, these neighborhoods were solid, attractive, clean, and quiet. This was the new, prosperous urban India, where work and play went on behind curtained windows, out of sight of passers-by.

Novelists like me enjoy finding symbols in the landscape, and two of them cried out to me here. One, at the Ashtalakshmi Temple end of the beach, was a colossal billboard rising on steel stilts from among the hutments' cocoanut-matting roofs. It pictured glittering Dubai harbor with its World's Tallest Tower, and was captioned "The Only Things Higher Are Our Dreams for India." Whose dreams for India? I wondered. Would the fishermen of Besant Nager want to live in the shadow of the world's tallest tower?

The other inescapable symbol book-ending the stretch of shoreline was a billboard that rose high into the sky above the Elliot's Beach end (where there's still an expanse of clean, pretty sand for the public to walk on.) "Thank the Lord!" the sign exclaimed, showing a girl's face floating like a zeppelin, her hands folded in prayer. Thanks for what? I asked myself. Approaching, I read the fine print (three feet tall): the appreciation was for supporting a charity that helped heart patients.

Though I'm not religious, I preferred the girl to the World's Tallest Tower. Especially when I discovered that, almost directly below her, the once-shabby little Kali temple had been enthusiastically painted, with bright red and gold cement lions guarding its roof. They looked like real killers, not about to be dislodged for anything.

The ultra-materialistic edifice glaring across the burning sand at the angelic face of the praying child—what writer could resist them? But of course, real contrasts aren't as simple to read as symbolic ones. Wealthy Besant Nager residents aren't building towers (some of them are too busy supporting important charities) and fisher-folk aren't all angels. Still, from the changed appearance of the place, I couldn't help seeing the two billboard as adversaries and wondering which side would win out.

Well, there's no stopping the spread of prosperous, urban India, and no one would want to. But if Besant Nager is anything like similar sections of Rio, or Nairobi, or Port-of-Spain, the answer to the question probably is: neither side can win. Temporary hutment-settlements have a way of becoming permanent neighborhoods, towns and even cities. The fisher-families of Besant Nager reminded me of the rough, defiant Martiniquan characters in Patrick Chamousoux's classic novel *Texaco,* who much to the annoyance of their more affluent neighbors, carried on as they damn well pleased as they hung onto their harsh territory for generation after generation.

Novelists tend to root for the underdog. History may belong to the victors but literature belongs to the suffering victims. If I'm not careful, I admit, I can romanticize Village India, where I did my first research in Rajasthan the 1980s. But when I first came to Madras, where did I choose to live? Not Village India. No, I preferred a pleasant apartment block with a view of—but not sharing—the grittier life below. Like my neighbors, I had the best of both worlds.

And I now realize that this is probably no longer possible—anywhere on earth.

FORESTS OF THE NIGHT

1.

I wasn't the ideal New Frontiersman. If I'd run into President Kennedy as I loped stoned through Greenwich Village with my shaggy hair and mustache, guitar hanging from one shoulder on a rawhide strap, would he have said: "Go out to those villagers in the developing world struggling to break the bonds of poverty, and pledge your best effort to help them help themselves?" Hell, no. He'd have rolled his eyes and strode on, surrounded by droves of genuine American idealists.

The spirit of the times did get to me, though. I'd marched in civil rights demonstrations, handed out leaflets, and once chained myself to a bulldozer to protest a building company's discriminatory hiring policies. But what I mostly wanted to do at twenty-two was have far-flung adventures, write about them, and learn more chords on my guitar.

One day, I saw a notice on a college bulletin board that announced a US government program for a one-year training course at a university in Uganda followed by a two-year teaching job. I'd wanted to go to Africa ever since working summers with a gang of friendly African students at a New York restaurant. They urged me to apply to the program. I did, and despite my peculiar personal history, somehow got accepted.

Arriving at Uganda's national airport in September of 1963, I helped raise high a *TEACHERS FOR EAST AFRICA* banner as flashbulbs exploded. In the newspaper photo we appeared a somberly purposeful group: ten fluffy-haired young women in calf-length skirts and loose blouses, nine clean-cut guys in narrow ties and creased slacks, plus me, a shaggy character with a clueless, hokey grin. We were part of a massive foreign aid package: America was flinging vast sums of money at Africa to train the first post-colonial generation of leaders who, armed with Western expertise, would guide the newly independent nations toward stability, democracy, and prosperity.

After settling into my dorm at Makerere University, I helped celebrate the first anniversary of Uganda's Independence as I rolled through Kampala, the capital city, playing my guitar on a parade float I'd help decorate with caps and gowns. I waved to cheering crowds whose national flags turned the streets to roiling streams of red, black, and yellow. Everyone shouted *Uhuru!*—the Swahili word for freedom. Ahead of our float, the African Methodist Army Band pummeled the air with its bass drums' thunder; behind us, warriors in leopard-skins boogied and thrust their spears in the air. *Uhuru! Uhuru! Uhuru!*

On its hilltop above the city, the Makerere campus was luxuriant, with rolling lawns, tile-roofed classroom buildings in the open tropical style, flowering bushes that exhaled clouds of fragrance. A blue swimming pool sparkled like a block of sunken ice; from behind the louvered theater windows came African-inflected dialogue from *As You Like It.* Young men in bold dashikis stood beneath flame trees chatting up co-eds in wrap-around print skirts, their dark, cheerful faces glistening in the heat. Above the chapel's mahogany doors a blue mosaic Jesus gazed into the wavy rays of a mosaic sun. Inside, I heard a choir sing hymns in English, in Swahili—East Africa's *lingua franca*—and in Luganda, the regional tribal language.

For the first week, I wandered happily around the university soaking up the colors, the warmth and vibrancy. Gradually, though, the place began to seem like a tropical version of a British university. The dorms were named for English explorers and statesmen like Livingston and Northcote. Many of the students seemed keen to adopt the customs and attitudes of their former colonial masters. As if at Oxford, they pulled on academic robes to eat in paneled dining halls; to be invited to join the professors at High Table was considered an honor. In the most popular club on campus, students danced sedate Scottish reels to the bleating of a recorded bagpipe. Though Makerere had electricity and running water, the families of the school's gardeners who lived in one-room huts near the campus had kerosene lanterns, charcoal fires, and hand-pumps; when a professor circulated a petition to improve their conditions, few students signed it.

I met some, though, who called all this elitist. They plastered walls with posters protesting against apartheid in South Africa and segregation in the American South. In the dormitory common room, African students asked me about my country's race relations. I admitted that they were shameful but also told them about changing attitudes and growing support for integration. They heard me out politely, probably figuring that if I'd come here to study, there must be a few Americans who weren't racists.

One of my new African friends was a member of a cattle-herding tribe in the far north of the Country; he had gone all the way through high school on correspondence courses, reading his lessons by the light of cook-fires. Another was planning to be the first member of his tribe, the Maasai of Kenya, to do anthropological studies of his own people. I also admired Okani, a guy whose left leg had been withered by childhood polio and now used a heavy pole to propel himself agilely around campus.

I liked the other American students, but was wary of them, feeling like an imposter among such natural ambassadors of good will. They all seemed to come from cheerful, liberal families—unlike my own distressed, conservative one. As undergraduates, they'd been student body presidents and deans' list scholars, while I'd barely roller-coasted through. In the program application's required autobiography, I'd glossed over my dismal, gilded childhood spent living in a servants' wing of a big country home with a housekeeper who passed on her bitter mistrust of my parents to me. I had to admit that my draft status was 1-Y: questionable fitness—due to a breakdown I'd had at nineteen and three months I'd spent in a private mental hospital. It had given me an even more skewed view of life than I'd already had—though hopefully, I wrote, a more compassionate one. I spent my summers and vacations from Cornell living with a friend in Greenwich Village, taking menial jobs to stay as independent as possible from my family. Though supposedly possessed of the best mental health money could buy, I still felt as if I were flying without a compass or a safety net.

At Makerere, I loved the African literature courses, but most of the professors who taught education were "colonial re-treads," as they jokily termed themselves, manning the university until qualified Ugandans could take over. These elderly British academics from African universities had been enticed by lucrative hardship bonuses, the "hardship" being that they were staying on in places where the Crown no longer protected them from the natives. Their lectures gave off clouds of mustiness; the topics were ancient Greece and England during the Enlightenment, with a nod toward Dewey's pedagogical theories. They seemed useless in preparing anyone to teach in modern Africa. But maybe I was the only one who didn't understand their relevance. If so, would I ever learn to teach? Frustrated and confused, I showed up at fewer and fewer lectures.

The linguistics professor, a wispy-domed Briton named Dr. Cary, spoke in lugubrious sentences as if intoning a roll-call of fallen military heroes. On the blackboard, he chalked their eccentric names in neat coffin-like boxes: Phoneme, Morpheme, Fricative, Glottal Stop, Plosive, Implosive, Litote. They were all, he said, elements of a logical system of sound and meaning. As he dictated, I often drifted into a fugue state in which I had to fill in crossword puzzles covering the walls of an endless tunnel.

When the Americans were invited to a party by Dr. Cary, I wanted to ask if they, too, had trouble understanding his lectures, but decided not to risk it. I expected the professor's house to look like his blackboard grid, each room meticulously furnished, immaculate floors geometrically carpeted. When we arrived, though, it looked as if demented crocodiles had just ravaged the place. I stepped around toppled mountains of books, tripped on a sprawled goose-neck lamp and edged between dusty, rolled-up rugs. In the dining room Dr. and

Mrs. Cary sat side by side at a table cluttered with half-full amber bottles and plates of crusted food. The professor gazed down into his glass. His wife silently wept, tendrils of white hair stuck to her cheeks. The other guests whispered embarrassed good-byes and left, but I stayed, accepting the professor's offer of a drink.

"Glad *you* stayed for the party, at least." Mrs. Cary smiled wetly at me. "Deserted us, the rest of your lot." After a while, she dried her eyes and poured out generous refills. When I finally tiptoed away, the two of them were chuckling over old times in the colonies, their fricatives and glottal stops slurred incomprehensibly—to me, but evidently not to each other.

I didn't realize it until years later, but one purpose of our year at Makerere must have been for us just to hang out, deal with culture shock, and acclimatize ourselves to Africa as best we could. One friend of mine did succumb to disorientation and flew home; he left me a beautiful Raleigh bicycle that helped saved my sanity during those first months in Kampala. I didn't feel any shock, myself, just loneliness and intolerable restlessness.

Only one of the Americans admitted that she was feeling adrift, too. Susan was an unlikely ally: a former sorority girl from Ohio with bouncy bangs and a freckled nose she wrinkled nervously when she laughed. She was the only other member of the program who had a fiancé back in the States. After I'd graduated from college, I couldn't bear to say good-bye to the first girl who'd ever loved me; worried that I'd never again find anyone who would, I asked her to marry me. We planned a wedding after she finished her master's degree at Cornell and came to join me in East Africa. When Susan spoke of her loneliness, I could commiserate platonically. Perhaps fortunately for her, she was religious. She'd contacted a local missionary priest about doing some volunteer work at a camp for Sudanese refugees.

"Are you interested?" she asked as we sat on the grass outside the student canteen, me smoking throat-scorching Sportsman cigarettes, she sipping a Coke through a straw.

I wasn't. My African friends at the restaurant in New York had told me that missionaries had been sent to the continent to soften up people so they'd submit to being exploited by the invading colonialists. "I'm kind of busy these days," I said.

"Oh, I can see that—always zooming that bike of yours everywhere." Her nose wrinkled, then her laugh cut off as she cocked her head at me. "What're you running away from, anyway?"

"I've quit running *from*," I said. "I'm more running *toward*."

"Toward what?"

"I'll let you know when I find out."

Already I was spending a lot more time exploring the city than I was at the university. Kampala's maelstrom of streets drew me deeper and deeper in, my bike wheels perpetually spinning over the rutted roadways. Along the tops of Kampala's seven hills, tall office buildings stared from rows of gleaming windows past the traffic circles and boulevards and down the slopes of deep valleys into the older sections of the city. There the streets were red clay, the roadsides ragged with green banana trees; mud brick and wooden houses sagged beneath rusted metal roofs. I liked swerving down one off-road after another with no idea where any of them led, letting gravity lead me around steep curves into the midst of kids' soccer games, fleeing chickens, snarling traffic where placid-faced women glided in and out with tall bundles on their heads. I coasted into a maze of palm-shaded stalls in Mmengo, the old capital of the ancient Buganda empire.

Dismounting, I squeezed through busy crowds, listened in on passionate bargaining sessions, inhaled spices so strong they resonated as colors. Dramas appeared around every turn. Hawkers shouted the prices of pants dancing like clowns on makeshift high-wires. Tiny girls prodded sizzling omelets for sale on roadside woks. A man led a lyre-horned steer past a mosque. I examined hand-woven cloths laid out on blankets on the ground, paused to eat fiery curries in tiny Indian restaurants. Along with roadside crowds I threw down coins to gamble on sidewalk checker games, my mind racing to keep up with the fingers scurrying over the board like mice on a stove-top.

Seeing me kibitzing, some players dusted off a low stool and invited me to try beating the neighborhood champ: entry fee, four shillings. Why not? I kinged three of my opponent's men in his back row and won the first game. The old man was duly consoled by his fans. The entry fee for the next game was ten shillings, still a small amount. I won it, too. Cheers and murmurs rose. Now money changed hands fast. The next game's entry fee was two hundred shillings, a day's wages in this neighborhood. Well, I had plenty of funds from my program stipend; I couldn't let these people down. I dropped my bills into the pot. The game was over in lightening *slap-slap-slap* leaps of my opponents' checkers—flicking my singletons off the board.

I'd been hustled. I stood up wearing a greenhorn grin. "Good game," I said to the old man as he raked in bills with both hands, and quickly remounted my bike.

On I rode. Sometimes I passed pockets of appalling poverty— men in rags straining to haul gigantic loads in tottering hand-carts, women nursing emaciated babies beside fetid sewage ditches. And fights, too—raw screaming anger and flying fists. I remember these scenes now, but how did I respond to them then? Did I pick up speed, pressing down harder on my bike's pedals as I passed? I'm afraid that's all I could do.

Chewing roasted goat at roadside stalls, I talked to every English-speaking customer I could find about the city's life—the prices at the markets, the lives of the truckers who slept in their dusty behemoths beside the highway, the adventures of country kids seeking their fortunes here as workers, students, thieves, and also as musicians in the dance halls.

As night fell, I heard the amplified dance music cranking up in clubs—the *Free African Star,* the *New Life Café,* the *Sporting Life* and others. I sat in on rehearsal sessions, trying out new melodies but giving back the guitars after a few numbers. I was more eager to listen and learn than to play. I loved the clever pop song lyrics that reflected the working people's family tragedies, their satirical or worshipful pictures of African political figures, their yearnings for riches and fast girls. The musicians roughly translated them for me.

"Malayika—my lovely angel—how can I ever ask her to marry a poor man like me?"

"Our leaders, our heroes, don't desert us for shiny-shiny Benzes!"

Every day I wrote down the lyrics as well as detailed 20- or 30-page letters to Jill, my fiancée. I missed her terribly, but, like Columbus, I was keeping double log books of my voyages—one for her, and a more intimate one for myself. For her I painted a rich, compelling picture of Africa which, though genuine, wasn't all-inconclusive; I wanted to make her eager to join me here. The contents of my private log, I feared, represented neither a place nor a person that any normal woman would give up her comfortable, familiar life for. I credited her normal upbringing with producing in her a warmth and openness I'd never known in anyone else. So concealing my entire self from her felt terribly wrong—but necessary. Necessary not only because of her but because, for years, my life had never felt fully real to me until I'd written it down in all its details. So I kept obsessively filling my letters and private journal with all the things I saw, did, and felt in Kampala, lest they drift away like handfuls of feathers in the wind.

Often I was the one drifting. More and more of my nights were spent with African students in the scruffy nightclub district where the air throbbed neon red and vibrated with the screech of electric guitars. Dance floors undulated, couples swayed and wriggled from midnight to dawn. Tall brown bottles of Nile Lager crowded our tables, girls in slinky dresses draped themselves over our shoulders groping for cigarettes. They sat on laps and tried on students' horn-rims, they squealed as they were fondled, they bounded to their feet to squirm the *Congo Cha-cha-cha*. As a university student, and as a white man—thus unmistakably rich—I had my pick of lithe young women. They were nurses, office workers, seamstresses, girls down on their luck in the big city, and—I have to admit it, though I didn't then—professional prostitutes. I lost track of how many bottles I gulped down, streaming sweat until my shirt stuck to my skin like a drowned man's. I danced and danced with the blurry girls as the room careened around me.

I'd always been a binge drinker in prep school and college, unlike my mother and my uncles who were steady, undemonstrative alcoholics. Now I was running wilder than ever—not just on weekend nights with the students, but two, three, four nights a week on my own. I'd stumble out of a dance hall long after midnight to collapse into a slow-roving taxi that took me back to campus, or to the room of a girl who'd clung to me the longest. When tsunamis of loneliness overwhelmed me, I clutched the inert bodies of drunk girls as close as possible until my empty feeling drained away. Then I'd skulk out into the night, leaving behind folded bills as "gifts" to buy a new blouse or a plastic radio or food for a girl's baby.

Taxis stopped trolling the district around 4:00 in the morning, so sometimes I'd trek the steep miles up to the campus. One night, just before dawn, a motorcycle ridden by three revelers slammed me off a roadside. If I'd rolled a few feet farther I'd have pitched down a precipice into a pen of grunting pigs which would have gobbled my cadaver before sunrise.

Back at the dorm, I had to bribe the watchman extra not to report my bloodied face and hands to the campus authorities. I hid out in my room for days waiting for my warpaint-like gashes to heal. I tried studying to distract myself, but, even sober, the words blurred to indecipherable swarms of black ants. The dreaded old symptoms were back—a terrifying inability to concentrate *just like the one that had triggered my breakdown years before.* My books were flung to the floor and kicked under my bed. In the bad old days, I'd always been hard on myself, staying one step ahead of even more scathing invisible accusers who might catch me acting with more confidence than I had any right to. Again I'd made myself defenseless against my demons; they dug their talons into my shoulders, roared into my ears: *Look at the drunken fraud, the unfaithful double-dealer, the neocolonialist sexual exploiter—*

Was this what I'd come to Africa to become?

2.

In Bombo, a village about an hour's bus ride from Kampala, I stood with Susan and four other Americans before the wire-mesh gate of the refugee camp. The residents—about forty high school boys who'd fled their boarding school in Sudan, the country north of Uganda—had hammered together three barracks-like dormitories and a dining hall that stood on a raised plank verandah. Behind it stretched a moonscape of terra-cotta stalagmites—filigreed termite hills that jutted up four or five feet high. A tall chain-link fence encircled the camp; behind it loomed a forest of gum trees and tangled vines. The sparse grass looked as if it had been trampled in a perpetual running game.

And so it had, I'd been told: for the past fourteen months, the refugees had had nothing whatsoever to do but kick a ball around and wait for something to happen. Crows cawed in the trees; cicadas shrieked incessantly. Nothing moved except two boys stirring a heavy, peeled branch in an enormous cauldron of *matoke,* the starchy banana gruel which was supplied, like the students' khaki shorts and shirts, by the Uganda government. A charred smell rose from the pit where a cook-fire crackled low.

I whispered to Susan, "Remember, I'm not promising anything here."

She rolled her eyes at me and handed me a canvas bag full of notebooks.

A bare-chested boy in shorts came running inside the parameter of the fence. He seemed to grow as he approached until, panting behind the gate, he stood nearly seven feet tall. His ropey muscles bulged in long, long, skinny legs. I'd never seen anyone so dark; his skin was a deep blue-black, reflecting the sunlight with a pewter-like sheen.

"Welcome...welcome!" He leaned forward, catching his breath. His eyes narrowed to crescents, and when his hand shielded them from the glare, the white ripple of a smile was all I could see of his features. "Father Murphy told us you would come...."

I heard voices from the buildings. Suddenly the camp swarmed with boys rushing out of doorways, sprinting toward the gate. They shouted and waved, they pressed against the wire fence until it bulged and creaked. A rumpled soldier appeared and slowly pulled some keys from the pocket of his uniform shorts. I was the last one to step inside the gate. *Click!* He re-fastened it and strolled away. I felt locked in, a familiar but uncomfortable sensation. The boys crowded close, all talking at once. They, too, had that midnight-black skin; many of them towered over us, waiting, watching.

"*Sijambo! Habari gani!*" I finally spoke, trotting out a newly-learned Swahili greeting.

The boys stared at me. Coming from Sudan, they didn't know Swahili.

"Hi! We're glad to see you." Susan stuck out her hand.

The boy shook it, then mine. "We are also glad. My name is Jabez."

In a moment, the Americans were shaking hands with every student who could reach us, nodding and answering questions about our health and the health of our parents and siblings. "Fine, thank you," I kept saying, my arm pumping up and down. Elaborate greetings, an important custom in Africa, took time but I could see their point; the long introductions broke down everyone's awkwardness. Biblical names were popular here: Bildad, Noah, Tobias, Nicodemus.

We all trooped toward the buildings. Jabez invited us into a dormitory to show us something: glossy photos of a smiling President John F. Kennedy that several boys had put up over their bunks. The metal beds stood in rows, evenly spaced, blankets threadbare but tightly tucked in as if ready for a prefect's inspection. Blades of yellow sunlight sliced between the cracks in the walls.

Several boys appeared with tin mugs of sweet milk-tea for us. We all sat cross-legged on the plank floor outside, the Americans facing the students. In tumbling-out, school-boy English they asked us about our university courses, our homes in America, our favorite cars and pop musicians.

Jabez hushed the boys. "We thank you," he said, "for coming here to start a school...."

School? I glanced around. None of the other Americans seemed surprised. All Susan had mentioned to me was seeing if the students needed books or maybe some sports equipment.

"Since our school in Sudan was destroyed," Jabez continued, "we have been too lonely for learning."

"Until you came," one boy said, "our minds are rotting like fallen mangoes in the sun."

Jabez focused on me. "What courses are you going to teach us?"

"Well...." I'd never taught anything in my life. I looked at the eager, waiting faces. "We're going to find out what you need. And see what we can do," I waffled.

"Today is just a sort of a meet-'n'-greet," Susan said.

"Tell you what," an American said to Jabez. "How about helping these guys divide into groups—history, biology, physics, math, English—and maybe find places for them to meet—"

"They can divide into groups!" Jabez snapped. "It is not for me to do."

None of the boys moved. Nobody spoke. Then the moment passed. We all scrambled to our feet, identifying our subjects. Eventually the boys padded after various Americans in search of shady spots around the yard in which to set up class spaces. I stayed on the verandah, the lone English major. Eleven boys remained with me, including Jabez and Nicodemus. Jabez's sudden resentful expression had completely faded.

"Okay....." I looked around. "What do you think you'd like to read?"

"Anything," Jabez said. "Father Mario—he was our English master in Sudan—said our minds should be open to all subjects."

"What books did he use?" I asked him.

"First, the Bible. All the priests and lay teachers taught it."

"How did you...like the Bible?" I asked Jabez.

"The Old Testament has many exciting stories. " A smile rippled over his face again. "But the New Testament has more lessons to help us."

"Help you?"

The boys glanced at one another. Nicodemus spoke in a whispery voice. "Help us to endure."

The others nodded. This, obviously, was not the place to question anyone's faith. "What else did Father Mario teach you?" I asked.

"We read Shakespeare," a boy piped up from the back.

"*Julius Caesar* and *Macbeth*." Another boy grinned. "They were too savage!"

"And Wordsworth...." Someone groaned.

"His daffodils." Jabez sighed. "They are yellow and grow in 'hosts.'"

"Tell us—what are 'hosts?' a boy asked. "Our dictionary said only that they are hospitable people. Or holy sacraments."

"Hosts are, um—groups. Yeah, clusters of flowers...." I felt a trickle of sweat drip into my left eye. "I think they welcomed the poet, the way hosts welcome guests. And maybe they were holy, too—Wordsworth thought loving nature was sort of a religion." I smiled as if I'd known that all along. Who knew daffodils could be so versatile?

"Father Mario was from Italy." Nicodemus said somberly. "This is why he did not know the English word. I wish we could tell it to him now."

The boys glanced at each other, smiles fading.

"The only book we have now is a Bible," someone said. "We held it with us on the journey all the way from our village to here—for five months, one week...four days."

"At the camp, one of us reads aloud from it every morning." Another boy spoke up from the back. "It makes our *matoke* breakfast almost eatable."

Most of the boys' expressions relaxed. But Nicodemus, frowning hard, stared at his fingers.

"'Food will not commend us to God,'" Jabez quoted. "'We are no worse off if we do not eat, and no better off if we do.' First Corinthians."

"This verse we recited very often, when we were fleeing our country," Nicodemus said, his voice rising. His poppy eyes gave him an unhinged look. "We had almost no food to eat! Except things we found. Some birds' eggs—and wild plants—and small animals we hunted."

"And beetles!" another boy piped up.

Faces contorted amid some uneasy chuckling. Had these kids really eaten insects on their trek from Sudan to Uganda? Why had they come here, anyway?

I glanced at my watch. "We've got to go in a minute. But maybe you'd like to write about your experiences," I said. "Something to do…keep yourselves busy."

"What should we write about?" Jabez asked.

"Well, you talked about Father Mario." I tried to sound upbeat. "You could write about him."

"Father Mario stayed with us on our journey." Nicodemus twisted a long piece of grass around his forefinger. "He was like Moses—he never quite reached the promised land. When we reached the Sudan-Uganda border—"

"Yes—" Jabez shot a sharp glance at him. "We will write about our teachers."

"Okay, then." I nodded.

"Do you know what happened to another teacher?" Nicodemus demanded. He winced as if the grass around his finger had turned to wire. "He was like an uncle to me!"

"Good," I said, "You could describe him in an essay—"

"Listen—when he was a boy he had been a believer in native spirits. Then the Arabs stole him. He was only ten years old. They made him a slave!" Nicodemus blinked away tears. "But later the priests from Italy came. They paid the Arabs to set him free! He converted to the faith of Jesus Christ, and the fathers educated him."

Jabez rested his hand on Nicodemus's shoulder. "All right…."

"No—I must *tell* it! The Moslems hate Christian converts! When the war came to our school—" He coughed, regained his voice. "The Arabs from the North—they took my teacher *away*. And they *crucified* him!"

I couldn't escape his stare. Around me, the students shifted their positions, frowned, whispered. Jabez spoke softly to Nicodemus in a language I didn't understand. The smaller boy rubbed his eyes.

Silence. Charcoal smoke drifted by, nearly making me choke. "Nicodemus?" I leaned forward. "I'm sorry."

He didn't move.

"You do not need to apologize," Jabez said.

"No, I mean—" What *did* I mean? How could I understand this kid's troubles? What he'd said about a slave, a crucifixion—of course it was mad, but there must have been some reason he'd blurted it out: maybe too many traumas, too much self-medicating with religion all these months in the camp. "Well, there's a Swahili word I learned—*polé*" I tried again. "It translates something like, 'I know that's hard for you. You don't have suffer it alone.'"

Several boys nodded. Nicodemus's eyes remained tightly shut.

"It is a good word," Jabez said.

I reached for my canvas bag and lifted out some exercise books. "Let's pass these around." I handed it to Jabez. "You want to help me?"

Jabez's face hardened. Then he wiped his mouth. "All of us can help."

"Right." I took out some more. "Hey, Nicodemus—give us a hand, will you?"

He took them from me. "Are there…biros?" he asked faintly.

"I think so…yes." I took a box of plastic pens from the bag. The boys all grabbed for them at once, a tangle of waving arms. "Hey, take it easy!" I protested. "There's plenty!"

They laughed but they kept reaching. Some immediately wrote their names in bold letters on the new books' inside covers; others tucked their pens carefully into the breast pockets of their shirts. By this time they'd taken all but one notebook from Nicodemus. He opened it, a pen poised over the first page. Then he frowned at me.

"If we write things in these books," he said, "will you read them? How do we know you will ever come back?"

Silence. The boys froze. So did I. Had Nicodemus caught a whiff of my earlier hesitation? He must have. Jabez was also watching me closely, eyes narrowed. Nicodemus's neediness and fragility resonated with me—or with an old self I was still sometimes trying to appease—but the impact of Jabez's expression was even more arresting. He wasn't making a plea; he shot me a look of determined hope, as if encouraging something to emerge from within me that I'd only vaguely sensed was there and badly needed to know better.

"I'll be back," I said, and managed a smile. I had no idea what I was getting myself in for.

3.

I wanted to ask the priest in Kampala why the Sudanese boys had been interred, but on the day we were to meet with him, he was down with malaria in a Nairobi hospital, and never returned. We were on our own. The Uganda government, nervous about hosting refugees from its more powerful neighbor, didn't allow its citizens into the camp. The Americans could visit two at a time on different days each week until the end of term, three months away, when we were to leave for Kenya schools to do ten weeks of practice teaching.

Information about the political situation in Sudan was scarce. Books in Makerere's library covering the country's history stopped at 1956 when the country gained independence from Britain. I did read about ethnic tensions between Arab Moslems in the North and Christian and animist blacks in the southern regions, but couldn't find many details. If people were being forced to flee the country, why wasn't the press covering the troubles? I looked through back issues of *The Argus,* Uganda's only newspaper, and Kenya's *East African Standard,* then searched British publications, but found no mention of any hostilities in Sudan. Inhaling the cozy scent of books on dusty shelves, I watched a student across the table from me read *Pickwick Papers.* This place and the Bombo camp seemed to be on different planets.

In my enthusiasm for *Uhuru,* I hadn't considered that Africa's problems might not all have been caused by the colonial powers. My friends at the New York restaurant hadn't mentioned any internal troubles. As I'd gazed out the bus window returning from the camp, an aura of sunlit red-clay dust coated the maize fields with a velvet benevolence. Hadn't Churchill famously called Uganda "the pearl of Africa?"

From some history texts, I read that trouble had flared locally between Moslem and Christian converts in Uganda, and tribal wars had been fought here during the 19th and early 20th centuries. But nowadays people in Kampala looked too determinedly busy—selling goods in marketplaces, building new shops and schools—to fight about anything. Uganda appeared to be an easygoing, stable country; it was governed by a democratically-elected parliament and a progressive president named Milton Obote, whose big, friendly hand I'd shaken at a State House reception for foreign teachers.

The only trouble reported in the press was the rivalry between the nation's federal government and the southern region's traditional monarch, or kabaka, of Buganda. I'd met Kabaka Mutesa II, too—known informally as King Freddie—a smiling, alcoholic Sandhurst graduate some of whose loyal subjects still prostrated themselves when he passed in the street with his entourage. One night he showed up briefly at a dance at Makerere and drove off in a magnificent open-topped 1927 Rolls Royce in whose back seat sat several radiant female Baganda students he had chosen—as was his time-honored right—to be his wives for the night. Inter-tribal rifts reportedly ended when the president married a Buganda aristocrat at an extravagant wedding in the capital's soccer stadium.

No one then—certainly not me—could have predicted that in eight years a former army boxing champion named Idi Amin would overthrow Milton Obote and plunge the nation into years of terror and carnage. I couldn't imagine times when troops would burn down King Freddy's antique palace and send him into exile in England to die in poverty, or when, afflicted by an AIDS pandemic, Uganda's people would struggle for years to re-build their once-prosperous nation. In 1963, the country's vibrant life offered me so much freedom to become someone new that I convinced myself that its own progress would rush on unimpeded forever.

But troubles were closer than I knew even then. One day I chatted with a student named Wanjiru, a young, plump-faced Kenyan woman who was studying law to help her family get back land the British settlers had taken from it decades earlier. Her country's independence, scheduled for December that year, had been won through a brutal guerilla war in the 1950s whose traumas were still being felt everywhere. The war had been termed the

What Can You Do

"Emergency" by the settlers, the "Mau Mau Rebellion" by the world press, and the "Freedom Struggle" by the finally victorious Africans, who'd suffered thousands more casualties than the British troops that were called in to fight them. During the conflict, these troops had set ablaze all the huts on Wanjiru's family's farm. I listened silently, nodding; I'd never met someone younger than me who had survived such trials.

"My father often preached in church about holding peaceful negotiations with Britain. But the guerillas didn't like his moderation. So just as he'd finished building up our shamba after the fire caused by the British, the guerillas burnt it to the ground!"

"That's awful!" I leaned forward. "What did you do?"

"What could we do? We're still re-building—again!" She bit her lip. "Sometimes I think I should be there, helping."

"But you're helping here—by learning to be a lawyer."

She smiled. "I hope I am...."

"Of course you are," I said. But what was *I* doing with my education?

I saw little of the American students these days, still avoiding many lectures and continuing my long cycling explorations. It surprises me now the way I assumed I could ride all over an African city without any danger. Secure in my own harmless intentions, I was sure that everyone would good-naturedly tolerate my blunders, reciprocate my friendliness, patiently satisfy my unrelenting curiosity about their lives. I never considered that people might want to rob a foreigner obviously richer than they'd ever be; and no one ever did. Nor did I consider that Africans who read headlines in local papers about Mississippi Ku Klux Klansmen murdering black activists might resent a pale young man breezing through their neighborhoods. I suspect that I was rolling along inside a bubble of white privilege, the one whose shiny membrane allows Caucasians—even in places where we're a minority—from seeing no more than we want to see in the darker faces around us.

After my talk with Wanjiru, my trips began to seem more and more like time-wasting, though I always found material for my letters and journals. One afternoon, I bought typing paper in an Indian stationary shop and saw on sale the same kind of exercise books I'd given the Sudanese students. I pedaled back to campus with packets of them strapped to my luggage rack.

In Bombo, as Susan and I walked from the bus stop toward the camp, I heard the boys' voices rising like a flock of birds flushed into the air. At the gate, the bored Uganda soldier took his time checking our bags. The students shouted their impatience through the fence; he waved his rifle at them. With its eroded stock and rusted muzzle, it could have been a Boer War souvenir, but the students shrank back. Nicodemus sprinted all the way to the dormitories. Jabez called him back outside. Finally the guard unlocked the gate for us.

Susan, a biologist, turned out to be tougher than she looked. She'd evidently given her students an assignment: "find" a chicken. They proudly presented her with one when her class convened under a tree near a hole in the fence the bird must have been lured through. It squawked its last as one of the boys wrung its neck with a quick snap of his wrists. Susan then commenced to slice the bird up with her Swiss army knife. She yanked out various innards, dictated their names and functions to the scribbling class. Later, the exhibit went into a communal stew pot.

All I had for my English students were notebooks and a selection of cheap, English-language adventure novels printed in Nigeria and occasionally sold on the sidewalks around the Kampala markets. My eleven students and I met on the shady verandah between two dormitory buildings, sitting cross-legged on the plank floor. The boys spent a long time asking me more questions about America. I should have taken more control of the discussion but didn't know how to. Finally I asked them to read aloud from the assignments I'd given them about their favorite teachers. Their 24-page exercise books were completely filled; final sentences covered back covers like squiggly, tightly woven twine. They looked like *samizdat* writings I'd seen from Siberian prison camps.

I thought Jabez would be the first to read, but he stared hard at his notebook as several other boys shot their hands up, fingers grasping the air as if trying to pull themselves into it. I called on a very skinny boy with diagonal scarifications on the side of his forehead. (Many of the students, including Jabez and Nicodemus, had one or two of these markings in their skin. Their foreheads had been cut, they'd told me proudly, as part of tribal puberty rituals. From my motorcycle debacle, I also had a forehead scar, which the boys were amused to point out. When they got to know me better, they commiserated with me about how quickly it faded away.)

This first reader, named Bildad, spoke in a clear, deep voice, describing life at the mission school where he'd boarded: the food tasted strange but delicious and the students slept for the first time on beds raised above the ground. Each bed had a mattress. The boys smiled, nudging each other as they listened to the details of their old life.

"We all wore smart uniforms of blue shorts and white shirts as well as leather shoes which distressed our feet too much. But after some months our feet learned them.'" Bildad stood at what looked like military attention, glancing over his notebook at me every few seconds to get my nod to go on. "'Everyone learned to speak English quickly because if we were heard speaking in tribal languages, we must be caned. But the priests and lay teachers were usually kind to us, especially Father Mario. I liked his beard like a black bush and his smile full of large teeth. He read to us about the Garden of Eden and we thought we must be in it except without any Eves.'" The boys chuckled. "'At first, some students did not respect Father Mario,'" Bildad continued, "'because the priest gave up his vow of chastity. He had an African wife who begat him three children.'"

One boy corrected Bildad. "We admired him for leaving his foreign customs behind. Even he learned to speak our language!"

"Nuer!" Nicodemus piped up proudly.

Some boys narrowed their eyes at him. The Nuer people and the Dinka—Jabez's tribe—were traditional rivals, I'd learned, but their common plight as refugees made them value friendship more than competition.

Bildad continued reading. "'One day, Arab soldiers came to our school from Khartoum, in the North. Father Mario tried to stop them from spoiling our education. But the soldiers decreed to us that from now, Arabic must be the only language spoken in the classrooms. Many of the teachers and students did not even speak it! And we must read the Koran and no more Bible so we would become Moslems." Bildad shook his head. "We could not agree. We protested loudly!'"

"Some villagers also protested with us!" Nicodemus spoke up, his voice shrill today. "We should not have asked them to do this! We knew that the Arabs had guns. The children in the village—" Nicodemus wiped his eyes. "They did not understand—"

"'The students—'" Bildad interrupted him, "' marched and shouted many angry words. We circled the school and refused the soldiers' orders to halt. Father Mario tried to warn us....'" Bildad stopped, as if he could feel Nicodemus's glare burning into his eyes. "I have written more, but I cannot read it just now."

I stared at him, trying to think what to do but nod. "You don't have to read," I said. The air had tightened over the verandah. Finally I saw Jabez raise his head.

"I also wrote about Father Mario. I can read it."

"Well, if you want," I said, "but if it's difficult...."

"Yes, for myself, it was terrible at first to write it." Jabez looked somber. "But as I started with my pen, some of the hurt was captured by the pages and stayed on them instead of in my heart. So I am grateful for the exercise book...." Jabez cleared his throat, hushing whispers. "'Father Mario could have fled back to Italy. But he desired to come with us from the school and bring his family as well.'" Jabez flipped through some pages in his notebook. What had happened at the school? He'd left that out. But I didn't want to stop him as he began again.

What Can You Do

"'We ran through the dark forest,'" he went on. "'Dozens of boys, as well as Father Mario, also his wife and his small children. I was carrying his daughter and trying to find her berries to keep her from crying.'" Now Jabez was reading in a rush, the sentences wrenching themselves out in a gravely voice I hadn't heard before. "We all feared the Arab soldiers too much. They were close behind us. I could hear them searching in the forest while we hid. It was hard to keep from crying but I forced tears down with two fingers in my eyes. Now I have seen so many things I think I can keep my eyes dry about anything, but sometimes I am so lonely I do feel weeping wanting to burst from me....'"

I dug my fingernails into the rough boards on either side of me. The boys around me were blinking, staring straight ahead. "'Our escape from Sudan was as the Israelite's flight from Pharaoh's armies,'" he read. "'Two boys died from snake bites. Another died from illness. Two boys were shot fleeing through a swamp. Then the soldiers stopped chasing us but we were lost in jungly places with thick clouds of mosquitoes. A crocodile came but I beat it to death with a rock and then we cooked it....'" Jabez took a long breath, and continued. "'Father Mario knew how to keep moving properly by reading the stars, because he had been a sailor as a young man. Now we had gone far south toward the Uganda border. One night we found a small fishing boat for crossing a river. But after we had succeeded, Father Mario came with his family and the boat turned over in the water. His wife and two older children drowned. He alone knew how to swim, but he could drag just his baby from the river. I took the child from his arms. But the tiny girl was dead when she was laid upon the bank. It hurt me to tell this to Father Mario. We prayed and buried the baby. Then we walked on for more and more days....'"

Jabez dropped his exercise book to his lap. I shifted my position, feeling queasy with sadness. I had expected affectionate remembrances of favorite schoolmasters, not a story like this. But the deep lines in the boys' faces told me that none of them wanted to quit now.

"'Father Mario walked with us but sometimes we carried him, for now he was lame and ill,'" Jabez continued. "'Finally, one night, I was overwhelmed by joy to see the electric lights of the border posts on the Uganda frontier. They were two metal huts with a wooden gate between them. Hiding in the bush, we searched fearfully for men wearing the berets of the northern Sudanese soldiers, but we saw only men in khaki uniforms—Ugandan border guards." Jabez turned the page in his exercise book and read on. "'Never I will forget Father Mario saying to us, "Boys, let me just go and talk to those soldiers. I will tell them our story and they will let us pass." He limped toward the border posts. But Uganda soldiers ran outside and made urgent signals to him to run away quickly—'"

"*Kabisa!* Class finished today!" The camp guard stood beside me, scowling down. Behind him I could see Susan and her students walking toward the gate.

"Hey, give us another five minutes, can't you?" I asked him.

Jabez stood up, speaking to him in Luganda; he was the only student, I would learn, who'd become fluent in the language. The soldier relaxed his sour face.

"He says you must leave us now, Sir," Nicodemus told me.

Who was this Sir? Me. I'd had to call masters at my prep school "Sir"—smug old farts with tweed, dandruff-flecked shoulders and pipe-tobacco-breath. How could I be a Sir? No time to fix that now. "Okay, what books do you want me to bring next time?" I asked.

"The authors we said before," Jabez said. "Also we like the poems of William Blake!"

"What is our new essay assignment?" Bildad wanted to know.

Some topic that would help them recall happier days. "'Life in My Village,'" I said, standing.

"Will you take our essays from today and mark them?" Jabez asked. "Our old English master always corrected our mistakes with his red pen. He shook it at us in class like a wand for putting knowledge into our heads." I heard hushed laughter.

"Sure, I'll mark the papers," I said, though I had no idea how I'd do it. Suddenly I remembered I hadn't handed out what was in my satchel. Squatting, I set it on the planks. A scene of unprofessional confusion followed: me pulling out new exercise books and the Nigerian paperbacks, the boys grabbing them and simultaneously trying to stuff their last week's notebooks inside. And the soldier marching around muttering, "*Twende-twende!*" at us.

Quickly-quickly! This was no way to run a class. I stopped scrambling and handed out the last of the new materials. When I finally started toward the gate surrounded by the boys, their notebooks full of essays shifted in my bag. They felt terribly heavy.

4.

When I overslept my lectures now, it usually wasn't from being hung over from late-night binges but because I was straying up until dawn reading the boys' papers and trying to figure out how to mark them. The problems weren't in their writing skills; many boys had picked up an antiquated but oddly eloquent style from a British schoolmaster some wrote affectionately about. "He was too strict with us but caring," one student wrote, and I crossed out "too" and replaced it with "very," making a note to explain the difference between the two words. That part of marking was easy.

From reading about their teachers, I could visualize the school run by Italian and African priests with a few British lay teachers. It was a compound of mud and brick structures with roofs of rusted corrugated metal. Boys slept on hard bunks in one long dormitory where buckets were set out during the rainy season to catch continuous drips. The students scrubbed floors and worked for hours weeding the vegetable garden. The bathrooms were long pit latrines.

Yet they'd loved their school. The classroom windows were "refulgent with glass." Boys ate three meals a day, many for the first time in their lives, and were served meat at least once every week—an "astonishing feast—" on benches at long plank tables. Reading this, I recalled the great slabs of roast beef I'd been served at my prep school dinners, and the platters of crisp bacon on Sundays mornings to go with butter-soaked pancakes…with sunlight streaming in the high windows of the gleaming, wood-paneled dining hall. This was the same hall where John F. Kennedy and other members of America's first families had eaten. How could I have taken so much there for granted, and been so miserable amid such opulence?

Jabez's paper described Father Mario's wife as "a slim Dinka woman young with graceful eyes." I wrote beside that sentence "good description." Jabez had baby-sat for the priest's children, feeding them "millet porridge in a small spoon which I carved from soft wood" and reading to them from an picture book, *Pinocchio,* "that made them to laugh from my pronouncing words in a foolish way." I smiled as I read his notebook. Then I froze: these were the children who had drowned with their mother during the escape from Sudan.

Another essay: "The soldier thrust a bayonet in the stomach of my good friend he cry when the blood squirted out." How was I to mark *that?* Well, semi-colon after "friend" and past tense for "cry." But picturing the blood stopped me. What could it be like to see a friend bayonetted? I read on: "One night, a lion dragged Father Barnabas into the bush. I wept to hear him scream as his organs torn by the lion." Organs *were* torn, it should be. But could I insert the "were?" I sat still, eyes closed tight. Then I thought: my markings would show the boy I cared about helping improve his English. I corrected the sentence.

On my desk were eleven notebooks, each twenty-four pages long—a total of 262 probably harrowing pages. Well, I'd asked for them. When I came to Nicodemus's book, the sentences rushed on from trauma to trauma as if he'd been weeping all over the pages. I did manage to find events that showed his courage, his determination to survive, though; my red pen double-underlined them.

I kept looking for information about the school strike, left out of Jabez's account at the camp, but it was well after sunrise now and I was too numb to read any more.

At Makerere's Education Institute, I found books on lesson-planning and syllabi that African high school teachers had used in their courses. Afternoon trips to Kampala now had an urgent focus: to find materials for my classes. The city's one bookshop stocked some literature paperbacks; I ordered some class sets of African novels plus Dicken's *Great Expectations,* which many boys had started but never finished. The U.S. Information Service library was full of good books but had none to give out, though I did pedal away with a dozen illustrated brochures about a cattle drive in Wyoming. The Dinka and Nuer peoples were cattle-keeping nomads; maybe the boys would enjoy reading about cowboys. The Alliance Françoise loaded me up with bi-lingual pamphlets depicting the lives of happy French fishermen; the British Council Library people were generous with brochures about League Football Heroes. At the Russian Information Service, I was given two beautifully illustrated volumes of folk tales I looked forward to reading aloud. In the university library I found anthologies of African and English poems and typed some onto cyclostyle stencils; fitting them onto the machine's purple-inked drum, I cranked it round and round to make multiple copies.

On one of my foraging trips into the city I heard incongruous music pouring out of a white stucco church. It sounded like…yes, American revival-tent singing. I'd listened to folky gospel songs in Greenwich Village coffee houses, but what was country music like this doing here in Africa? I stepped into the vestibule. Inside, beaming Africans raised their voices to the beat of a guitar and conga drum. They swayed back and forth, they clapped their hands above their heads, they shouted "Halleluiah!" and "Amen!" Up front, a white evangelist reached his hands high in the air, fanning the singing to a crescendo. A glossy golden pompadour rose from his forehead; his close-set eyes scanned the room, cheeks bulging in a cherubic smile as the song ended. Strutting back and forth on the platform in a powder-blue suit, he yelled into a hand-held microphone, "My brothers and sisters—are you *saved?*" A short African man, also wielding a mic, shouted the same question in Luganda. The congregation shouted back—"*Iye! Iye!* Yes!"

It was one thing to listen to "Will the Circle be Unbroken?" being sung by a hip, stringy-haired guy in New York—I'd never heard any real Appalachian congregations singing hymns—and something very different to hear the fundamentalist sermon that went with the music: *"I tell you folks, the Lord <u>hates</u> sinners—<u>yes,</u> he does!—but He don't condemn <u>nobody</u> who throws down his pagan ways and bathes hisself in the Blood of the <u>Lamb!</u>"* And here came a dumbed-down Bible story delivered in a Southern twang, all of it translated phrase-by-phrase by the pastor's African sidekick. Even as I tapped my feet to the background guitar, I grew enraged at the pastor for getting his converts to parrot his pie-in-the-sky platitudes. Many years later, I would become even more angry reading how extensive networks of American evangelicals had preached hatred of homosexuals, some of whom were hunted down and murdered by newly-converted African Christian zealots.

I'd been raised on tepid Episcopal sermons delivered to congregations of corporate executives—a more restrained but scarcely more convincing form of worship than the fire-and-brimstone sermons I was hearing here in Kampala. By the time I graduated from prep school, years of similar sermons had droned religion completely out of my head. At the Bombo camp I'd shelved my secularism. Who was I to criticize religion if it helped the boys keep their sanity? And I could appreciate the heroism of priests who'd helped their students make the terrible trek out of Sudan. But I couldn't listen to any more horseshit from this cornpone evangelist, and started to duck out the door.

Then a glossy booklet in a rack grabbed my attention like a fist clutching my throat. I stared straight at a photograph of a crucified man. A flesh-and-blood human hanging on a cross. A nearly naked black man. With his arms outstretched, hands nailed. My stomach clenched. According to this booklet, these public executions in Sudan were committed by brown-skinned, Moslem Arabs as a warning to black Christians not to support a guerilla movement advocating an independent southern region.

This was the sort of information I'd searched in vain for in the university library. But could I believe it? The booklet was printed at the church's headquarters in Georgia, a state where pastors used Biblical passages to preach racial prejudice that justified mob violence. Now the same sort of church was urging its members to—to save black people? Evidently so. Its information tallied with what I'd learned at the Bombo camp; the outburst I'd heard from Nicodemus about a crucifixion had not, in fact, been brought on by an hallucination.

Apparently he hadn't exaggerated about slavery, either. According to the booklet, Sudanese Moslems had been capturing and selling slaves for centuries, and the practice was still thriving. More photos: men with ropes around their necks, a young girl holding up one hand with a finger hacked off, reportedly because she'd tried to flee her captors. Some American congregations were collecting funds to allow missionaries to buy and set free enslaved men and women. Others argued that paying slavers would only encourage them to capture more victims.

I'd once thought that my Midwestern ancestors had been free of the taint of holding Africans in bondage. But a year ago, visiting the home of relatives in Ohio I'd never met before, I was shown a four-poster bedstead they were proud to report had been hand-carved for a great-great-grandfather on his sugar plantation in Jamaica in 1847. *Oh shit!*

Still trying to fathom what this hillbilly American church was doing in Kampala—the joyful hymns pouring out the door, the tambourines jingling in my ears—I wobbled away on my bike.

As the boys walked with me to the verandah at the camp, they eyed my canvas bag as if it were giving off heat; I opened it and handed back their notebooks, all of them corrected. The students flipped through the pages, reading my red-inked comments, murmuring to each other. Finally one boy spoke up: "But you have given our essays no grades."

True, I hadn't. Could I tell them that their stories had been too upsetting to attach evaluations to? No—I had to appear to know what I was doing. On the other hand—the students had written their papers with such honesty that I was ashamed to waffle. "I didn't know how to grade them," I confessed. "I need...more experience before I learn that."

The murmuring ceased. "You are a student, too, Sir," Jabez said.

"True," I said. "And so—well, I can do without the 'Sir,' if that's okay with you." I told them my last name, but they couldn't get their mouths around it; finally we settled on "Mr. Edward."

Nicodemus had kept his head down, frowning into his notebook; I hoped he wasn't upset by my written comments. But he had something else on his mind. "Last week," he blurted out, "the guard came before Jabez finished reading his essay about Father Mario."

"It is all right." Jabez turned toward him. "We all know what happened."

"Here is what I wrote, myself!" Nicodemus scrambled to his feet. "'Father Mario told us, "Let me just go and talk to those soldiers."'" I recalled that the group of boys had been hiding near the Uganda border wondering if it was safe to cross. Nicodemus snapped the page as he turned it, making himself wince.

The boys turned away from him, faces tensed.

"'Sudanese soldiers with berets rushed from one border post. They raised their rifles. We heard the shots. Then we saw Father Mario fallen dead on the road.'"

Jabez reached up to rest his hand on Nicodemus' arm. "That is enough."

Nicodemus shook his head. "'And we fled back into the bush! We just *left* him!'"

"We had no choice," Jabez said.

Nicodemus stared at him. "I was among those who left him—who fled!" The exercise book fell from his hand.

I dug my fingernails into my palms. Finally I said, "I can see...you must feel awful."

Jabez shook his head. "Father Mario's death, it was *my* fault."

"No!" The boys suddenly spoke in their language, voices rising chaotically.

Why did Jabez blame himself? This wasn't the time to ask. I raised my voice. "I know these essays have to be painful to hear," It surprised me the way the boys reacted to my voice; they were suddenly silent. "Let's try something else just for now! I've got poems...." I pulled some cyclostyled papers from my bag. "The first is by Gabriel Okara, a Nigerian writer—"

The air flapped with a frenzy of hands. "There's plenty!" I shouted. The boys kept pushing forward, grabbing sheets of paper. When they finally sat back, I asked Bildad to read an Okara poem aloud—"Piano and Drums"—about trying to reconcile new Western ideas with older African ones.

"...And I...keep / wandering in the mystic rhythm / of jungle drums *and* the concerto," he concluded his reading. The boys loved talking about their traditional music and their first exposures to Western music—both the classical piano pieces played by their teachers and the blues, rock, and country-western songs they'd heard over their school's short-wave radio.

Everyone had ideas about what Okara's lines meant. Their forefingers pecked the paper as they made points, their eyes widened. All I had to do was look at one student after another as if conducting a small orchestra. Now and then I'd pipe up—"But what if....?" or "Yes, and how about?...." and the current of ideas would flow headlong off in another direction.

Did the two kinds of music, I asked, necessarily produce the confusion of cultures the poet talked about? Was it all right to remain "lost in the morning mist," as the poem said—stuck between two cultures—until you figured out how different ideas might live together in some sort of harmony? Arguments surged again. I told them how I'd struggled to fit African chord progressions to American folk melodies.

"Perhaps you can make changes in your own music," one boy spoke up. "So the African sounds can come into it better."

I nodded. "That's what I want to do."

Next, I asked Nicodemus to read a poem from William Blake's "Songs of Experience" called "The Clod of Clay." He blinked hard—it was nervous tic he had—yet his voice sounded calmer than before: if Love seeks *not* itself to please, it "builds a Heaven in Hell's despair" but if Love seeks *only* itself to please, it "builds a Hell in Heaven's despite."

I asked the class which definition of love they thought was right. Given their recent ordeals, I would have expected them to agree that a Hell had been built in their lives. I was dying to say it, but somehow knew enough not to press my views, and let them try to decide. Arguments ensued. The consensus was for Heaven.

Two hours had sped by, but I hardly noticed the hardness of the planks beneath me as I sat listening, questioning, commenting—teaching.

We read the "Life in my Village" assignment the following week. The boys asked Jabez to read his essay first. He shook his head and hunched his shoulders as if to make himself smaller, but he was too tall to hide. Finally, he began: "'When I was a boy, we all herded the animals and played fighting games with sticks. We gathered together to eat evening meals with our father and his wives. We slept in our mothers' huts. It was a happy time for me.'" I saw the boys begin to smile at the cadence of Jabez's voice. Then his tone deepened. "'These were the days when our land was a British colony. One day, a Christian black man from the government appeared in our compound wearing Western clothes. He demanded each family to send one son for education at the mission school in a distant village. The sons were needed to become clerks in the colonial offices.'"

The boys nodded. This was apparently a story much like their own.

Jabez took a deep breath. "'My father refused the man. Our family was loyal to our traditional beliefs. But the man said the government would fine my father many cattle if he did not cooperate. And in the end, a boy would be taken, anyway. Finally my father had to agree. I was the youngest and the least useful. So he turned to me and said, 'You are the one who must go to the school.'" Jabez glanced around. "'I was trying not to cry out. My mother and sisters were wailing. I asked my father, "Why you are loving me so little that you should banish me from my home?" Even I cursed him for giving me to the government man. But somehow he did not punish me for this terrible disrespect.'"

"How could he?" a boy asked. "He must have seen you could not help yourself!"

"Yes, he was wise, he saw this." Jabez leaned over his exercise book to squint at his words. "'Finally I went to the school. In the beginning I hated it—the stiff uniform, the strange rules, the new food. But soon I was surprised because I began to love the lessons and the games and new friends. I learned to love reading the English Bible and all the books I was given.'"

He paused. "'Then, after several years and I had grown very much, my father arrived to the school.'"

No one spoke. I sensed a pressure in the air.

"'He had become a member of the tribal council. He told the headmaster that the council ruled I no longer had to remain at the school. I was free to go home, with no penalties or trouble for my family. My father ordered me to leave with him.'" Jabez's eyes narrowed to slits, and in the building's shadow, all his features seemed to fade into a hazy, blue-black mask of grief. "'But that day, I betrayed my father. I told him I did not want to return home. I said, "Now I am learning many new things. I am a Christian, not the same boy I was. So no longer I am fit for living my old life of herding cattle. I must continue being educated!"'" Jabez sighed. "'My father tried to pull me,'" he read. "'I pushed his hand away.'"

Jabez cleared his throat, then read on slowly. "'When I refused my father, I saw his wretchedness. He had lost his son.'" The boys looked down, pushed their knuckles into the wood. This was evidently their story, as well. "'Is this not the worst thing a father can endure?'"

As I listened to the students' murmurs, I realized that to them, the answer was clear. But not to me—I had no idea what was the worst thing my own father had known. Or the best thing, for that matter. I hardly knew him. I couldn't recall the expression on his face when he'd seen me off at the train station for boarding school. Or when I'd gone away for college, or for Africa.

"'I stood in my uniform beside the school flagpole.'" Jabez read, his voice sunk to a whisper, "'and I watched my father walk away into the countryside. My heart was feeling almost to explode. For all that next year, I made plans to go home and visit my father and try to heal his heart. But then the Arab soldiers came to my school, the violence broke out....'"

Jabez stared down at the floor for a moment. "'I have never seen my father again. I cannot write letters to him for fear of bringing danger to my family. My father does not know where I am. He may think I have just run off. He may think I no longer love him....'"

Jabez closed his notebook. He sat back, blinking hard. I couldn't speak.

The boys gradually looked up at me. "Was the essay good?" Bildad asked finally.

I cleared my throat several times, and finally said, "Yes" in a scratchy voice.

"Why?" someone asked,

"Because it made me understand something...about how Jabez felt."

"Did you betray *your* father?" Nicodemus asked.

"In a way, I did. I defied him," I said. "Sometimes you have to do that. I wouldn't be here with you if I hadn't. So I'm glad I did. But I didn't know I was sad about it, too."

"You did not know until you heard me read?" Jabez asked.

"That's right." Overhead, the tree branches shifted in the breeze; I heard their leaves rustling. "If you don't know what you're feeling, it's like there's a big hole inside you, and you're scared of it. But when you know there's something in there after all—even if it's sadness—then you're less…empty. And less scared."

Jabez looked at me and nodded. Several students exhaled.

I pointed at the boys' notebooks. "So let's keep going. Who wants to read now?"

Hands waved in the air.

5.

Fast footsteps approached my room along the dorm corridor at Makerere. The racket swelled, rattling the transoms. Rushing to open my door, I heard a high pitched cry—a barefoot man stumbled past me—gone so fast that I saw his face only in a splash—terror-bulged eyes, a bloody gash splitting one cheek—but a face familiar from somewhere. A mob of students hurtled full-tilt past me, panting, bellowing in rage.

"*Thief! Thief!*"

"*Get the bastard!*"

I'd never seen grown men running so hard in furious, headlong pursuit of a person. I fast-walked after them, then—catching a blast of adrenaline that made me wince—ran hard behind the echoing voices. The stink of sweat and something even more acrid filled the hall. I heard a clump-clumping behind me—the stick of Okani, my friend with a polio-withered leg.

"Hey—what's going on?" I slowed, my heart slamming.

His face gleamed. "We caught him—the man who was thieving our shirts from the line!"

"What—what are you going to do?"

Okani poled himself on down the corridor. "We have to punish him! He is a thief!"

Shouts of rage erupted in a little courtyard outside the common room. Holding tight to its doorframe, I leaned forward, craning my neck for a view. The barefoot man's face rocked backwards. With a long shriek he collapsed in the scrum. Fists pummeled his torso, his blood-smeared face. Everyone crowded close to get in a blow, a hard kick. Okani, balancing against the wall, raised his heavy stick, snapped it down—*whomp!* The man's jaw exploded open in a spray of red. I spun away from the mob.

Rubber-legged, trembling, I lurched down the hall and out to the driveway. The air hummed like a furnace. I blinked open my eyes. A flame tree spread its red-pedaled branches over the gravel, creating an eerily soft net of dappled shade. I leaned against its trunk and heaved up everything in my stomach until nothing was left but the burnt-rubber taste of bile.

Still shaky, I walked along a path that led outside the dormitory, arriving at the little courtyard where the students had beaten the man. I'd been too shocked—scared?—mesmerized?—to try to help him. But at least I could try to get him medical attention—call an ambulance—bring a doctor.... The air still seemed to reverberate in the courtyard. Bloody footprints smeared the tiles. But incredibly, the man was gone. He must have crawled over the low wall I was standing at. The ground at my feet was indented from the impact of his body; drag marks showed his escape route into the underbrush through a strip of loose dirt. Suddenly I knew who he was: one of the kneeling, bare-chested men I'd seen planting flowers around the dorm wall. He was one of the small army of university laborers who lived in the mud huts down the hillside. I'd often greeted him as I parked my bike outside the dorm.

Voices rose in the courtyard doorway—angry-faced students. I picked up enough of their Swahili to know some of them were arguing that the thief should not have been beaten; it was *"kikatili."*—bad, brutal. Others insisted that this was what you always had to do with thieves.

I returned to my room, locked my door, paced, smoked. I thought of the gardener who'd glanced up at me as I passed—*"Jambo sana"*—with my bicycle. I pictured his terror-stricken eyes, his blasted face. I'd never witnessed such violence before. The attackers were my dorm-mates—friends I'd sat around the common room with and joined for meals in the dining hall. None of them had seemed remotely capable of doing what I'd just seen them do. I heard them again up the corridor—murmuring, chuckling, slamming doors, making all the usual dormitory sounds. Nothing had changed.

Except Africa. Except me.

I don't know how many hours I spent wandering around the campus. I seemed to wake up sitting in the conversational Swahili class I'd joined. All I could do was shove the dorm scene out of my mind as best I could and get on with my life. It's amazing, how you can do that.

Two years later, I saw a mob chasing a wild-eyed thief down a Nairobi street and prayed he'd escape. By then, I'd been told that motorists who hit pedestrians in rural areas were sometimes dragged from their cars, beaten, even killed by villagers. Foreigners said that this violence represented the dark underside of African culture. I didn't believe it: by then I knew about atrocities committed in other parts of the world, some of them in my own country. Yet I was tempted to tell myself: Here's an example of a cultural difference that, no matter how long you stay in Africa, you will never understand.

It took me years to connect myself with what I'd witnessed in my dormitory at Makerere. The connection was not in acts others had performed but in what I'd felt and done. A wild blast of adrenaline had propelled me up the corridor. Something much like it had kept me standing at the edge of the mob, leaning forward, twisting my face back and forth to get a better look—and simultaneously trying to turn away from the beating. Minutes afterwards, I threw up. My eyes filled with tears picturing the gardener's bloodied face. And yet, and yet—I'd stayed to watch the violence, and had come away trembling. What had kept that trembling alive in me? Horror and sorrow, yes, but also something else I couldn't—was afraid to—identify. Eventually, though, I had to face the cruel demon grinning back at me from my memory like a ghost in a mirror.

Then my sense of estrangement from my dorm-mates abated. I began to understand how it's possible both to enjoy cathartic cruelty and to desire fervently to stop it, to feel both a rush of viciousness and an urgent need to fight it whenever one can with compassion for its victims.

Who, after all, is most soothed by compassion?

I was no longer so shocked by the harrowing events I read about in my Sudanese student's essays, but they still saddened me; their authors were people I was getting to know and to worry about. On the bus back from Bombo that week, I asked Susan how she always managed to stay so cheerful about her classes there.

"I just teach my subject," she said. "Chicken organs, weed roots systems, photosynthesis. The guys love it. We plant stuff, too. Have you noticed the way their garden's coming back?"

I nodded. "But what about the things the boys tell you—about their lives?"

She sighed. "Well, they don't tell me much. I suppose I keep them too busy to."

"I should do that, too. Assign the boys more essays about poems and folk tales."

"I'm a scientist, not a therapist." Susan patted the cyclostyled notebook of diagrams in her lap. "By the way, a lot of those 'boys' aren't boys at all." She explained that when they first showed up for primary school, the officials asked their ages, and they knew that if they admitted they were older than ten, they'd get sent away. That would shame their families. "So they said 'ten,'" Susan said, "even if they were fifteen or eighteen or whatever."

"None of their teachers figured this out?"

"Oh, probably. But the teachers wouldn't get paid if they couldn't find students, so…." She shrugged. "Once in school, the guys zipped through the primary grades in a few years into high school. I've got students in their twenties. Some married, some fathers already."

"They might be older than us."

She nodded, her blond bangs bouncing. "You know, that giant, skinny guy in your class—Jabez, the sort of head honcho in the camp? One of my students told me he's twenty-two—or about that. A lot of Africans don't have birth certificates."

Damn—*I* was twenty two. How was I going to talk to Jabez now? Probably the same as I had before. The students weren't blowing my cover—they treated me like a real teacher. I wouldn't blow theirs.

"Now is when I go to my job outside the camp," Jabez told me after our next class. "A farmer has employed me. His family sometimes feed me, too. Do you want to greet them?"

"Sure." I was curious to see the village and meet its people. We walked toward some bushes with deep shady areas behind them at the back of the compound. There, before the start of the forest, the fence had been wrenched up from the earth to leave a space it was easy to slip through. I ducked and followed Jabez out of the camp. Many boys passed in and out here, Jabez said, his voice low; there were a few, though, who were afraid to leave the place. Some of the villagers, unused to seeing people different from them—so tall and deeply black—stared at them suspiciously. "As if we were witches," Jabez said.

"Even in broad daylight?"

Jabez nodded. "Yes. But it is something you can get used to."

"I know," I said, and for a moment recalled the wary looks I'd gotten from townspeople when the mental hospital staff took me and other patients off-grounds on weekly shopping trips.

Some of Jabez's wages, he said, went to bribe the guards not to repair the fence. "But truthfully, the Ugandans do not care if we vanish from this place," he said. "The reason most of us have not left is that we have nowhere else to go." Farming was supposed to be below the dignity of cattle-keeping nomads, he told me, but these were different circumstances; learning agricultural skills kept the camp life from driving him crazy. "I must be always busy—moving here, moving there," he said. "It was my nature even before I came here." I understood what he meant, though I hadn't been brought up moving herds of cattle from one pastureland to another.

The village's main street was of red clay, with more footprints than tire tracks on its dusty surface. Some huts were white-washed; others were clay-colored with roofs of corrugated metal or stiff thatch that sloped down to bristly edges at shoulder-level; adults had to stoop a little coming in and out of doorways. In the yards, women leaned over, buttocks pointed to the sky, sweep-sweeping with short, straw brooms that left swirly patterns in the dirt. Bare-chested men in shorts returned from the fields swinging machetes at their sides. I passed a brick church with a wooden cross on the wall over the doorway. Farther along was a primary school where small children screamed high-pitched recitations of numbers—until they spotted Jabez and me. Then they clustered curiously around the glassless windows. Smiling, we waved to them as we passed.

Jabez stopped before a hut's open doorway where spicy scents mixed with the hazy red dust from the street. It was a tiny shop. I admired the filigreed patterns ants had made in the dried mud behind the wooden door frame. Jabez introduced me to the proprietress, a woman named Wangena who was the cousin of his employer. She was a chubby, cheerful-looking woman, barefoot in a long skirt, loose blouse, and head-cloth. I shook her hand and tried out my Luganda *asee-bya-teno* greeting, which made her cover her mouth to keep back a laugh. *"Balun-jee!"* she returned my greeting in a pretty sing-song voice. She sat down on her stool surrounded by open sacks of rice, grain, and seeds.

"I often stop here for a cigarette and tea." Jabez sighed. "But today I forgot my money."

"Let me—" I reached into my pocket.

Jabez shook his head. "Please, no! I don't need anything."

Since I'd left my cigarettes back at the camp, I was dying for a smoke, and handed the woman a shilling coin. Slowly she extracted two Sportsman cigarettes from a pack for us. Spotting some packets of cookies on the Dutch-door shelf, I bought two and handed one to Jabez.

"But you have bought those Nigerian books," he protested. I'd left another packet of reading materials back at the camp. "And you pay your bus fare here from Kampala each week."

He couldn't have imagined what a lavish stipend my government was giving me; I'd even arranged to buy a used car with it. But explaining this to Jabez would just widen the gap between us. Wangena came outside dragging metal chairs. We helped her set up a table, and soon we were sitting around it drinking sweet milk tea. She refused to take any money for it.

In the heat of the afternoon, the tea made me sweat, and the moisture on my skin cooled me. I asked Jabez about his farm job, his plans. He could tell me about chopping brush, sowing seeds, tending the farmer's rows of coffee bushes. But plans? I stopped asking; he lived with total uncertainty about his future.

I looked forward to my trips to the Bombo camp all week long, spending more and more time planning lessons. I brought the students poems, stories, books, also some stationery they needed to write to schools they'd heard of in Uganda and Kenya that might admit them after the six of us from Makerere stopped coming to the camp. The walls of the Sudanese students were filling with glued-on pictures from the magazines and brochures I brought. John F. Kennedy and Martin Luther King, Jr. were popular subjects; Miriam Makeba, Elvis, Satchmo and other entertainers also appeared above bunks—anything to cover up the stark, bare walls.

Each week after class, now, I walked with Jabez and sometimes another boy or two out to what had become the little village's tea-stall, where several tables and chairs were now set up outside Wangena's shop. Her little girl padded out the door in a pink dress to wriggle up onto Jabez' lap. He let her nibble at a corner of his biscuit after he'd soaked it in tea. She climbed on my lap and, with her nose inches from mine, reached out and fingered my straight, straw-colored hair. Her fingers tickled. I smiled back at her. Her mother watched us and laughed.

One week, Jabez brought Nicodemus with him as we left the camp. I could see that the boy—he was only fourteen, according to other students—was more agitated than usual. At one point after we'd sat down at the tea stall, he started to stomp away. Jabez grabbed his arm.

"*Let go!*" Nicodemus tried to kick him.

Jabez, turning sideways, caught his bare foot and could have flipped him onto his back. But he took hold of his shoulders and half-carried him back to the chair. Nicodemus sat hard, glaring straight ahead. Wangena put a mug of tea down on the table in front of him. Her hand rested on his shoulder for a moment before she slipped away.

"Nicodemus is talking about running off," Jabez told me. "He wants to go and join the *Anyanya*. They are the rebel forces in southern Sudan fighting the Arab government."

"Why should I not go?" Nicodemus's lower lip puffed out. "I cannot stay here rotting while my people are being tortured and killed!"

Jabez leaned forward. "If you go join the rebels, the Arabs can find your family and do bad things to them."

"My family has already left our village. No one will find them."

"You must wait!" Jabez' voice was quiet but urgent. "Like the rest of us."

Deep furrows appeared in Nicodemus' brow. "You have no right to tell me this!"

"What do you think?" Jabez turned to me. "I brought Nicodemus to hear your opinion."

Me? The perpetual hum of village life swelled around my ears, then sank away. "Nicodemus...." I started, but my mind stayed blank. At that time, I didn't have any idea what "join the rebels" would have entailed for Nicodemus. I hadn't yet heard about child soldiers in Rwanda, Sri Lanka, Kosovo and other strife-torn places around the world; I couldn't have envisaged Nicodemus being forced to club babies to death or do unspeakable things to women with a machete. But I did realize how badly he'd fare in a bush war; he was too awkward and gentle to survive long.

"I wish you'd stay here, where you're safe," I finally said. "At least until you're older."

"You have not seen what I have!" he blurted out. I felt his saliva spray against my cheeks. "The Arabs who came to the school—to the village next to it—the gunfire...."

I glanced at Jabez. But it was *my* authority as a teacher that I needed somehow to assert. "Listen, Nicodemus," I said, "I know it's hard to be penned up, to feel so helpless. But if you run off and fight, you could easily get yourself killed."

"It doesn't matter—"

"The hell it doesn't!" I grabbed his forearm. "Don't run your mouth like that!"

Nicodemus's muscles hardened in my grip. Eyes narrowed, he glared at my fingers.

"Don't you owe it to Father Mario and Jabez—everybody who helped you—to keep yourself alive?" I demanded.

Jabez leaned forward. "Listen to what he says!"

Nicodemus sighed. Slowly, the tense features of his face relaxed. "All right...I will stay here a while longer." Pulling his arm free, he started to get to his feet.

"Sit and take tea with us! Show some—" Jabez glanced in my direction. "respect!"

Nicodemus slouched into his chair. "Sorry...."

"It's okay," I said. "You have homework to do for next week. And I'll have new poems."

Nicodemus slowly turned to me. "Which ones?"

I had no idea yet, but I grinned. "You'll see," I said.

The following week, though, I would be in no mood for poetry.

6.

Very late one night in the Mmengo section of Kampala, I sat drunk and barefoot on a bed beside a young woman who called herself Sweetie. In the dance hall, she'd looked graceful in a silky blouse and tight mini-skirt. Her breasts had bounced frantically in the blue neon glow, but now when she flopped onto her back, they lay deflated along the sides of her narrow chest. She'd told me she'd once been a nurse, but the old, hand-me-down European-style dresses hanging on her wall suggested she might once have been some foreigner's servant. A whining cloud of mosquitos hovered; I saw raw bumps where she'd scratched her forehead. She stared wide-eyed at clouds of nothing floating above the corrugated metal waves of her ceiling.

"You...okay?" I asked her. I'd lost all desire to take off my clothes.

Shivering, she turned sideways, knees hugged to her chest. "I do not want to be...."

I leaned closer. She smelled of sweat and beer. "Be what?"

"Any...thing." Her voice was flat.

A mosquito's needle vibrated in my ear. She talked in whispery gasps about losing jobs because her brain "became empty" as she worked, she said; for long minutes, the world went blank and suddenly started up again, loud and demanding and bewildering.

"That's no good," I mumbled, shaking my head. Before my hospitalization, I'd been fired—once from a supermarket, once a restaurant—for the same reason. Silent again, she looked as hopeless as I'd still be if I hadn't been a lot luckier than her.

"I c'be your housegirl," Sweetie whispered. "Please, I am not lazy, I am not bad...."

Against my hip I felt the heat of her shoulder. It, too, was covered in bumps. I pulled the sheet over her. This was the first time, I realized, that I'd talked more than a few drunken words to—or listened to—a girl I'd picked up. She lay on her side facing me, eyes blinking slowly as if to fend off images flickering in the low flame of her kerosene lantern. Finally her eyelids fell. She began to snore.

I wished I could sleep, too, vanish under some darkness for a while. I stood up, hopped as I put on my shoes. From down the street, the bouncy beat from the New Life Café mocked my clumsy movements. On my way out, I dropped all the bills in my wallet onto the cloth-covered crate she used as a table. But they weren't enough.

Along the hill leading to the university, the air hung moist and heavy; this was the bleary hour before dawn when a purple heat was poised to roll over the city from behind the jagged silhouettes of palm trees. I walked with care, still unsteady on my feet. Hardly any streetlamps illuminated the road; most stood dark like a row of tall flower stalks. So I was startled to turn a corner and look up into the orangish halo of a single dim light. I heard footsteps. Out of the shadows an emaciated old man in a suit shuffled toward me. I stopped. He stopped, squinting at me. We faced each other. The lamp's glow illuminated the whites of his eyes, made caves of his cheeks. I saw his jawbone's outline beneath his ashy skin.

The jaw moved—"I am...very sorry," he said.

"What?"

He nodded slowly. "I am sorry for the death of your president."

I rocked sideways, holding out one hand for balance. "My—president?"

"He was shot." The old man's voice sank to a whisper. "In a place called Texas. President Kennedy. He was a great friend of the African people." The orange light seemed to throb. "I am very sorry...."

He shuffled away and dissolved back into shadow. My heart was slamming. I pressed my fist against my chest. Had that skinny man really appeared in the road to tell me such impossible news? I walked faster, sober now, disbelieving with all my might.

❧

The dining hall gave off a white glare beneath the still-starry sky. Usually the building reminded me of a dark, empty fish-tank when I came in late; now, with its windows pulsing bright, I could see movements behind the glass. The door, usually locked at night, was wide open. Twenty or so students, African and American, were sitting around a long table where a short-wave radio was set up, crackling and hissing.

"Is President Kennedy....?" I was panting too hard to finish my question.

"He's dead!" An American woman—Susan—turned her face to me. Her eyes shone wet. Strands of hair stuck to her cheeks.

I collapsed into a chair, my face in my hands. Suddenly I felt wretched for not having been with these people, my own people, when this—this *thing*, this murder had happened. Ashamed for having been getting drunk, dancing, groping poor Sweetie—or whatever I'd been doing at the moment when the gunshots had been fired on the other side of the world. I'd never felt so far away from my country before. "I didn't *know* until a few minutes ago," I panted.

No one heard me. The Americans, some in jeans and t-shirts, some wearing bathrobes over pajamas, stared out the windows, smoked cigarettes, wept silently. The news, I learned, had come over Radio Uganda at about eleven forty-five: the American president had been shot while riding in a motorcade through Dallas. The last report before the station shut down at midnight was that he was being rushed to a hospital. Students had dashed from room to room to find a short wave radio, the one now set up in the dining hall. By the time someone found a signal in English, the president had been declared dead, his skull shattered by a high-powered rifle bullet.

None of the Americans wanted to leave each other to return to rooms where sleep would be impossible. I sat at a table beside Susan. What could I say?

"How are you doing?" I asked finally, my voice sounding hollow.

"Okay, I guess. Everybody keeps asking everybody that." Susan rubbed her eyes. "It's so goddamn *sad!*" Her voice cracked. "It's too much to...."

"To take in," I said.

Biting her lip, she nodded.

We all stayed up well past dawn. Breakfast—pineapple, cornflakes with warm milk, toast—was available at the counter, but only the Africans ate anything. Gradually the Americans wandered away in small groups. I sat on the grass with Susan and several others, sometimes silent, sometimes talking in snatches about what we remembered of Kennedy.

In America, I later learned, every citizen had stayed transfixed in front of their television set for days, watching replays of the motorcade in Dallas, of the funeral with the caissons drawn by white horses through the streets of Washington. The dead president's widow and children, the tight-suited little boy standing at attention to salute—everyone knew them now, and had a chance to grieve for them privately and publically. But Uganda had no television service; the only pictures I saw were a few grainy black-and-white photos in the morning's newspaper. I felt as shaky as I had on the day after the gardener was beaten in the courtyard. My confusion about the assassinated president hovered over me with a sad, futile urgency. He was gone before I'd been able to figure him out.

I said to the other students that Kennedy's speeches about changing the world had helped inspired me to come here, but I could never manage to see him as the romantic figure the press presented to the world. My friends glanced worriedly in my direction. But hell, I needed to just talk, the way they did, and couldn't have censored myself if I'd wanted to. I said I'd admired Kennedy's idealism, yet he was responsible for the Bay of Pigs fiasco, and he'd terrified me during the Cuban missile crisis. "The first political act of my life was when I carried a placard at a demonstration at the Cornell student union," I said. "There were signs that read *NO BLOCKADE OF CUBA!* and *NO NUCLEAR ANIHILATION!*"

Most of the students stood up and wandered away; they looked as if they were moving under murky water. Only Susan remained, chewing on the ends of her yellow hair.

"Maybe this is the wrong time to talk like this," I said. "Shit, what's the matter with me?"

"It doesn't matter." She lay on her side on the grass. "I'd rather listen to you than feel—I don't know…hollowed out, numb. When you talk, it feels like he's still around to argue about."

I rambled on, telling her that during my senior year at Cornell, I'd met the author James Baldwin, whose every essay I'd read. Before giving a lecture, he talked informally with the staff of *Epoch,* a small, national literary magazine of which I was the student editor. He'd just come from Washington where he, Lena Horne, and Harry Belafonte had tried to impress on John and Robert Kennedy the need for them to lend government support to civil rights organizations in the South. A slightly-built, intense man with a powerful voice, Baldwin—he asked us to call him Jimmy—spoke in our office with a kind of despairing eloquence I'd never heard anyone use before. "The Kennedy brothers—they're so incredibly *ignorant* about what Negroes are facing!" he'd exclaimed, looking as if he might either break out weeping or smash a window with his fist. "It's not that they don't care—I think they probably do—but they just don't know *half* of what we're up against!" I asked if he though his visit had helped wise them up. "*I* don't know! Oh God—I hope so!" he'd answered.

"He must have gotten through," I said to Susan. "Kennedy eventually did move decisively. I admired him for that."

"Me, too." Her eyes were closed, the fingers of one hand pulling at the grass.

Later my senior year, I said, with Kennedy's support of integration, his charisma started to resonate with me again. I'd listened to his famous civil rights radio broadcast during one of my rare visits to my parents' house in Connecticut. For the first time in

What Can You Do

over three years, since leaving the hospital, I argued with my father—defending Kennedy's assertion that the federal government should play an active role in guaranteeing racial equality. Since my breakdown, my parents had been tiptoeing around me, avoiding controversial topics—afraid, I supposed, that they might set me off again and have to send me back to the funny farm. This time, I found myself pounding the dining room table and shouting "Yes, you *do* have to try to force people to give up their prejudices—it won't *just happen gradually!*" My father, a self-made businessman, fumed at any government interference into private citizens' lives; he loathed Kennedy, whom he considered a spoiled member of an élite East Coast family. (It was my more socially ambitious mother who'd insisted on sending me to prep school). My tirade rendered my parents speechless.

"It felt good to tell them how strongly I felt about something." I said to Susan. "I never thought I'd be defending Kennedy to them."

"My parents always loved him, like I did," Susan said. "They were thrilled when I got into this program. Do you think we might be sent back to the States now?"

"No. I'm sure they'll want us to finish what Kennedy started." Was I sure? I wasn't certain of much any more. But it felt good to say it.

Susan looked up slowly. "I never felt so awful before."

I had, often. But I said, "I know," and the squint-lines beside her eyes faded a little.

"Everything's sort of been pulled out from under me," she said. "What am I supposed to believe in—care about—if the president can just be...*annihilated?*"

"Yeah, it's scary." I hated feeling a void was gaping beneath me, too. "You know, I'd wanted my previous life to vanish completely when I came here. Now, in a way, I've gotten what I wanted—but not in any way I could have imagined."

Susan sighed. "I wish there was something I could *do* about all this! I can't just traipse off to lectures and everything, as if nothing's changed."

"Well, I've got essays correct for when we go to Bombo this week."

"The guys at the camp!" Suddenly she sat up straight, brushing off her skirt. "Oh, Lord! I told them I'd have an anatomy chart for them this week!"

I scrambled to my feet. "They're still there."

By now, I knew I couldn't make grammar corrections on especially violent parts of papers, but I found other places to mark and sentences to underline with "good" and "well-written" in the margins. After the president's assassination, the whole world sometimes seemed to be seething with violence, and all I had to combat it with were plastic pens, exercise books, and cyclostyled poems. How could I ever help these students keep up their will to survive?

At the camp, Jabez was the first to meet me at the gate. "I am very sorry for the murder of your great president," he told me in a whispery voice. *"Polé."*

Other students crowded around, their murmured condolences surrounded me as I walked with them toward the verandah.

"We feared you would stop coming," Nicodemus said to me.

"No—all the more reason to be here," I said.

Jabez and the others led me into their dormitory, a long shadowy room that smelled of raw wood and sweat. Several students drew me to their bunks to see photos of President Kennedy glued to the wallboards. We walked up and down the row of bunks solemnly, stopping as I stood to pay my respects before each picture.

"Thank you for this," I said, turning to face them.

Susan wanted to hold a service in honor of the president, and the Sudanese students set up a makeshift chapel with crates for an altar beneath a gum tree. She read aloud from the boys' Bible, and they all sang a hymn whose familiar melody resonated both nostalgically and gloomily with my childhood memories of church. I couldn't see what good sending prayers from Uganda to America would do for anyone except perhaps the senders. But that wasn't nothing: standing beneath the tree with the refugees did calm us all a little.

The following week, I came with my canvas bag full of poems. One of them, by popular request, was Blake's "The Tyger." This beast was less common in Africa than a host of daffodils, but the boys didn't seem to mind.

"'Tyger, Tyger, burning bright,'" a student read aloud, "'In the forests of the night, / What immortal hand or eye / Could frame thy fearful symmetry....'" How *was* it, I demanded—with more vehemence than I'd planned—that the same immortal blacksmith could, if he existed, fashion such beauty and, at the same time, such horror? If anyone would understand this, I thought, they would. All right, he *could* fashion it, they agreed, as the first stanza asked. But how did he *dare* to?—as the poem's last line demanded—especially after we had so enthusiastically adored his other creations? I wanted to know about his Tyger: "When the stars threw down their spears, / And watered heaven with their tears / Did he smile his work to see? / Did he who made the Lamb make thee?" Neither the boys nor I arrived at any definitive answer, but at least we recognized the need to face both creatures' presence in the world.

The next week I lightened things up singing American folk ballads and playing my guitar. The boys crowded close, mouthing the choruses. I brought in four sets of African novels I'd ordered; we spent the rest of the class discussing *Things Fall Apart*. Later, on my walk into the village, Jabez and I talked about our families—his in the Sudan, mine in America—and about our childhood and adolescent adventures; these were the topics of the essays the boys were now writing. They were more cheerful than earlier ones; at the end of many came the boys' gratitude to have their memories of home preserved on paper.

"Without our notebooks," Jabez said. "I might have forgotten who I was."

His papers were well written but strangely detached, as if the things he had done while younger were too far from his mind to recall in detail. I was still curious about the pages he'd skipped reading aloud from his first notebook, but decided not to ask him about them as we sat at a table outside the village tea-stall. He told me that some of the boys had learned how to build a short-wave radio from parts the American physics teacher had brought. Now they could cluster around it late into the nights finding distant stations that brought them music from all over the world. The Beatles! B.B. King! Aretha Franklin!

" But we picked up Radio Khartoum last night," Jabez told me in a somber voice. "It said the Sudan government is putting pressure on Uganda to close this camp."

"But where would you go?" I asked.

"Wherever I could." He sighed. "I do not like to ask you for things. But we need more stationery and stamps to write to schools. I must write to Southern Rhodesia, myself."

"I can bring them," I said. "Have you had replies to the letters you've already mailed?"

"No. None of us has received any." Jabez smoked his cigarette down to a stub. Wangena brought us a saucer ashtray. After she left, he looked up and said, "I have to ask you one more thing. A different matter."

"All right."

He lowered his voice. "I must go the clinic in the next town. For an injection of penicillin."

"What for?" I leaned forward in my chair. "Are you sick?"

Jabez sighed. "I have caught gonorrhea."

"Oh...." I glanced at the furrow in the dust he was making with his toes.

"I was going some nights to Kepuria, near here, to a bar for dancing." He looked up, his eyes tilted at the corners. "I was ashamed to ask you...."

"Well, never mind." I said, remembering poor Sweetie with her mosquito bumps. "I've been to those bars."

Jabez's eyes widened. *"You?"*

"It's just dumb luck I haven't caught a dose of the clap, myself." I was relieved not to be the only sinner around here. And that Jabez wasn't so noble as I'd sometimes imagined him. "I'm not proud of it. But sometimes it seems like the only way to get as close to someone as you need to."

"This is true. The loneliness...."

"The loneliness." I took out my wallet and handed Jabez some bills: U.S. taxpayers' money at work.

I began writing to everyone I knew in the States, telling them about the refugees, including some poignant excerpts from their compositions I'd typed, and asking for contributions to help them continue their education. I still wondered, though, if funds would help them. In those days, only about one percent of primary school graduates found places East Africa's few secondary schools. What chance did a non-citizen have for admission? I made copies of old high school exams I found in the university library; the Sudanese students did exceptionally well on them, and my appeals included their scores. Jill collected funds from her friends and professors at Cornell. After several weeks, checks started coming in, twenty dollars here, fifty there—a great deal of money in Uganda.

Though my parents had paid for my hospitalization and expensive college tuition, I hadn't asked them for anything in a long time. I decided to risk it. "Being among these boys, who are cut off from their families and miss them so badly," I wrote, "has made me realize how sad I've become, without admitting it to myself, about having cut myself off from you." It took me a long time to get to that sentence right. I'd begun to understood that whatever mistakes my parents had made bringing me up hadn't been due to their rejection of me but to their own personal troubles—which, I saw, weren't so very different from the ones my doctor had helped me deal with, myself. Despite our difficulties getting along, my parents had done the best they could to be good to me. As I read my letter aloud to the students, I was conscious of a certain weight lifting off me and blowing away past the camp's stark wire fence.

My parents sent a generous check. With it came an awkward note. At the bottom, my father wrote, "We wish you well with what you are doing there." That gave me a shot of elation I'd never felt before.

I had enough money to cover several boys' fees. But their letters to headmasters still hadn't been answered. How would I find any schools to accept them? I had no idea.

7.

The following week, I arrived in Bombo in my new used Renault "Roho"—meaning "heart" in Swahili—a cheap, small version of a Land Rover with a heartless suspension on rutted dirt roads. The car had space in back for my bike, though it was so battered by now I planned to leave it behind when I left for Kenya to start my practice teaching assignment in a few weeks.

As I pulled up at the camp gate, the wooden buildings looked bleaker than usual, the grass pocked with dark, bald patches. I squinted through the wire fence. Only about a dozen students appeared to meet me. Where were the others? Several uniformed soldiers milled around with rifles strapped to their backs. I told one I was the teacher from Makerere. He stared at me, waiting. For a bribe? Identification? I reached for my new Uganda driver's license.

My sudden movement made him shift his gun from his shoulder to his chest, its muzzle slanting at my feet like the long snout of a suspicious animal. I let my hand fall to my side.

"Your class finished," he said. "Camp, soon it will close."

"But why?" I demanded.

"No problem." The all-purpose explanation of things unexplainable.

"We're not done here! We have to—to graduate the students—"

"Bas!" the soldier shook his head. "Finished!"

"Where are the other boys?" I asked. "Have they been sent back to the Sudan?"

"Sudan? No...." He strode away to inspect my car.

Jabez and Nicodemus approached the gate. Nicodemus grabbed the wire, fingers wriggling through its diamond-shaped openings as he fixed his gaze on me.

"Take me!" two boys shouted, crowding him.

"What—leave *now?*"

Jabez stood behind Nicodemus. "You can transport some students to schools in your car." He gestured toward the soldiers, and I got a message: take advantage of their good mood. But the lesson I'd planned…never mind—

"I'll be taking some boys now," I said to the soldiers. They nodded. I never did learn why they let the boys leave; perhaps they were glad to have fewer refugees to guard. One unlocked the gate and waved the first two through. I thought Nicodemus would be among them, but he stayed back, close to Jabez.

"Jabez, come on!" I called to him. "We can make room! You and Nicodemus."

"Not this time." Jabez poked some bills through the wire. "But here is the money you lent me—for cigarettes, tea."

Just a few shillings, less than an American dollar. "No, no! That's okay—"

"*Please!*" His eyes burned. "I promised it! You must take it!"

I did, stuffing the money into my pocket. "All right—but why aren't you coming?"

He pushed two more students forward. "After these boys have found schools, perhaps."

The soldiers were peering into my car windows. I jumped into the driver's seat; the students clambered in after me—one in front, three in back. "See you soon!" I called to Jabez, my voice scratchy. It occurred to me I might never see him or Nicodemus again.

Now that I had four students, where the hell did I think I was going with them? I headed for Kampala, took money from my bank account for gas, food, and supplies. Then, armed with my road map, I drove off in search of schools.

The country's dirt roads punished my Renault over the following days; in several villages, we sat around tea stalls for hours while men with acetylene torches repaired its ravaged underside. At night, we stopped in all-but-deserted government rest-houses built decades earlier by the British for traveling officials. Sometimes we ate brazier-charred market meat, sometimes bought food to cook over our own makeshift fires. We slept on blankets beneath broken roofs, defenseless against choirs of mosquitos. Several boys woke up screaming from nightmares. I woke once with tiny feet—a rat—scurrying over my face. A boy was bitten by a tarantula; we had to wait a day for him to recover before driving on. In the car, the tall, gangly students seemed to grow extra knees and elbows; they (and I, probably) stank of sweat and cooped-up tension. But I always felt a powerful sense of momentum as I drove, grinning as I focused on the road ahead without knowing what might be around the next turn

At each town, I asked local people where the secondary school was, and presented myself there. Two of the students had written to headmasters in advance, two hadn't. At each stop, a boy went in with me while I made my pitch: just take one boy, just one, and I would contribute as much of the school fees as I could.

I have no idea why I thought I'd be able to get places for any of these boys; the schools were already crowded to bursting and my students had no transcripts or identity papers. But all I could do was keep going. Several Anglican and Catholic priests—most of Uganda's schools were still run by missionaries in those days—gave us tea and listened with concern as a boy told about his harrowing escape from the Sudan. But they apologized and told us they could not squeeze one more student into their classrooms. Finally, though, I met one old priest who recalled receiving a letter from the camp from a boy named Paul. By sheer luck, Paul was the student standing beside me, almost a head taller, stick-figure thin.

"I was down with malaria," the headmaster explained, "and then I'm afraid I never quite caught up with my correspondence." He still looked ill, his face deeply lined, eyes rheumy.

"That is all right." Paul smiled. "Now we are face to face!"

The man sighed. "So we are, so we are...." He invited us into his study, a musty room lined with home-made plank bookcases and old texts. I nudged the boy, who handed the man the examinations he'd recently passed. The priest frowned as he read, and took a long time over the boy's appeal on lined notebook paper—the story of his perilous flight from southern Sudan. "Terrible, terrible," he muttered. He looked up at Paul, balanced on the edge of his chair. "We have no extra room here," he said. "But I'll find you a place somehow."

The boy smiled. "Thank you, father."

The priest lumbered toward the door "We'll have a uniform made—if we can get enough cloth." He turned to me. "Where on earth do you find such big ones?"

"They're all like that." I grinned.

"Good at games, I reckon." He turned to Paul. "Play football, do you?"

"Yes, father!" Paul kicked an imaginary ball with the side of his foot. He looked as if he were improvising a dance-step.

I drove away with tall plumes of dust rising in celebration behind the car. The boys were elated about their friend's success, but still anxious about their own chances. Then we had a run of luck—two schools in a row accepted students. A day later, I placed the last one, and, the car moving light as a gazelle, I headed back to Bombo.

The scene at the camp was the same as before: sagging fences, milling soldiers, boys sitting around. They swarmed toward the gate. I pressed my forehead against the fence and saw Nicodemus.

"Where's Jabez?" I asked him through the wire.

"I do not know. Perhaps working for the farmer." Nicodemus's eyes tilted sadly.

"All right. You come this time!"

He backed way. "No! I must wait for Jabez!"

I packed four more students into the Renault and rolled away. At school after school, they showed their exam results to headmasters and read aloud from the accounts of their escapes from soldiers, starvation, illnesses, crocodiles. After eleven stops, all the boys were accepted. Back at the camp, I sent Nicodemus searching for Jabez. He returned alone. Susan had taken some students, but Jabez wasn't among them. I didn't want to leave without him. By now, a lot of students had convinced the soldiers to let them go in search of education on their own; they'd vanished into the countryside. Perhaps Jabez had gone, too. Finally I loaded my dinged-up Renault and drove off. Two cracked side windows were crisscrossed with tape, and I'd lost a front bumper to a galloping cow. How many more trips could I take? I felt as if I were conducting a kind of triage with the remaining boys. I was glad to have Nicodemus this trip, at least, though I knew he'd be a hard sell.

At each school where we stopped, Nicodemus slumped down in his seat, unwilling to face an interview with a headmaster. Mile after mile, he stayed silent, teeth gritted and stare fixed out the window. What was he seeing? Thinking?

I'd stared through some windows that way, myself. "Hey, Nicodemus," I called into the back seat. "What's up?"

Silence.

"Come on—how're you doing, my friend?"

He glanced at me in the rear-view mirror. "I miss the camp. I fear for Jabez."

I squeezed the steering wheel. "So do I."

In seven days, three of the boys and I convinced headmasters to take them in. I was driving farther and farther out in the countryside now on roads whose surfaces were eroded like dried-up river beds. We stopped outside a school compound of mud and brick buildings surrounded by flame trees.

"Let's go," I said to Nicodemus, who was now sitting in the seat beside me.

"I do not belong in one of these schools." He spoke in a whispery voice. "The boys will see that I am a refugee."

"Listen, I know what it's like to be scared like this," I said. "But you can't go back now." I slanted the mirror toward him. "Look."

He squinted at it, scowling. "I look like a deranged person."

"Well, not quite. But is that the way you want to meet the headmaster?"

He pressed down his hair, wiped his face hard with a handkerchief. Finally he managed something like a smile. "Do I seem a little better?"

"You look great," I said.

Weeks before, Jabez and I had coached him for school interviews: speak up, control the tremble in your voice, don't glare off into space. Nicodemus managed to look cheerful and determined as he spoke to this school's headmaster, a balding Scotsman in patched khakis and short-sleeved shirt. He had the splotchy skin and haunted eyes I'd noticed some white men got when they'd lived too long out in the bush. He nodded as Nicodemus told him about the good grades he'd received in my class, but then stopped him, sighing.

"I'm very sorry, lad," he said. "We truly have no room here."

I had a strong feeling that Nicodemus wouldn't do well at another interview if he failed this one. Suddenly I started talking fast. "Excuse me, but this boy deserves—he needs a chance to continue his education!"

"Of course he does, but...." The headmaster started to stand up.

"Just read what he's been through!" I shoved Nicodemus's essay into his hands.

The man sat again. His lips moved as he read, but he continued to shake his head. From a classroom outside his office, I heard boys reciting a grammar lesson—so tantalizingly close! The priest finally raised his sad eyes from the paper.

"Nicodemus," I glared at him. "Tell him about the reading group you started!"

"I—" He glanced wildly at me. "I lead a Bible study group every evening at the camp!"

The priest closed his eyes.

I kicked Nicodemus under his chair. He talked about his favorite Bible stories. As his voice rose in pitch, I clamped my teeth together and decided I was not going to leave this office until Nicodemus had a place in the school. This was like nothing I'd ever done before. On occasions when people in authority had turned me down, I'd rushed away quickly, figuring that they'd only get impatient to see me gone if stayed longer. But I had to do better today—

"What Bible verse gave you the most...inspiration?" I asked Nicodemus.

He cleared his throat. "It was the Sermon on the Mount. May I say it, father?" He smiled. "'Blessed are the poor in spirit, for theirs is the kingdom of Heaven—"

"Yes, I seem to recall those verses...." The headmaster began standing again.

But I prodded Nicodemus to keep going. He quoted faster and faster, fixing a cobra stare on the priest. The man blinked hard, shaking his head. Nicodemus hardly paused for breath. "Blessed are the meek-for-they-shall-inherittheearth—"

"All right!" The priest sighed. "D'you think you'd be active in the chapel if—"

"*I will, father!*" Nicodemus's head bobbed, eyes bright with tears.

The priest stood, smiling wearily. "Well, come along with me, then...."

Nicodemus wanted to walk with me to the car, but I told him to stay where he was—taking no chances. "You'll do fine!" I said, grinning. Would he? I shook his hand, trying to coax a smile from him. He didn't want to let go. Finally I released him.

As I walked to my car, I turned to see him standing stiffly on the school office's porch. He raised one hand in the air. I waved back. It was a long, lonely journey back to Bombo.

Jabez was still not at the camp. "Where did you see him last?" I asked three students standing inside the gate. "Did he go into the village?" They didn't know. I wanted to walk all over Bombo, but the students were staring at me, anxious to leave. Soldiers paced around my car. I drove away with the three, going farther afield into some of the remote towns bordering Congo and Kenya. One night, we had to find a village headman and, with hardly any words in common, explain that we needed some food and a place to sleep. As soon as he and his wives understood our situation, *matoke* was heated over a fire and an empty storage hut was cleared for us. We left with many good wishes, also many fleas. I was out of leads now, just following my frayed map from village to village. At the schools we visited, my pitch began to sound stale, at least to me, but the boys' presentations remained fresh and enthusiastic, alive with the urgency of people fighting for their lives. After many stops, all three students were taken.

Again I returned with an empty car, but this time to Kampala: my exams were only a few days off; I had to pass them to be certified to leave for my practice teaching. Susan lent me her lecture notes and some of the other Americans brought library books to my room. Now the British system of education I'd railed against—saving all evaluations until one grueling set of papers at the very end of term—worked in my favor. I sat up night after caffeinated night, swallowing theories and key phrases. In a blur of energy, I filled the blue exam books. When the results were posted, my name was nowhere near the top of the list, but I'd passed.

8.

Since my Renault was being repaired, I took the bus to Bombo, anxious to find Jabez. Its engine started coughing on the way, and finally stopped altogether beside the road. Cursing under my breath, I sat in the shade of a spreading acacia tree with the other passengers—women nursing babies on their laps, men holding chickens in homemade wire cages. A half-hour went by; the driver, lying on his back under the engine, clanged a wrench and poked a screw-driver. I paced around, going over my plan to bring Jabez to the mission school where I'd been assigned; once there, I'd work on my new headmaster to admit him. If I could find him today.

The clanging noise had stopped. Was the driver asleep in the shade under the engine? I walked over to the rusted loaf-shaped bus and squatted to talk to him.

"Petrol-line *liki*," he said. "Repaired now."

"Okay...." A gas line leak. I considered hitch-hiking.

"No problem. *Liki kidogo* only."

Oh, only a *small* leak. Which had nonetheless emptied the tank. The driver carried a jerry can into the bush. Where the hell did he think he'd find gas out here in this landscape of fields and scrub trees? No problem—he was back in minutes, and we were on our way again.

Today, no one stood behind the fence to meet me. I shouted into the camp. Silence. The gate hung open. I walked in. Across the compound, the tall pointy anthills stood watch over the emptiness like terra-cotta guards. I stepped onto the verandah we'd used as a classroom; planks creaked under my feet. The dormitories were bunkless sheds, the walls turned to patchworks of magazine and brochure pictures. The air here was too close; everything smelled of hot planks. Outside a window some chickens clucked like tiny motors.

Worn out, I sat on the verandah with my back against the dormitory wall. This had been one of the most peaceful, happy spots I'd found in Uganda—or anywhere else I could think of— but now its emptiness registered as a dull ache inside my chest. The cicadas set up a steady rasping whisper. Gradually the sky turned a hazy purple. I must have dozed for a while.

Opening my eyes, I heard a crunching sound—footsteps on dry leaves. A tall figure approached me, loping along, arms swinging: Jabez. I scrambled to my feet.

"You're here!" I called to him.

Grinning, he picked up his pace. "Every afternoon I come to see if you have come back!" His white teeth gleamed.

The deserted camp made us both uneasy; we walked out the gate to the little shop in the village where metal tables and chairs were set outside. We sat, and Jabez held out a squashed pack of cigarettes to me. I took one, lit it and his, and breathed in the harsh smoke I was now used to. Wangena padded out of the shop and set a glowing kerosene lantern down on a table for us. Jabez and I stood to greet her, shaking hands. As night settled over the village, I told Jabez about my journeys around the country and he nodded, smiling. The milky tea had never tasted so sweet.

He was wearing long pants and a checked shirt given to him by the farmer and his wife with whom he'd been staying. He talked of the work he'd done in the man's fields, the nights he'd spent playing with the family's children. No longer did he seem like a schoolboy. Talking here in the darkness, we seemed suspended in a cone of dim light that radiated from the lantern's globe and spread down to the clay at our feet. Cook-fires flickered in the huts around us; the scent of the charcoal smoke blew past on the breeze. When Jabez and I paused in our conversation, I listened to the sounds of children laughing, goats baaa-ing, cattle lowing in a faraway kraal.

Jabez had often written his essays at this table, and kept his notebooks in the shop. He brought them out, one with some loose pages poking from the cover. "I skipped reading these pages many weeks ago. I want to read them to you now."

What Can You Do

I tensed, reluctant to interrupt our peaceful evening. "You sure?"

"Yes—I must." Jabez smoothed the notebook open flat on the table top. He took a deep breath and started reading. "'On my last day at my school in Sudan, a politician from the Khartoum government ordered us to an assembly and told us we must change our language at school to Arabic and learn the Koran instead of the Bible. The boys were very restless and angry. When the man left, we gathered together. I stood on a stool and told the students that we must organize for a strike. I was too proud, shouting and demanding—wanting to lead....'" He sighed and turned over the page. "'I wrote a list of demands. The fathers urged us not take them to the government office in the village. But I insisted that we would march there.'" Jabez's voice was strained. I sat forward, holding the edge of the table. "'We shouted in front of the government building until some men in berets and military uniforms came to the doorway. I read the demands. The soldiers returned inside.'"

Jabez started at the notebook. "I did not write much more, but I will tell it."

"Okay...." I drank the last of my tea, the flakes sticking to my tongue.

Jabez closed the notebook. "We waited, whispering. Finally the soldiers came out. They raised rifles to their shoulders. I heard the cracking of the guns. The dirt at my feet was bouncing with bullets. I shouted at the boys—run! They fled scattering and screaming. Several boys fell, bleeding. I dragged one of them away. The soldiers rushed after us...."

I gripped my mug with both hands. He focused on my face.

"We ran toward Father Mario's house. He told us, 'Hurry out the back door!' Many boys and priests ran with us. The soldiers kept chasing, firing rifles. Now some villagers were hit with bullets. They were screaming in voices I can still hear in my head." Jabez paused for breath. "The villagers fled. Some of them fell, wounded, bleeding. And dead I think. I ran down one path, pushing the boys ahead...." Jabez wiped his face on his sleeve, staring out into the night.

"Did all of you escape?" I asked, my voice feeling scratchy in my throat.

"Not all. Two were killed. Some were wounded and got captured." Jabez stared down for a moment. The scar above his eyebrow shone strangely raw. "Many of us hid in the forest that night as the soldiers searched for us," he went on. "One boy with a bullet wound to his chest died. I had to lie still beside him as I heard his breathing stop."

Jabez sighed. The flame in the lantern globe flickered low. Wangena watched us from beside the shop door.

"The next morning a villager came and told us...." He paused. "The—the soldiers had nailed a Christian man to a wooden cross. As a warning to others like us not to oppose them."

My breath caught in my throat. I felt my chest muscles contract.

"Father Mario had hurt his foot, he could not lead," Jabez continued. "So I did. I said, 'We will go south from here, toward Niruba.' And that is when we started walking and walking for so many months."

"Did anyone help you?" I asked.

"Some gave us food and water. Many were afraid of being arrested or shot."

Jabez sat far back in his chair. Sounds from the nearby huts seemed to have stopped.

"If I had not been eager to lead the strike at the school, to be a big man...." Jabez's eyes gleamed with tears. "If I had not led the boys to the government building with our demands...."

"It sounds like they all wanted to go, anyway."

"They did." He nodded. "Then we all wanted to flee the country."

"I think more people might have been hurt if you *hadn't* led them toward the border."

"I can never know." His voice dropped. "But when I remember the villagers...and some of my friends left behind, I feel as if I had led them to their deaths. Do you understand?"

I swallowed hard. "Yes," I said finally.

"Good. I had to confess." He let out a long breath. "The memories will not all leave me, but they are not too heavy to hold me back now."

The murmuring sounds of the village rose around us again. Wangena spoke to Jabez in Luganda as she took away our empty tea mugs. He shook hands with her and the people who came out of the nearby huts. I heard them wishing him *Weeraba*—good-bye, safe journey. I was sad to learn Jabez was leaving Bombo tonight, but when the people clutched my hand in theirs, I smiled and pumped my arm up and down.

Jabez took a small woven basket of personal items from inside the shop where he'd evidently been storing it. He and I walked toward the bus stop. Though his legs were longer than mine, I had no trouble keeping up with him tonight. Several children followed behind on the path. We stood under the tin roof of a wood-frame bus stop on the roadside where other people were waiting as well.

"Is there an address where I can write to you?" I asked.

"Yes, of course! When I arrive, I will mail it to you at your university."

"Where will you go, Jabez?"

"Father Mario once gave me the name of his friend in Southern Rhodesia, the headmaster of a school. I have been writing to him. This week I received word that he will admit me for two terms, without fees—long enough for me to take my final examinations and graduate."

"That's great!"

Jabez nodded. "I have only to find my way there. He posted a map with his last letter."

"Did he send you money for bus tickets?"

"No. I have saved some shillings, but I doubt I will take many buses. I may hitch-hike. Mostly I will walk. Along the way—well, I think you know about African hospitality."

"Yes." I smiled. "But let me at least give you some money. I haven't got much with me, but when we get to Kampala—"

"No." He set down his basket. "But I thank you."

I didn't press him; he might change his mind after a while. While we waited for the bus, I calculated that he'd have to somehow go around Lake Victoria from Uganda into Kenya, then trek south all the way across Tanganyika into Northern, then Southern Rhodesia—a distance of well over a thousand miles.

Jabez must have seen the worry on my face. "I walked for many, many weeks to come to Bombo," he said. "The countryside to the south of here is much safer."

"Then…no problem." I said the mantra.

I heard the rumble of the bus coming. Two headlights appeared in the dark, jiggling above the rough road. The beams grew brighter; several people shielded their eyes. Now the rounded shape of the vehicle was visible, slowing with a grumbling of gears. Fat jute sacks strapped on the top rack swayed as the bus listed like an old drunk. Finally it stopped and rested under its load. Engine fumes swam in the amber light from the windows.

Jabez picked up his basket and turned to me. "I need to make this journey to the school on my own." He smiled.

"I understand."

The bus door swung open. Assuming that he'd ride with me as far as Kampala before heading south, I got on. There was a double empty seat part-way back; I waited for him to come along. But more people crowded past me in the aisle. Craning my neck, I couldn't spot Jabez among the boarding passengers. Finally I sat and gazed out the front window. Up ahead, a tall figure appeared in the bus's headlight beams, casting a long shadow as he strode down the road.

A few days later, after saying good-bye to Susan and other friends at Makerere, I drove my Renault into Kenya and up the gradual slope of Mount Elgon to a school in a village which, years later, would be the setting of my first novel. The area was cool and lovely, with views of long, green valleys dotted with clusters of huts. Footpaths led all over the mountainside; I spent my weekends exploring them. The classrooms reverberated with eager boys who, like the Sudanese students, soaked up every assignment I gave them and clamored for more. Teaching felt more exhilarating than ever.

When I returned to the university, I studied hard, storing up African literature to teach during my permanent posting. I felt no compulsion to rush off to the dance halls; that part of my African journey seemed to be over. Final examinations were difficult, though Dr. Cary, perhaps remembering that I'd stayed late at his party, gave me a higher mark in linguistics than I deserved. With my sketchy knowledge of Plato and John Dewey, I received only a second-class diploma. Never mind—I was now fully qualified as a teacher.

On the day before I left Kampala for a two-year posting in Nairobi, a pale blue aerogramme arrived from Jabez. I rushed to my room and tore it open.

Dear Mr. Edward,

I have arrived in Salisbury after a long and slow journey. My feet are very sore. Many people gave me food and places to sleep. Lorry drivers let me ride with them. Often I spent time working on farms or in market shops to earn money for food along the way.

The school here is very good. Each student has his own classroom desk and the dormitory has running water toilets and even a shower which gives hot water. We will be studying William Blake but here no one knows about new African writers yet. I have been playing on the school football side and have been elected captain.

I hope you are well. I send you my very best wishes.

Your student,

Jabez

I wrote Jabez from Nairobi, and during the two more years I lived in Africa, received several letters from him. One contained a sad report: Nicodemus had left school in Uganda and returned to southern Sudan to fight with the SPLA, the Sudanese People's Liberation Army. He was only fifteen, and the war was raging more savagely than ever. Neither Jabez nor I heard any more about him.

Bildad and another Bombo student who were enrolled in Uganda schools stayed with Jill and me at our house in Nairobi over Christmas holidays. They asked to go to mass at the cathedral in Nairobi; I told them I wanted to stroll around and would meet them afterwards. As I walked, I took a fresh look at the city where I'd first settled on my own. I'd helped to start a recently-built school here and had begun to live as a fully competent adult. Passing Nairobi's university, a campus of crowded gray buildings, I thought how lucky I'd been to live among the lawns and flame trees and tiled roofs of Makerere on its hilltop overlooking the city. I wouldn't come to love Nairobi as I once had Kampala, but I was enjoying Kenya's capital in new ways. Life with Jill was happier than I'd ever have imagined a marriage could be. I'd made friends who had jobs, salaries and homes like mine; I'd even found work singing in small clubs with my guitar and backing a sextet of exiled South African singers I'd gotten to know.

Today, Nairobi's streets were nearly deserted for the holiday. The sunlight shone warm along the wide boulevards and even made the shops' corrugated shutters ripple gaily like sheets of ribbon candy. When I returned to the cathedral, the doors were open wide; the blurry outline of a crucifix floated ghost-like in a haze above the altar. As crowds streamed onto the steps, I could hear the waterfall rush of organ music from deep inside, and I recalled the memorial service for President Kennedy we'd held at the Bombo camp. It occurred to me that if I hadn't know Jabez and Nicodemus and become so involved with learning to teach the refugees, I might not have made it to where I was today. I had more to be grateful to them for than they would ever know.

Just for a moment I wished that I could believe in the sanctity of the organ music I was listening to. Then I spotted the two Sudanese students, so tall in the new slacks and dress shirts they'd unwrapped on Christmas eve. The way they stood there at the top of the steps, gazing around with bright, curious looks on their faces—those expressions were plenty for me. Who knew what sadness lay behind them? But for now the boys appeared safe and content to trust that I'd arrive. I waved to them, and they came running down the steps, and we went off to join Jill and my South African friends for Christmas curry at an Indian restaurant.

9.

I've continued to follow events in Sudan. For a time, American magazine articles and television shows featured stories about "The Lost Boys" who, like my students, wandered all over the country's southern region before being rescued. These stories had happy endings, with the kids being sent to Europe or the United States where friendly families welcomed them. I've read no reports about the majority of boys who have remained behind in refugee camps for months and years, or have simply disappeared. Rivalries have broken out between tribes in south Sudan, the Dinka and Nuer, who lived in peace in the Bombo camp. Jabez and Nicodemus, had they stayed home and never met in Uganda, might be shooting at each other as the fighting escalates toward civil war.

Years ago, Southern Rhodesia's white minority government's army slaughtered African rebels, who turned into an army which ousted the settlers from power and slaughtered rival tribesmen to take over the government of the nation now called Zimbabwe. My letters to Jabez's school there were neither answered nor returned. But more than a decade later, I received a battered aerogramme that had been forwarded from several addresses in Uganda and Kenya.

Dear Edward,

I finished my university studies years ago and am now in Sierra Leone on the West Coast of Africa. My journey took years with many stops along the way, living and earning money and moving on. Fourah Bay College has hired me as an English lecturer. My wife and son and I have moved into campus housing which is very beautiful.

I remember the Bombo camp as a lonely "Hell in Heaven's Despite" for the first year— until you and your friends came. Now I have happy memories of the time we were all there together. Those months changed my life, and I hope to do well here so that I can think of you remembering me with pride.

Your friend,
Jabez

Two years later I travelled for a magazine assignment to Freetown, Sierra Leone. Fourah Bay, Africa's oldest university, had a lovely, palm-fringed campus built into a mountainside overlooking the ocean. Its tile-roofed buildings reminded me of Makerere's. But it was a sad place now. The country was ruled by a ruthless dictator; many teachers and students had fled, fearing persecution from the government. The few teachers I spoke to said the campus bookshop had recently been looted by soldiers, and the only texts the students could find were tattered editions sold on city sidewalks.

News stories I'd read years earlier reported that Makerere had been nearly emptied by Idi Amin's rampaging soldiers; afterwards, with valiant efforts, Ugandans gradually got the university thriving again. In the campus bookshop at Fourah Bay, fluorescent tubes flickered above empty shelves and loose pages lay strewn around the floor like leaves after a storm.

When people told me that Jabez was no longer in Sierra Leone I was at first disappointed, then relieved; a month after my visit, the nation broke into civil war. I've never seen Jabez again, but whenever I recall him striding in the bus's headlights along Bombo's dusty road toward his new life, I know I have no cause to worry about him.

Uganda, like Sierra Leone, is well along on its recovery from dictatorial misrule, though going through the troubles all developing nations are still facing. They're the kinds of problems I was too innocent to see as I careened over the country's surface—bedazzled by its beauty and energy during those first, golden post-colonial years.

The southern region of Sudan, after nearly a half century of war, has finally broken away from the northern part of the country that oppressed it so brutally. A negotiated settlement resulted in the establishment of the fully independent, though not peaceful,

Republic of South Sudan. Do brass bands and leopard-skin-clad warriors march through the capital's streets to commemorate each anniversary of independence? If I were there, would I be riding a float and flailing away at my guitar to the melody of the new national anthem?

Probably not. You never get to re-live times like those—when you're twenty-two and believe you can do anything, go anywhere, and find all your discoveries fascinating. But I'll always be grateful that I had the chance to live among the people of Africa who helped me learn to trust the person I was then, and the one I was to become.

AFTERWORD

Inspired by my son Dan, the artist who designed my web site (www.edwardhower.com), I decided to try writing an artist's statement of my own - something about how I started writing and why I keep at it. Then I remembered that I'd already published an article in 1983 that summed up my ideas about what I do. It was a brief homage I paid to Tennessee Williams who had recently died, an artist who was enormously important to me many years before.

I hope my own writing will always have some of the luminous compassion and the sense of wonder that I first discovered in his work.

When I was fifteen, a film of one of Tennessee Williams' plays changed my life.

I wanted to be like everybody else then, and was tormented because I wasn't popular. With persistence, I managed to get a date with the most sought-after girl in school and go to the Wednesday afternoon movie, not only with her but with the two most popular couples in the ninth grade. They were the sons and daughters of corporation executives who, like my father, owned some of the biggest homes in my colorless and odorless suburban town. Fortified by zoning laws and high hedges around their lawns, the townspeople had put their struggling paths behind them and, in middle age, had decreed that no Unpleasantness of any sort was to penetrate their sanctuary. Unpleasantness not only included poverty or dirt, but any strong human emotions expressed directly: exhilaration or despair, love or loneliness. Only the middle range of feelings was permitted.

What Can You Do

The executives commuted on the train past the tenements of Harlem on their way to work every day; they rode the bus through the raucous canyons surrounding Grand Central Station, but when they came home every evening, they seemed determinedly untouched by the lives they had seen out their windows. Theirs was a world of beach club dances, church building drives, historical society meetings, and catered cocktail parties on the terrace. It was a clean, cheerful, purposeful world, one that I had been trained from infancy to take my place in. I had only just begun to notice that I hated it.

But on the Wednesday afternoon of the movie, I had finally been accepted by the in-crowd. My date was daffodil-pretty: blonde, wide-eyed, well brought up to be quietly amused by the banter of ninth grade boys. The film I took her to was Tennessee Williams' *The Rose Tattoo*.

For the first few minutes inside the theater, I concentrated on edging close enough to my date to drape my arm around her shoulder. Then I stopped edging. I watched the screen. While the other two boys made clever comments that got their girlfriends giggling, I sat with my mouth half-open throughout *The Rose Tattoo*. I had never seen anything like it. I was amazed. And I stayed amazed.

Afterwards, we walked along a wide, tree-lined street toward my date's house. I couldn't speak. My new friends were still making amusing comments about the film. They'd thought it boring and "grungy." I told them they were wrong.

"You mean you liked that sweaty guy with the tattoo?" they asked. "You liked that big woman who was always moaning and walking around in her slip?"

"Yes," I told them. "Yes - I thought they were great." I had no other word to express what I felt, and if I had, I would have kept it to myself. I was in love with Anna Magnani. I was in love with art.

I dawdled along behind the others now, and when my date turned around to ask what was wrong with me, I just stared at her. Beside Anna Magnani, she looked vapid and soulless to me, a blonde ghost who would never walk around her house in a slip, who would never have those beautiful lines in her face, who would never wring her hands over anything more than a messy table-setting.

I knew then, that afternoon, that I was not like her or her friends, that I would never be, and that it was a waste of my time trying to be. When they made funny remarks about my strange behavior, I simply didn't care. I didn't go to my date's house to play records, as was the Wednesday afternoon custom. I said I didn't feel like it, and just kept walking.

I wandered all over town. For the first time in my life, I knew I belonged somewhere: in the world of my imagination. I was not the only one there, as I had previously thought. I had company. Others, like the man who had written *The Rose Tattoo,* had explored their own murky feelings and had made something wonderful out of them with words. It was all right now to feel that my private world was realer than the one that surrounded me. It was all right to think up people I preferred to my friends and my parents, and to imagine these characters laughing and shouting and grieving and touching each others' lives intimately. It was all right to be the kind of person I was. I was happy. I began to write dramas of my own.

Tennessee Williams was not famous for making people happy, and yet he was an immensely popular playwright. His haunted vision touched millions of lives. When his lonely and wounded characters spoke, they reached behind the masks we wore and awoke those parts of us that were most vulnerable, delicate, fearful, and gave us permission to experience them in hopes of finding something much more alive and sustaining than the masks we thought protected us.

He was accused of writing about only of the extremes of human nature—the pathologically sad, the sexually driven, the obsessed—but in fact he wrote about the infinite capacity of the human heart to feel everything and to feel a kinship with others who have also allowed themselves this freedom. "Nothing human disgusts me, unless it's unkind, violent," Hannah in *Night of the Iguana* tells us.

Because we have been moved by her story, her compassionate vision becomes ours. If she has survived the extremes of her loneliness, and can think of her chaste encounter with a pathetic salesman as a "love experience," then perhaps we can view our own extreme predicaments with as much sensitivity and dignity.

Like every good artist, Tennessee Williams made us see the world as a place populated with people like ourselves at our most human moments. He helped us feel a common bond with them. The moments of connection in his plays were often painful, even tragic. His characters had to work through tortured social rituals in order to reach each others' hearts, and then the exposure of their shared vulnerability was sometimes more than they could endure for long. But these brief moments of connection were always worth the suffering. As the characters' lives were transformed by them, so the lives of the audience were illuminated and given meaning. In *The Glass Menagerie*, we can understand Laura's Wingfield's exhilaration and grief when she shows her glass unicorn to "the gentleman caller," a warehouseman her brother Tom has invited to dinner.

"He loves the light," she says of the unicorn. "See how the light shines through him!" But while she dances with the man in the living room—her one wild fling in life—the unicorn is knocked to the floor, its tiny horn broken.

"Now it is just like all the other horses," she says sadly, hopefully, knowing that she has at last made contact with the herd, with the world she had feared to approach and the high-school boy she had once loved from afar. For this one moment, she has allowed him to share her private, delicate life, and he has found it beautiful.

"You're pretty," he tells her, "in a different way from everyone else.... They're one hundred times one thousand. You're one times one.... You're—Blue Roses!"

"But," she says, referring to this name he had given her in high school, "blue is wrong for roses."

"It's right for you," he says. We in the audience know that this contact will be brief, and that what makes Laura special—like the unicorn's translucent horn—is too fragile to survive for long. But we also know that she is pretty not in spite of her uniqueness but because of it. What Laura comes to understand about herself, we in the audience can value about ourselves as well.

I kept writing and kept straying as far as possible from the kinds of towns where I was raised, working in Africa, England, Los Angeles, New York. I saw the plays and films of Tennessee Williams wherever I could. And finally I met him at a party in Key West, Florida, in 1981. I had recently read a story of his in a literary magazine whose editor we both knew. When I told him I'd liked it, he was very pleased; few people had admired his recent work. I didn't plan to gush, but I was as drunk as he was, and began telling him the story of how he had influenced my life at fifteen. Who can resist a fan? He was seventy then and not in good health, but that night he looked slim and tanned, dapper with his gray mustache and a fisherman's cap pulled down at a jaunty angle.

"And did you become a writer?" he asked me when I'd finished.

"Yes," I said, "for better or worse."

"Or both," he said, grinning.

During the rest of the party, I kept looking back at him as his friends introduced him around and settled him at a table. I was very glad I'd had a chance to tell him how much his writing had meant to me. I wish he hadn't died alone in a hotel room. I prefer to remember him as I saw him at that party: sitting with his arms around two friends, smiling, surrounded by his admirers-pretty but aging middle aged women and beautiful young men. They could have been characters from his plays, come back from the stage to keep him company. One of them could have been Tom's and Laura's mother out of *The Glass Menagerie*—or, for that matter, my mother.

I have to remember the rest of the scene, though. It was a far cry from the backwater Key West of *The Rose Tattoo* I had first seen on the screen many years before. The party was at a beach club on a terrace looking out on the Gulf of Mexico, a setting not all that dissimilar from the ones where my parents and their friends socialized. Most of the people here were about the same age as my parents had been when I was fifteen. So was I, now.

What was I doing here? What was Tennessee Williams doing here? Never mind, never mind, I thought—we're both still writing. At least the party guests were people to me, now, not pale ghosts. They had lives; I had learned that. Perhaps that fifteen-year-old date of mine had grown up to be a woman with beautiful lines in her face, after all; perhaps she had learned something, too.

"Nowadays the world is lit by lightning," Tom says at the end of *The Glass Menagerie*. It is a fearful thing, this lightning. We have all seen it and felt its shudder pass through us. But the world is lit by a stronger light, as well, the one that shines through Laura's glass horses, the one Tennessee Williams has left behind to keep us company.

ACKNOWLEDGMENTS

The names and some physical characteristics of some of the people in these essays have been changed.

Many of the essays originally appeared, sometimes with different titles, sometimes with minor changes, in the following publications:

"What Can You Do" – *Alaska Quarterly Review,* 2012
"Echoes" – *Blackbird,* 2014
"Gratitude" – *Five Points,* 2013
"Writing Dangerously" —*Cornell Alumni Magazine,* 2011
"Belize: A Laid-back British Colony in Central America" – *Grapevine,* 1979
"El Sapito" – *The New York Times,* 1999
"Queens, Demons, and Saints: India's Folklore Heritage" – *The Pomegranate Princess and other Tales from India, RBSA Publishers (Jaipur, 1988), Wayne State University Press(Detroit) 1994, Indian Illustrated Books (Jaipur, 1999), Authors Guild Backinprint.com (New York, 2004)* "The Song of Naina Bai" and "The Flying Prince" also appeared in *Columbia, a Magazine of Poetry and Prose,* 1993
"Ananda's Dove" – *River Styx,* 2011
"The Witch Temple" – *American Scholar,* 2011
"The Village Artist" – *Epoch,* 2009
"Children of the Maze" – *Five Points,* 2011
"Explorers of the Spirit World" – *Smithsonian,* 1993
"Along South India's Coromandel Coast" – *The New York Times,* 2008
"A Village on the Bay of Bengal" – *Indian Express (Chennai),* 2011
"Afterword" – *Ithaca Times,* 1983; www.edwardhower.com, 2013